Leisure & Tourism
for GCSE

This book is

SSL

SSL

Lindsey Taylor

     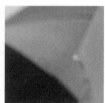

Collins

CONTENTS

Acknowledgements

The author would like to sincerely thank Graham Bradbury, Kay Wright, Melanie McRae and Tony Wootton for their expert guidance, advice and support during the project. Special thanks as always to Nick, Lucy and Alice for their unending patience and good humour at being left to fend for themselves whilst 'work was in progress'.

The authors and publisher would like to thank the following for permission to reproduce photographs and other material:

Alvechurch Waterways Holidays: 71
Avis: 59
Big Bus Company: 46 [bottom left]
Brighton & Hove Visitor &
Convention Bureau: 60, 183
Britain on View: 198 [top]
British Airways: 130
British Tourist Authority: 8-9,61,63,155,158,173
Butlins Holidays: 87 [centre]
City of York Council: 69
Cloud Nine Photography: 109
Corbis: 10 [bottom], 31, 42 [top], 72, 84
[top right], 100, 104, 110 [top left], 143 [right],
144, 148, 164, 172 [centre], 174, 200 [centre],
216, 217, 223
Coverdale Sports Centre: 221
David Towersey Photography: 44, 132, 133, 134,
135, 191 [top], 191 [centre left], 191 [centre right]
Dean Court Hotel: 197
English Heritage: 67 [bottom], 112 [centre left]
English Tourism Council: 151 [top left]
Frames Rickard: 43
Getty Images / Creative: 176
Getty Images / Hulton Archive: 84 [top left]
Getty Images / Imagebank: 195 [top right]
Getty Images / Photodisk: 46
Getty Images / Stone: 32, 39, 50, 186, 208
Getty Images / Telegraph Colour Library: 68, 158,
168, 193 [top left]
Goodwood Racecourse: 12 [top]
Guild of Registered Tour Guides: 196

Helen Evans: 103
Jaco Wolmarans Photography: 10 [top]
Jorvik The Viking City: 116
KFC: 190
Legoland: 111
Lindsey Taylor: 14, 111
Mark Dudgeon: 16 [top]
Mark Watson Photography: 30, 38, 92
My Travel (formerly Airtours): 50 [bottom right],
56 [top], 57 [top]
Nickelodeon: 17
North Sea Ferries: 50 [bottom left], 58
PA Photos: 12 [bottom left], 12 [bottom right], 136
Pizza Hut: 127
Popperfoto: 34 [bottom]
Rex Features: 97 [top], 126 [centre], 143 [left],
151 [top right]
Ryanair: 56 [bottom]
Sarah Clarke: 50 [top left], 51, 172 [bottom], 213
The Mail on Sunday: 37, 110 [bottom]
Thomson Holidays: 161
Tiger Electronics: 86 [top]
Warner Cinemas: 22 [top]
www.blockbuster.co.uk: 27

Every effort has been made to contact copyright holders but if any have been inadvertently overlooked, the publishers will be pleased to make the necessary arrangements at the first opportunity.

The purpose of this book

The purpose of this book is to help you to develop the knowledge and understanding that you will need to complete a Leisure and Tourism for GCSE course. The book has been written specifically to cover the topics in each of the three units that make up your course.

Leisure and Tourism for GCSE units	
Unit 1	Investigating leisure and tourism
Unit 2	Marketing in leisure and tourism
Unit 3	Customer service in leisure and tourism

I've tried to write a book that helps you to gain a good, clear understanding of a range of leisure and tourism topics and also to give you a taste of what to expect from a career in the leisure and tourism industry. Taking a Leisure and Tourism for GCSE course gives you an opportunity to decide whether this is an area of work that you are suitable for and interested in pursuing. Hopefully, you'll think about taking your interest in leisure and tourism further when you've worked through the book and completed your GCSE.

How does the book work?

The book is organised in the same way as your Leisure and Tourism course. There are three main units and these are divided into double-page topics. For example, the topic 'UK tourist destinations' is covered on pages 66 and 67. The topics covered in each unit are listed on the contents page at the start of the unit. You can also find the topics that you are looking for by using the index at the end of the book.

Every topic has a number of features. These include topic information as well as **Case Study**, **Stop and Think** and **Over to you** activities. You should try to complete the activities as you come to them because they are designed to help you to learn and understand the topic information more clearly. Each of the units also includes questions on the **revision pages**. These provide you with an opportunity to revise what you know and to test your understanding of the topics that you should have learnt about. Completing the activities and the revision sections will not always be easy, but it will help you to learn more. It is worth making the effort if you want to achieve the best grade that you are capable of.

What is different about this qualification?

Leisure and Tourism for GCSE is a **vocational qualification**. This means that it is work-related. It aims to provide the basic knowledge, skills and understanding that you will be able to use in a workplace or as the basis for further education or training in this area. The content of the course and the work that you do will all be related to the leisure and tourism industry in some way. For example, you will look at the types of leisure and tourism organisations that exist in the United Kingdom, the range of people who provide these services, explore the different ways that organisations use marketing and learn how to deal with customers by providing excellent service. This means that all of the leisure and tourism topics you cover will be related to people who use or provide these services, and to the ways that these services are organised and run.

What will my Leisure and Tourism for GCSE cover?

All GCSE-equivalent vocational subjects are composed of three compulsory units. The titles and general focus of your three compulsory units are set out below.

Leisure and Tourism for GCSE	
Unit title	**What is it about?**
1 Investigating Leisure and Tourism	The facilities, products and services that make up the industry and how they are linked and work together to meet the needs of a wide range of customers
2 Marketing in Leisure and Tourism	The key ways in which leisure and tourism organisations use marketing tools and activities to ensure that they are successful
3 Customer Service in Leisure and Tourism	The reasons why customer service is important to leisure and tourism organisations and the ways in which you can provide good service to meet the needs of all customers

The content of each unit is set out in detail in a course specification that your teacher should have and may give you.

How will my Leisure and Tourism for GCSE course be assessed?

Leisure and Tourism for GCSE requires you to work at the same level as any other non-vocational GCSE, such as history or mathematics. The qualification that you'll receive when you complete the course will be graded on an A* to G scale. However, Leisure and Tourism for GCSE is a double award. This means that you will receive the equivalent of two GCSEs at the grade you are awarded when you complete the course. Your grade will therefore be somewhere between A*A* and GG.

To gain a graded GCSE qualification you will need to complete an assessment of your learning in each of the three course units. You will have to complete assignments set by your teachers for units 2 and 3 and you must also sit a test set by the Awarding Body (examination board) for unit 1. You will need to complete each of these three assessments to gain a Leisure and Tourism for GCSE award.

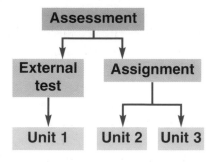

What can I do with my Leisure and Tourism for GCSE?

A Leisure and Tourism for GCSE qualification can help you progress into further education, training or employment. For example, alongside other GCSEs, your leisure and tourism qualification could give you access to AS and A level courses at your school or at a local college or an AVCE in either Leisure and Recreation or Travel and Tourism. Alternatively, a Leisure and Tourism for GCSE qualification could help you to obtain a Modern Apprenticeship or an NVQ training course in leisure or tourism. A third option could be to use your Leisure and Tourism for GCSE award to gain employment in a junior or trainee position within the industry.

Whatever your career plans, a Leisure and Tourism for GCSE course should provide you with an opportunity to explore and develop your knowledge and understanding of this interesting vocational area. I hope that this is an enjoyable experience and that the book is useful in helping you to achieve the best grade that you're able to.

Investigating leisure and tourism

This unit introduces you to the important part that both the leisure and tourism industries play in today's society. You will learn about:

- the range of leisure activities and facilities provided in a wide variety of situations
- the key components of the leisure industry, how they are interrelated and the variety of organisations and facilities providing them
- how leisure provision has changed in the last twenty years and how both local and national services are provided
- home-based leisure facilities
- the products and services provided by leisure facilities
- factors that influence and affect how people choose to spend their leisure time
- the range of employment opportunities in the leisure industry
- how tourism is defined and the purpose of visits
- the key components of the tourism industry and the different types of holiday available
- the costs and merits of travel methods used both to get to a destination and to travel around once there
- popular tourist destinations for both domestic (UK-based) and incoming (overseas) visitors
- the social, economic and environmental impacts of tourism and sustainable development
- the range of jobs available in a wide variety of tourist organisations
- the links between leisure and tourism.

Unit 1 of this book covers Unit 1, Investigating leisure and tourism, of the GCSE Leisure and Tourism award.

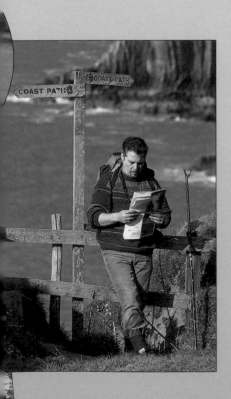

We all spend our leisure time taking part in a wide variety of activities. Some of us may go with friends to the cinema, play sport together or go to a fast-food restaurant. Others may stay at home and watch television, listen to music or play computer games. Alternatively, we may go with our families on holiday or to visit a theme park or watch a football match. If we kept a record of everything that we did in our leisure time over a year, we would probably find that the list would contain lots of different activities.

The leisure and tourism industry provides the facilities, products, services and activities that let people enjoy their leisure time.

Leisure time may be spent doing something simple, such as reading a book, or more daring, such as paragliding ▲ ▶

There are a number of different organisations within the leisure and tourism industry, ranging from theatres and leisure centres to travel agents and transport providers. Many of these are linked when providing products for customers. For example, a package holiday includes organisations such as a tour operator, accommodation provider and a transport organisation. It is important that they work well together to make sure that all aspects of the product meet customers' needs.

TOURISM INDUSTRY

England's domestic tourism spending, 1999

Breakdown	Spending (£ billion)	% of spend
Accommodation (non-package trip)	4.0	31
Eating and drinking	3.3	26
Travel	2.3	18
Entertainment (including sport)	0.7	6
Buying clothes	0.6	5
Other shopping	1.2	8
Package trip	0.5	4
Service or advice	0.1	1
Other	0.1	1
Total	12.8	100

▲ England's domestic tourism spending, 1999

People spend varying amounts of money on leisure and tourism products. The table shows just how important the leisure and tourism industry is in terms of the amount of money that it earns: £12.8 billion pounds was spent in 1999. This also means that the industry creates a lot of jobs.

In this chapter you will learn about the characteristics of the leisure and tourism industry and the facilities, products and services that they offer. You will also study a number of popular destinations in the United Kingdom, and find out:

- where they are
- what they offer visitors
- their main transport routes.

Conduct a survey

In pairs, carry out a survey to find out what people do in their leisure time. Ask a range of people of different ages. Ask each person whether he or she:

- takes part in or watches sport
- goes to the cinema or theatre
- goes to restaurants
- visits tourist attractions
- watches television or videos
- goes on holiday.

When you have completed the survey, draw a graph to show the results.

Do you...	(name/age)	(name/age)
play sport?		
go to cinema or theatre?		
go to restaurants?		
go to tourist attractions?		
watch television or videos?		
take holidays?		

THE LEISURE INDUSTRY

Leisure describes the range of activities that people do in their spare time, in other words, when they are not at work, school or college.

It is not always easy to see the difference between work and leisure because what may be work to one person might be a leisure activity for someone else. For example, a mother rushing home from work to prepare a meal for the family might see cooking as work. However, many people see cooking as a leisure time activity and may go on cookery holidays or attend classes.

The range of leisure activities offered is always increasing. People are always looking for new ways to spend their leisure time. Activities may include:

- reading
- sport (participating and spectating)
- going to the cinema or disco
- going for a walk
- watching television or listening to the radio
- eating out
- playing computer games
- visiting a tourist attraction.

A sport, such as racing at Goodwood, is a spectator sport ▼

▲ Some sports, such as football, attract people as both participants and spectators ▶

Sport is clearly an important leisure activity for many people. It may be seen as two different activities: sports participation and sports spectating. The biggest spectator sports tend to be those that receive a lot of television coverage.

Classify leisure activities

Look at the list of popular leisure activities shown in the table. Would you see each activity as work or leisure? Tick your choice.

Activity	Work	Leisure
DIY		
Gardening		
Reading		
Watching television		
Aerobics		
Playing football		

Sport	BBC1	BBC2	ITV	CH4	Eurosport	Sky	CH5	Total (%)
Football	4 800	650	7 475	2 930	29 725	102 765	2 815	16.54
General sport	935	295	215	7 705	10 610	76 106	16 610	12.31
Golf	1 485	3 548	0	60	2 160	83 900	90	9.98
Motorsports	390	1 680	5 620	0	26 065	31 945	645	7.26
Cricket	3 042	9 327	135	0	0	44 970	0	6.29
Tennis	1 130	2 466	0	0	21 035	15 955	0	4.44
Motorcycling	175	90	0	0	14 880	11 310	0	2.89
Horse racing	2 581	1 161	60	7 635	0	13 460	0	2.72
Boxing	95	0	140	0	7 845	16 260	0	2.66
Rugby league	40	160	0	0	0	22 910	0	2.53

Source: RSL Research Services, RSL Sportscan July–December 1998

▲ Television coverage of sport, 1998 (Top ten, in viewing minutes)

Some sports may be mainly participation, that is, they do not attract many spectators. For example, netball and darts are not often shown on television but large numbers of people play them.

Many factors influence what people choose to do in their leisure time. We will look at these in detail on page 30. The amount of time and when it is available for leisure is often a key factor. For example, shift workers who finish work at midnight may be limited in their choice of activities at this time. They would certainly find it difficult if they wanted to go to a theme park or museum. Likewise, hotel employees who have Thursdays and Fridays off may not be able to go and watch a live football match.

Identify sports

Using the table, list some sports for each category.

Mainly spectator	Mainly participants	Both spectator and participants

The term 'leisure' includes a wide range of different facilities and activities. Broadly speaking, the leisure industry can be split into the following components or sectors:

- Sport and physical recreation
- Arts and entertainment
- Countryside recreation
- Home-based leisure
- Children's play activities
- Visitor attractions
- Catering.

These components are often interrelated.

Sport and physical recreation

The Council of Europe's European Sports Charter defines sport as:

All forms of physical activity which, through casual or organised participation, aims at improving physical fitness and mental well-being, forming social relationships, or obtaining results in competition at all levels.

It is estimated that 25 million English people take part in some sport or active recreation at least once a month. The top ten participation sports are shown in the table.

Banana-boating has become a popular physical recreational activity ▼

Sport and physical recreation covers a wide range of different activities, including:

Archery
Badminton
Bowling
Cricket
Croquet
Cycling
Fencing
Fishing
Golf
Gymnastics
Hockey
Horse racing
Jetskiing
Martial arts
Netball
Orienteering
Polo
Rugby
Sailing
Skating
Skiing
Squash
Surfing
Table tennis
Tennis
Volleyball
Weightlifting
Windsurfing

Top sports participation facts			
Adults participating at least once a month, 1996		School children participating at least once a year, 1994	
1 Walking	44.5%	1 Swimming	85%
2 Swimming	14.6%	2 Cycling	79%
3 Keep fit/Yoga	12.3%	3 Athletics (track and field)	81%
4 Snooker/Billiards	11.3%	4 Gymnastics (Gym)	69%
5 Cycling	11.0%	5 Football	77%
6 Weight training	5.6%	6 Rounders	75%
7 Soccer	4.8%	7 Tennis	67%
8 Golf	4.7%	8 Walking (>1hr)/Hiking	62%
9 Running	4.5%	9 Cricket	59%
10 Tenpin bowls/skittles	3.4%	10 Cross Country/Jogging	51%

Source: Office of Population Censuses and Surveys, 1996; Sports Council, 1994

Interest in sport and physical recreation has increased as people have become more aware of the healthy benefits of taking exercise. Many realise that they do not have to be expert at a particular sporting activity to join in. For example, the number of people taking up cycling or running as a hobby has increased hugely in recent years.

Many people also enjoy the social side of sport and recreation. They enjoy being part of a team when playing football, or meeting fellow golfers or tennis players in the club bar after a game.

Arts and entertainment

The arts and entertainment component of the leisure industry includes:

- cinemas
- nightclubs
- theatres
- concert halls and venues.

The arts and entertainment industry covers a huge range of different types of entertainment from pop concerts and seaside variety shows to classical offerings, such as Shakespeare's plays, ballet and opera. Different types of entertainment will obviously appeal to different types of customer. For example, opera tends to be popular amongst older people while pop concerts attract a younger audience.

▲ The York Millennium Cycle Route

The Arts Council

The Arts Council is the government body for art and entertainment in England. They give grants to art organisations and artists. In 2001–02 the total grants allocated was £252 million.

OVER TO YOU

Conduct a survey

The table lists the top ten films of 2000. In pairs, carry out a survey of friends and relatives and find out which of the films they saw at the cinema. Make a note of the age of each person you interview.

When you have finished your survey, discuss which age groups seem to go to the cinema more often.

Top ten films in 2000				
Rank	Film	Distributor	Country of origin	Box Office Gross (£m)
1	Star Wars Episode 1: The Phantom Menace (U)	20th C Fox	US/UK	50 928 328
2	Notting Hill (15)	Universal	US/UK	30 765 273
3	A Bug's Life (U)	Buena Vista	US	29 310 536
4	Austin Powers 2: The Spy Who Shagged Me (12)	Entertainment	US	25 772 822
5	The World Is Not Enough (12)	UIP	US/UK	23 375 037
6	The Sixth Sense (15)	UIP	US	20 449 726
7	Shakespeare In Love (15)	UIP	US/UK	20 407 662
8	Tarzan (U)	Buena Vista	US	17 469 366
9	The Mummy (12)	UIP	US	17 439 339
10	The Matrix (15)	Warner	US	17 279 897

Source: British Film Institute

Countryside recreation

Countryside recreation refers to any recreational activities that take place in the countryside.

Countryside recreation might be based on land, on water or in the air.

Land	Water	Air
walking	sailing	paragliding
cycling	swimming	parachuting
orienteering	water-skiing	gliding
caving	fishing	hot air ballooning
abseiling		flying

▲ Walking is a recreational activity that attracts all ages

Water sports are popular in many areas, such as Sunderland ▼

Walking in the countryside has become a favourite recreational activity for many people. The Ramblers' Association sums the reasons up well.

Britain is perfect walking country, with a temperate climate and an impressive variety of landscapes crammed into a relatively small space. And with an extensive network of off-road footpaths, this beautiful countryside is easily accessible to all walkers. From the remote highlands of Scotland and bleak West Country moors, through the gentle landscapes of the south-east to the bustle of world-famous cities, there will be a walk to suit you.

Some of the main areas that concentrate on countryside recreational activities are the National Parks. We will look at these in detail on page 62.

Match activity and user

Read the two diary extracts. List the types of home-based leisure activities that each take part in. Describe the type of person that you think wrote each diary, including, the age and gender.

Extract 1

Saturday 15th November
Car would not start so abandoned plans to go shopping and swept up leaves from drive before pruning back the Wisteria. Peaceful afternoon spent doing The Times crossword and watching bits of the rugby on TV. Son and wife came for dinner so I cooked my famous Chicken Mexican before we settled down for an exciting game of Monopoly – I lost as usual! Fell asleep watching the late night news.

Sunday 16th November
Busy morning spent repainting the bathroom door while partner cooked roast beef – lovely meal so we spoilt ourselves with a bottle of good red wine and listened to some of our Frank Sinatra records. Completed my 10 000-piece jigsaw in the late afternoon – must buy another one. Good evening on telly – Heartbeat, my favourite – but needed to write to some friends so missed the programme.

Home-based leisure

A large amount of our leisure time is spent at home and there is a wide range of activities to choose from. Home-based leisure includes:

- watching television and videos
- gardening and DIY
- take-away meals
- crafts
- entertaining friends
- listening to music
- computer games
- reading.

We will look at some of the organisations that provide home-based leisure products and services on page 26.

Watching television is one of the main home-based leisure activities for many people. The average person watches 3.25 hours of television a day! It is interesting that some of the most popular programmes on television at the moment are ones that encourage us to take up other home-based leisure activities. In recent years there has been a huge increase in programmes on:

- DIY – *Changing Rooms, Better Homes, House Doctor*
- gardening – *Ground Force*
- cooking – *Master Chef, Naked Chef, Good Food, Ready Steady Cook.*

▲ The digital, cable and satellite channel Nickelodeon is popular with the youth market

OVER TO YOU

Extract 2

Saturday 15th November
Boring, boring, boring! No money so can't go shopping in town with friends. Fortunately, Mark and Lucy could not either so came round to chill out. Listened to Shaggy's new album – great, and danced to the best bits. Beat Mark at 'Who wants to be a millionaire' on the Playstation. Nothing good on TV in the evening so e-mailed some friends and went to an online chat room.

Sunday 16th November
Slept in very late which made family cross, so made up for it by cleaning the car. Went to Sarah's house for the afternoon, which was great – played table tennis and darts, then watched the new Friends video. Relatives came for dinner so I had to be home and wearing 'sensible' clothes – so boring. Crept away after the meal to read Sugar in my bedroom. Sent text messages to Sarah and Louise, then watched late-night horror film on TV – not very scary at all!

Children's play activities

While many leisure activities involve the whole family, there are others that are aimed purely at children. Examples of children's play activities may include:

- adventure playgrounds
- playschemes
- children's activity centres and holidays.

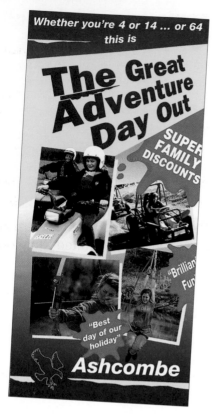

▲ Children's play activities at Ashcombe Park

CASE STUDY

Waltham Forest children's play scheme

Play provision and activities for 5–12 year olds

Summer or winter, inside or outside, children love to play. Activities and games form an essential part of a child's development, helping them to make friends, develop social skills, and encourage imagination, creative thought and physical coordination. Arts & Leisure provide a wide range of play activities and facilities for 5–12 year olds. There are playschemes for 6–12 year olds and Teatime Clubs with games and sports for 5–11 year olds.

Most playschemes have outdoor playgrounds with fixed equipment and kick-about areas. Many of the facilities and activities run throughout the year with added extras during school holidays.

All play staff are carefully appointed and are trained to help the children under their care get the most out of their time. But please note, the playschemes provide an 'open door' service and staff are not responsible for children remaining at the centres. Children are free to come and go as they like.

OVER TO YOU

Discuss

Read the details of the Waltham Forest Playscheme. As a group discuss what you think the main attraction of the scheme might be to:

- parents thinking about sending their children on a playscheme
- children going on the playscheme.

Visitor attractions

The Department of Culture, Media and Sport (DCMS) defines a visitor attraction as a:

Permanently established excursion destination, a primary purpose of which is to allow public access for entertainment, interest or education, rather than being a primary retail outlet or a venue for sporting, theatrical, or film performances. It must be open to the public, without prior booking, for published periods each year, and should be capable of attracting day visitors or tourists, as well as local residents.

The DCMS calculate that there are more than 6100 visitor attractions in the United Kingdom, which include:

- museums
- art galleries
- historic buildings and sites
- cathedrals
- gardens
- wildlife sites
- country parks
- farms
- steam railways
- visitor centres
- leisure parks
- theme parks.

Catering

The catering industry is the single largest component of the leisure and tourism industry. Catering outlets include:

- pubs and bars
- restaurants
- cafés
- take-away restaurants.

While there are a large number of small independent catering outlets, the catering industry is dominated by large restaurant chains.

In many situations, catering is the main product being offered, for example, you might go to Pizza Hut for just a meal. Catering services are also a large part of many leisure and tourism organisations. Visitors to a theme park or a museum expect to be able to buy food and beverages during their visit. We will look at further examples of catering on page 23.

OCT 01–FEB 02

THE NATIONAL MUSEUM OF PHOTOGRAPHY, FILM & TELEVISION

NMPFT 2002

the Human Body

▲ Visitor attractions include the National Museum of Photography, Film and Television

Did you know...?

In 1998, the latest year for which statistics are available, more than 395 million visits were made to attractions in the UK.

- Alton Towers
- Blackpool Pleasure Beach
- Blackpool Tower
- The British Museum
- Edinburgh Castle
- Giant's Causeway, County Antrim
- Hadrian's Wall
- Hampton Court Palace
- London Zoo
- Offa's Dyke

OVER TO YOU

Visitor attractions in your area

Collect a range of leaflets on visitor attractions in the area from your local Tourist Information Centre. As a group make a display board showing the variety of visitor attractions available in your area. You might include a regional map and show where each attraction is located.

In the last three sections we have looked at the seven main components of the leisure industry. There are a range of organisations and facilities that fit into each of these components. These might include:

- leisure centres and health clubs
- community centres
- libraries
- museums and galleries
- video rental shops
- sports venues
- cinemas and theatres
- theme parks
- pubs, restaurants and take-away restaurants.

Each organisation or facility tries to ensure that its products and services meet the needs of the customers that it aims to attract. Here are some examples of specific leisure organisations and the way that they satisfy the needs of their customers.

Leisure centres and health clubs

A wide range of people visit leisure centres and health clubs. Customers may include the elderly person who has taken little exercise but wants to get fit, and the professional sportsman or woman who uses the centre for intensive training. Because there is such a wide range of customers, centres and clubs need to offer a variety of products and services to meet their individual needs.

CASE STUDY

LivingWell

LivingWell are a chain of national health and fitness clubs with 82 clubs throughout the UK. They offer a range of classes, including fitness classes. These classes are classified for beginners, intermediate and advanced levels so members can choose the right class for their needs.

LivingWell offer a range of general facilities ▶

Libraries

Many people see visiting libraries as a leisure activity. However, people do not visit libraries just to borrow a book. Most libraries offer a lot of other services to meet the needs of different customers. Read the case study on Brent Libraries.

CASE STUDY

Brent Libraries

Brent Libraries aim to meet the needs of all of their customers. Here is their Mission Statement:

We aim to be a focus of community access to knowledge, information, works of the imagination, culture and heritage.

Brent Libraries meet the needs of their customers through the huge range of services that they offer. They include:

- books, CDs, cassettes, videos and DVDs for loan
- reference books and magazines
- newspapers and magazines
- access to multimedia CD-ROMs
- desk-top publishing
- holiday activities for children
- pre-school literacy and numeracy project
- senior citizens drop-ins
- arts exhibitions, displays and workshops.
- large-print and talking books
- newspapers and information
- toy loans
- public internet access
- word processing
- photocopying
- under-fives story times
- children's library clubs
- homework support
- visits from school classes
- writers' groups

Video rental shops

Video rental shops have changed in the last 20 years. When they first appeared in the 1970s they tended to offer one product – videos. However, as the market has developed, so have customers' needs. Spending an evening watching a video has become a regular leisure activity for many people, but other products are frequently involved in this activity. For example, video rental may be accompanied by a take-away meal and perhaps a bottle of wine. Video rental shops are usually near to take-away shops that offer food such as Indian, Chinese, pizza. They are also near to off-licences. It means that customers can choose their video while their take-away order is being prepared. Video shops have been quick to identify additional products that they could offer to help customers enjoy the 'video experience'. Many now stock a range of popcorn, confectionery, soft drinks and quality ice creams, in fact, everything that you would expect when watching a film at a cinema.

Did you know...?

- If the all the shelves of books at the British Library were laid end-to-end, they would reach from the British Library in London to the National Library of Scotland in Edinburgh.
- Visiting libraries is more popular than going to the cinema.
- More people visit museums than go to theme parks and pop concerts.
- More than 60 per cent of adults are library members.
- People in England pay 303 million visits to public libraries every year and borrow 480 million books.

Source DCMS

OVER TO YOU

Leisure services

Look at the list of services offered by Brent Libraries. As a group, discuss which specific services might be of interest to the following groups:

- general public
- students doing research for course work
- families
- tourists visiting the area
- special interest groups
- businesswomen and men.

Cinemas and theatres

Cinemas and theatres aim to attract a wide range of customers by offering a variety of entertainment to meet the needs of different customers. For example, a multi-screen cinema such as Warner Village Cinemas will think carefully about the films that they screen at any one time to ensure that there is 'something for everyone'.

Likewise, a theatre tries to provide different types of live entertainment to appeal to different types of customer.

WARNER VILLAGE CINEMAS

08702 406020

BASINGSTOKE LEISURE PARK

Where cinema comes to life

book online: www.warnervillage.co.uk

From Fri 25th to Thurs 31st July

Pearl Harbor (12)
Thurs only Preview 11.45, 12.15, 12.45, 3.30, 4.00, 4.30, 7.30, 8.00, 8.30

One Night At McCools
(15) (11.30 Sat/Sun) Daily 4.10, 6.45, 9.00 Fri/Sat Late 11.25

The Mexican (15)
(11.40 Sat/Sun) Daily not Thurs 2.45, 5.35, (8.30 not Tues) Fri/Sat Late

The Dish (12)
Daily 3.25, 4.30, 5.10,

All The Pretty Horses
(15) (12.40 Sat/Sun) Daily 3.15, 6.00, 8.40 Fr/Sat Late 11.20

15 Minutes (18)
Fri-Wed only 7.10, 9.50 5.35, Fri/Sat Late 11.10

Bridget Jones Diary
(15) (11.10 Sat/Sun) Daily 1.30, 3.50, 6.20, 8.50 Fri/Sat Late 11.10

The Mummy Returns
(12) Daily 2.10, 3.25, 5.10, 6.40 (8.30 not Tues)

The Dish (12)
Daily 3.25, 4.30, 5.10, 7.00, 9.20 Fri/Sat Late 11.50

Rugrats In Paris (U)
(12.20 Sat/Sun) Daily 2.30

Spy Kids (U)
(12.10 Sat/Sun) Daily 2.40

See Spot Run (PG)
(11.20 Sat/Sun) Daily 1.45, 4.05, 6.35,

15 Minutes (18)
Fri-Wed only 7.10, 9.50 5.35, Fri/Sat Late 11.10

▲ A range of films at Warner Village Cinemas

© TM 2002 Warner Bros

OVER TO YOU

Discuss and match

Look at the range of entertainment offered by The Grand Opera House. Discuss which type of customer each form of entertainment is aimed at. Be careful – *The Sooty Show* might be popular with very young children but it is unlikely that they would go to the show on their own.

GRAND OPERA HOUSE YORK

www.ticketmaster.co.uk
BOX OFFICE 01904 671 818
TICKETMASTER 0870 606 3595

Pubs, restaurants and take-aways

Pubs, restaurants and take-away restaurants are a major part of many people's leisure time and have therefore become very competitive. They all try to identify the needs of specific customers and provide products and services that meet these needs. In recent years there has been a big increase in the number of families that go to pubs for meals. As a result, many pubs adapted the products and services that they offer to meet the needs of the family market. Many now have special family areas, children's menus, play equipment and games.

▲ Terminal 4 at Heathrow Airport

OVER TO YOU

Matching people to eating places

Travellers at British airports want to be able to buy food and beverages at any time of the day. Terminal 4 at Heathrow Airport offers a range of catering facilities, some of which are listed. Identify to which outlets the following people might go:

- a family with young children wanting a meal
- a student on a tight budget wanting a snack
- a business woman and man wanting a relaxed dinner
- an elderly couple wanting breakfast
- two young adults wanting a drink and light meal.

Outlet	Description	Customer
Wetherspoons	Traditional English pub	
Starbucks (two outlets)	Coffee bar	
Costa Coffee	Coffee and snack bar	
Arbuckles	Waitress-served American-style restaurant	
Caffe Italia	Coffee bar	
AMT Espresso	Coffee kiosk	
Seafood and Oyster Bar	Island-site, circular restaurant	
Costa	Coffee and snack bar	
Garfunkel's Bar	Cocktail bar and savoury snacks	
Garfunkel's	American-style restaurant	
Coffee Republic	Coffee and snack bar	
McDonald's	Fast food burger bar	
Pret á Manger	Sandwich and coffee shop	
Metro Café	Savoury snacks and coffee	
Caffe Uno	Italian style cafe and pizza restaurant	

Community centres

Community centres are set up with the aim of meeting the needs of the local community. They usually offer a range of different leisure activities. Some may be aimed at specific people within the community, such as the young and they may have a Youth Club that uses the facilities.

Museums and galleries

Museums or galleries have changed from housing dusty exhibits in glass cabinets. Nowadays there is a vast range of different museums and galleries aimed at different customers. A large number are interactive and use advanced technology to help bring the exhibits 'alive'.

Many museums have stopped using the label because it is felt that the word has an old-fashioned image. Instead they use names such as 'Experience'. Many museums are based on a specific theme, such as:

- food
- the environment
- transport
- sea life
- science.

Sports venues

Sports venues include a variety of different types of venue, from local football and rugby clubs to national centres, such as Lords Cricket ground, Epsom Race Course, Wimbledon and Silverstone. Clearly the type of sport that takes place at each will appeal to those people who are interested in the sport. While some venues such as St Andrew's Golf Course will focus on just one type of sport, other venues may stage a variety of sports to appeal to a wider proportion of the public.

Museums meet the needs of different types of customers through using different themes ▶

Identify sporting venues

OVER TO YOU

In pairs, try to identify two sporting venues (other than ones mentioned above) that host the following sports. Fill in your choices on the table.

Sport	Venue 1	Venue 2
Football		
Rugby		
Golf		
Athletics		
Motor racing		
Horse racing		

Theme parks

Theme parks are big business in the UK. In fact, we go to theme parks more often than any other European country. Favourite theme parks include:

- Alton Towers
- American Adventure
- Blackpool Pleasure Beach
- Camelot
- Chessington World of Adventures
- Drayton Manor
- Flamingoland
- Lightwater Valley
- Thorpe Park.

Theme parks appeal to a large number of people from children and young adults to families, couples and older adults. However, different customers will have different needs and expectations. While teenagers and young adults might visit a theme park for its 'white-knuckle rides', a family with small children may be more attracted to the zoo, picnic areas and children's rides and entertainment.

White-knuckle rides are often used by theme parks as an attraction for people to visit. Each theme park tries to introduce new rides that are the biggest, fastest and scariest. Such rides include:

- The Black Hole, Alton Towers
- The Big One, Blackpool Pleasure Beach
- The Corkscrew, Alton Towers and Flamingoland
- The Depth Charge, Thorpe Park
- The Detonator, Thorpe Park
- The Katanga Canyon, Alton Towers
- The Missile, American Adventure
- The Nightmare Niagara, the American Adventure
- Nemesis, Alton Towers
- Oblivion, Lightwater Valley
- The Rattlesnake, Chessington World of Adventure
- The Shockwave, Drayton Manor
- The Skycoaster, the American Adventure
- Submission, Alton Towers
- The Terrorizer, Flamingoland
- The Ultimate, Lightwater Valley.

▲ Rides attract visitors to Lightwater Valley theme park

Big rides do help to attract customers, and most expect more services and products while they are at a theme park. Thorpe Park offers the following services and facilities to visitors:

- Toilets/toilets for the disabled
- Telephones
- Cash dispensers
- Nursing mothers
- Baby changing
- Drinking water fountains
- First aid
- Happy Memories
- Guest lockers
- Lost and found (people or property!)

Home-based leisure

Home-based leisure has always played an important part in the way we spend our leisure time. However, the types of activities that are included have changed considerably over the last few decades. During the 1950s people might have spent their time at home reading, listening to the radio, playing board games and watching television if they had a set.

These activities are still popular today, but there are a vast number of other activities that have also become available. Even an activity such as watching television has changed. Forty years ago you could choose from two black-and-white channels that screened programmes for part of the day only. Now 24-hour colour television is available on five terrestial channels and many more satellite channels. You are also able to record programmes on video and watch them when you like.

The increase in the range of home-based leisure activities has meant that facilities have been created to satisfy customers' needs and include:

- take-away restaurants
- video rental shops
- bookshops
- libraries
- shops that sell computer games.

It started with fish and chips ▼

1780	'Chippers' appear in Northern England
1819	first fish and chip shop opens in Yeadon
1890s	hamburgers introduced in USA
1920s	first chains of USA hamburger bars arrive
1940s	modern-day pizza introduced in the USA
1950–70s	Chinese, Indian and other ethnic take-aways open in the UK
1955	First Wimpy Burger opens in London and Kentucky Fried Chicken is introduced in the USA
1965	Kentucky Fried Chicken opens in Britain
1974	McDonald's open first outlet in UK in Woolwich, London
1980s	widespread appearance of pizza take-aways in UK
1990s	drive-thru take-aways introduced in the UK
1990s	rapid expansion of ethnic take-aways, including Japanese and Mexican.

Take-away restaurants

Take-away food outlets can now be found on every main street in the UK. The range includes fish and chips, burgers, Chinese, Indian, Italian and kebabs.

The UK take-away industry is thought to have started over 200 years ago with the original fast food – fish and chips. Since then, the take-away market has expanded considerably.

Video rental and computer games shops

As we saw on page 21, video rental shops now stock a wide range of products as well as videos. Films on DVD are becoming increasingly popular and most outlets stock both video and DVD. Many video rental shops encourage customers to use them by promoting forthcoming releases through advertising on television and in newspapers, or by giving customers monthly magazines.

There has been an interesting change in the types of films offered by video rental shops in the last 20 years. In the 1980s most shops offered a wide range of films but only stocked a limited number of copies of each. Now the trend is towards having a smaller range of films but far more copies of them. In fact, *Blockbusters* stock so many copies of popular new releases that they offer a night's free rental of the top films if they cannot supply it on the night that you want it. This change is because film production companies want to make as much money as possible from each film that they release. Films are usually released in the following order:

- premiere of the film at selected cinemas
- general release of the film to all cinemas
- film available through video rental shops and to buy
- film sold to satellite television such as Sky Box Office
- film shown on other satellite film television channels
- film shown on terrestrial television channels such as ITV or BBC.

▲ Blockbusters' magazine promotes the big October video release – *Bridget Jones's Diary*

Bookshops and libraries

Reading has always been a popular home-based leisure activity that is provided for through bookshops and library facilities. Books are also available through an increasing number of outlets, such as supermarkets and gift shops at visitor attractions.

Identify home-based leisure outlets

OVER TO YOU

The next time you visit a local town or city centre make a list of the outlets that sell products for the home-based leisure market. Compare you findings with the rest of the group. The outlet does not only have to specialise in home-based leisure, such as a computer game shop. A shop such as Woolworth's has a large number of products that are designed for home-based leisure.

In the last few sections we have looked at some of the specific products and services offered by leisure providers. Many of these providers offer a wide range of different products and services to meet the needs of their customers. A leisure centre might offer:

- sports activities
- lessons and classes for different groups of people
- functions
- food and drink
- special rates for members or groups
- purchase and hire of equipment.

It is important that a leisure centre is able to offer sufficient products and services that meet all of the needs of their customers. Customers may visit a leisure centre mainly because they want to go swimming. They will probably also expect to be able to buy refreshments and perhaps some equipment, such as a swimming cap. Likewise, adults who usually go to the centre to play squash may want to book a birthday party for their children at the centre.

CASE STUDY

Doncaster Dome – Europe's largest indoor leisure complex

The Dome is a unique entertainment and leisure complex, the like of which is rarely seen outside the USA and Germany. With spectacular sports facilities, first-class dining, luxurious health studios, state-of-the-art conference halls and a superb programme of live entertainment, it's an ideal haven for all ages. The Dome is arguably the best venue in Britain for combining business and pleasure.and workshops.

Facilities
Activities on offer include:

- Five-a-side football
- Volleyball
- Basketball
- Badminton
- Table tennis
- Short tennis
- Indoor bowls
- Netball

Equipment hire is available.

Wet, wild and wonderful
Splash into the geysers and fountains, zoom down the flume rides, relax in the spa pools or brave the rapids and the stepping stones at a magical seven-pool water world. Classes available for all ages.

The Dome Dippers Scheme
Tuesday and Wednesday at 11.00–11.30 a.m., 11.30–12 p.m., 12.00– 12.30 p.m. and 12.30–1.00 p.m. There are three grades and award stages all with certificates and badges for children aged four years and under. The scheme is aimed at increasing confidence and skill development in the water through a number of fun activities. This is a great way to introduce your children to the water. Each person on the scheme will receive a passport.

Graded Swimming Classes
Available for grades 1 to 5.

Private Functions @ The Dome

Making Your Special Day Extra Special

The Dome has a variety of function rooms on offer. Our experienced staff can help you organise your own function, from room design to choosing menus and drinks packages. We have a range of rooms to accommodate all parties, small and large:

- The Icebreaker Lounge can accommodate up to 150 people.
- The Sports Bar can accommodate up to 70 people.
- The Conference Room can accommodate up to 130 people.

Food and drink

A Ribena party at The Dome is special for everyone – problem-free for Mum and Dad, and maximum fun for all the kids. With an extensive range of activities to satisfy every child's needs, The Dome adds the finishing touches to make your child's birthday one to remember.

Party package

Location – Mall Diner
To include – Chosen activity – Dome Kid's Meal and Ribena drink – Party Bag – Birthday Card
You may upgrade your meal or add an activity for an additional fee.

Identify products and services

Get a selection of leaflets from some local leisure facilities such as sports centres, theatres or visitor attractions and share them out amongst the group. In pairs, identify the range of products and services each one offers. Present your findings to the rest of the group.

Different people choose different activities during their leisure time. Six main factors influence their choice:

- age group
- special needs
- gender
- culture
- type of household
- social group.

These factors are looked at in detail in both the Marketing (page 82) and Customer Service (page 154) sections.

Older people may enjoy activities such as crown green bowling more than younger people ▼

Day	16-year-old	74-year-old
Mon	Local youth club in evening	Amateur dramatics society club in evening
Tues	Tenpin bowling with friends in evening	Crown green bowling club in afternoon
Wed	Cinema to see new horror film	Theatre to see Noel Coward play
Thurs	Night in playing computer games	Night in reading
Fri	Take-away pizza and video at friend's house	Dinner party at home with friends
Sat	Day at local theme park	Day at local art gallery
Sun	Listening to music and watching Sky television	Gardening and DIY

▲ Different age groups often choose very different activities in their leisure time. Compare the weekly leisure activities of a 16-year-old and a 74-year-old

Age group

In the table, both the 16-year-old and 74-year-old took part in similar types of activity, such as clubs, sport, going to a visitor attraction, entertainment and home-based leisure. However, the actual activity was very different. Although this example is a generalisation, it is useful to recognise that different age groups may find different leisure activities appealing.

Culture

When we talk about **culture** we mean the traditions, tastes, opinions and behaviour that influence us. Young people are strongly influenced by 'youth culture', in other words, the behaviour, tastes and opinions of other young people. This may influence the type of music they like, the sports they take part in or watch, or the types of films that are popular. Likewise, many leisure activities are seen as part of the British culture. Americans and others view take-away fish and chips, pigeon racing and caravanning as quaint British pastimes.

We are influenced by the behaviour of those around us ▼

OVER TO YOU

Match age groups to the advertisement

Use a copy of your local paper.

- In pairs, identify as many examples of advertisements for leisure providers and activities as you can. Include sports facilities, visitor attractions, catering, art and entertainment.

- Decide which specific age groups might appeal to each. You may find that some providers offer products for different age groups, For example, does your local cinema have a Saturday morning children's film and then other films in the afternoon and evening?

Special needs

Many people have special needs that affect the leisure activities they choose. For example, someone with a mobility or sensory impairment will find some activities more accessible than others. In recent years there has been a growing realisation that people with special needs should be able to enjoy as wide a range of leisure activities as everyone else. Sports centres frequently offer specific sessions for customers with special needs. Most visitor attractions try to ensure that their products are accessible to customers with mobility impairments and many offer special facilities and services to meet the needs of these customers. Likewise, many theatres offer signers and hearing loops so those customers with sensory impairments can enjoy productions. However, there are still areas of the leisure industry where people with special needs seem to meet barriers.

◄ Young disabled people have the same right to enjoy leisure activities as everyone else

OVER TO YOU

Sponsorship for the disabled

Read the case study on Sport and disabled youngsters. As a group, discuss what you think the main barriers are to young disabled people taking part in sport. Sport England say that they are 'pumping millions of pounds into improving opportunities for disabled people'. Based on your discussion of the main barriers, what do you think these millions of pounds should be spent on?

CASE STUDY

Sport and disabled youngsters

Disabled youngsters take part in less sport, research reveals

Young disabled people across the country take part in less sport than young people overall – according to a new survey out today.

The results of the first English survey of young disabled people's participation in, and attitudes towards sport have just been revealed in a report commissioned by Sport England. Young people with physical, learning, sensory, and/or multiple disabilities between the ages of 6–16 were surveyed.

Running throughout the survey is the fact that, overall, sporting participation rates for disabled young people are much lower than for young people in general. Although Sport England is pumping millions of pounds into improving opportunities for disabled people, this survey shows that much more needs to be done to bring sporting participation rates among young disabled people up to the same level as the general population of young people.

The *Survey of Young People with a Disability and Sport* identified that:

- Over a quarter of young disabled people had not taken part frequently, i.e. at least ten times, in any sports, either in or out of school, in the last year. This compares to 6 per cent of the overall population of young people.
- Ten per cent of disabled young people had not taken part in any school sport at all during the past year.

- Outside of school the proportion of young people with a disability taking part in sport at least ten times in the last year was just 56 per cent compared to 87 per cent of young people in the general population.
- The young people surveyed offered several reasons why they did not take part in more sport.
- Only 10 per cent of all young disabled people gave lack of motivation or desire to do sport as one of the reasons or the main reason that prevented them taking part in sport during the past year.

Barriers to taking part in sport identified by disabled young people included:

- Lack of money, health issues, and the unsuitability of local sports facilities were all cited by 37 per cent of respondents.
- Unwelcoming staff and sports clubs were cited by 21 per cent of respondents.
- Local sports clubs not providing for people with their disability was cited by 3 per cent of respondents. This, coupled with the above 37 per cent who cited the unsuitability of local facilities for their disability, demonstrates that there are large gaps in sports provision for disabled young people.
- Discrimination from the general public or their own inhibitions was cited by 19 per cent of respondents.
- Lack of other people's time, e.g. to take them to sports clubs, was cited by 21 per cent of respondents.

Source: Sports England

Different types of household

On pages 30–31 we looked at how the age of customers can influence their choice of leisure activities. People often participate in leisure activities with others, usually friends and family. Therefore their choices may not be based on only their ages or individual interests but also the people that they spend their leisure time with. The type of household that people live in will have a direct influence on their leisure time and includes families, single people and couples.

For example, a woman aged 35 years might have specific and individual leisure activities, such as yoga classes and going to the cinema with girlfriends. If she has a partner she might choose leisure activities that both can enjoy together, such as playing squash and going to restaurants. If she has two young children her choice of leisure activities might be totally different; it might include going to theme parks and zoos with her children or perhaps the pantomime and children's films at the cinema.

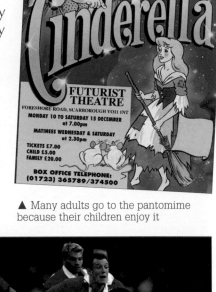

▲ Many adults go to the pantomime because their children enjoy it

By gender

Most leisure activities appeal to both male and female customers. However, there are some that are clearly more attractive to one gender than another. Aerobics tends to be more popular amongst women, whereas rugby tends to attract more men. Some leisure providers aim their products and services at just one gender.

▲ Rugby tends to be a male-dominated sport

Identify leisure activities

Each person in the descriptions lives in a different type of household.

■ Read the three descriptions.

■ In pairs, identify five different types of leisure activity that you think would be suited to each person. There are 15 in total. For example, do you think that Wayne would enjoy going to Art Galleries?

'I'm a Business Studies student at University and have a flat with three of my mates. We share all of the chores and try to cook a meal together in the evenings – but it's not good when it's Dave's turn as he can only cook toast. We all have our own friends but sometimes go out together for a drink or ask mates back to the flat. At weekends I like to chill out and sleep late then do something in the evenings.'

Wayne

'I am 55 years old and live with my mother. I work in a local bank so have evenings and weekends off. Mother gets very bored being stuck at home on her own all day so I try to take her out as much as I can. We try to keep fit but, of course, Mother can't do as much as she used to.'

Dorothy

CASE STUDY

The Sanctuary Spa Group

The Sanctuary, in London is a private health, exercise and beauty club for women only.

Britain's premier day spa – exclusively for women

Take the time to lavish some attention on a Very Important Person ... You or someone special!

Indulge yourself at The Sanctuary, Britain's original and most comprehensive Day Spa located in the heart of fashionable and vibrant Covent Garden. Pamper yourself in the unique and luxurious surroundings whilst experiencing some of the most effective treatments currently available.

Relax and have fun in the famous and beautiful Atrium swimming pool, share time with friends in our large whirlpool or simply unwind in the therapeutic warmth of our Steam Room or Sauna. There is also a Gymnasium and an Exercise Pool for use during your visit.

The Sanctuary's atmosphere is one of harmony and tranquillity, a wonderful haven away from the pressures of everyday life. We look forward to welcoming you and your guests.

Source: www. thesanctuary.co.uk

- Identify the ways that the club is described which will appeal to women.

OVER TO YOU

'I'm a marketing manager and my husband is a doctor, so we work very long hours. When we are not at work we like to spend our time with our two children, Tom (5 years) and Grace (8 years). We believe that families should do things together so most of our leisure time is spent with the children. However, in the evenings we like a little time together.'

Megan

Different social groups

The different social groups are explained in detail on page 91 of the Marketing unit. The social group that we belong to often influences the type of leisure activities that we take part in. For example, skiing and golf may be more popular amongst higher-income social groups than, say, darts and football.

Other important factors

Many other factors can influence people's choice of leisure activities. How much any or all of these factors influence someone's choice of leisure activities will vary according to individual circumstances. For example, some young adults might enjoy music and be interested in attending pop concerts. However, if they cannot afford the ticket price, do not have transport to get there or simply live too far away from a concert venue, then they are unlikely to choose this as a leisure activity.

Availability of local facilities

The facilities that are available locally will have a strong influence on how people spend their leisure time. For example, if there is no local tenpin bowling facility then clearly the local population is unlikely to participate in this activity. However, they might well choose to do so if there was a bowling facility.

▲ London has a very large local transport network

Availability of transport

Transport includes both private cars and public transport, such as buses, taxis and trains. Although people who have a car are generally more able to get to leisure facilities easily, factors such as parking can have an effect. Many local councils have introduced disc parking which allows people to park for a limited length of time, such as two hours. If such a scheme operates in an area surrounding, say, a cinema where the average film screening lasts two-and-a-half hours, then people may be put off going to the cinema because they cannot park nearby.

The availability of public transport can also have a strong influence on people's choice of leisure activities. Issues such as cost, transport routes and the frequency and times of services are important. People may decide not to go to the theatre if the last bus home leaves before the end of the show.

Personal interests

People's interests are going to have an influence on how they spend their leisure time. Those who have a very strong interest in a particular activity may devote a large amount of their leisure time to it in a variety of ways. For example, a football fan might spend time going to matches, watching football on television, reading football magazines, or playing computer games based on the sport.

Fashion

Many people are strongly influenced by fashion, particularly young people. Music is an obvious example of how fashion can influence our choice of leisure activities. A few years ago the Spice Girls were very fashionable and had a huge following amongst young people. They have since been replaced by performers such as Craig David, Westlife and Shaggy.

The influence of friends and family

We are all influenced by what our friends and family do in their leisure time because many leisure activities are done with them. This might even persuade us to choose a leisure activity that we would not usually choose.

Money

Money is a key factor when it comes to choosing a leisure activity. The amount of disposable income that people have will determine what they can afford. **Disposable income** means the amount of money that people have left over to spend on what they like after they have paid all their bills such as rent, food and electricity.

STOP & THINK

How often have you gone to a particular fast-food restaurant because that was where all your friends were going, when in fact you would rather eat somewhere else?

Westlife can fill any stadium on their tours – but how long will they remain fashionable? ▶

Tracking leisure activities

OVER TO YOU

Think back to all the leisure activities that you took part in during the past three weeks. Now answer the following questions:

- Which activities did I mainly take part in because they were available locally and easy to get to?
- What activities would I like to take part in but cannot because it is not available locally or transport is not available to get to it?

- Which activities did I do because my friends or family were doing them/ What would I rather have been doing?
- Which of the activities are particularly fashionable amongst my friends?
- If I had more money, what other activities might I have taken part in?

Discuss your ideas with the rest of the group.

The leisure industry offers a wide range of employment opportunities including:

- leisure assistants
- fitness instructors
- lifeguards
- ground staff
- park rangers
- restaurant managers.

The skills and qualifications that you need for these jobs will vary but all staff in the leisure industry need to enjoy working with people and be good at meeting and satisfying customer needs.

Leisure assistants

Leisure assistants are employed in leisure centres and carry out a range of tasks depending on the nature of the centre. The example here outlines the requirements for a leisure assistant at a Sports Centre. Similar examples can be found online at:
www.leisureopportunities.co.uk

▲ There are many job opportunities for trained fitness instructors

Charles A Nelson Swimming Pool and Lindisfarne Sports Centre, Alnwick

We are currently seeking an experienced Leisure Attendant / Duty Officer to assist with the supervision of two facilities ensuring compliance with relevant legislation and the supervision of staff.

Duties include taking bookings, collecting and accounting for cash, lifeguarding, setting out and dismantling equipment, cleaning and associated pool duties.

You will provide full cover for the Duty Officers as and when required, therefore you must have three years relevant service experience combined with a current National Pool Lifeguard Qualification and a First Aid at Work Certificate.

A National Pool Lifeguard Trainer/Assessor qualification and a Pool Plant Operators Certificate would be a distinct advantage, along with one year's supervisory experience and coaching qualifications. You will need to demonstrate a track record of achievement in leisure services provision and have excellent communication and customer care skills.

We welcome applications from people with disabilities who will be granted an interview if the essential job criteria are met.

Fitness instructors

With the growing interest in health and fitness there has been a large increase in the range of job opportunities for fitness instructors. Such jobs might involve designing and supervising individual customer fitness programmes, taking classes or acting as a personal trainer.

Lifeguards

Lifeguarding skills are needed for many jobs within the leisure industry. Staff working in a leisure centre that has a swimming pool would usually be required to hold a life-saving qualification. There are also opportunities within the industry for people wanting to be employed only as a lifeguard and there is a range of training courses and qualifications available.

Ground staff

Ground staff covers a wide range of different jobs and usually refers to staff that work around a facility, on the 'ground floor' such as cleaners, maintenance staff and gardeners. While some of these jobs may be seen as quite basic, leisure organisations value such staff highly and the contribution they make. For example, the Disney Corporation recognises that the staff that are most frequently approached by visitors are the cleaners who collect litter and keep the park clean. Therefore these staff are given extensive training in customer service skills and product knowledge so that they can answer visitors' questions.

Park rangers

'Park ranger' is a general term for staff employed in countryside recreation areas. The job is ideal for anyone who likes to work outside and covers a variety of duties, including forestry, conservation and dealing with the public.

Restaurant managers

Restaurant managers tend to have formal catering training and qualifications. Most will have worked their way up to the position having started as a waiter or waitress. There are many different job opportunities in a variety of different restaurants, from a five-star hotel to fast-food restaurants.

Ranger Service at High Woods Country Park in Colchester, Essex

'There is no such thing as a typical day. However there are a few things we may be asked to do. These include walking around the park, checking fishing permits, collecting litter, carrying out small-scale practical work, such as replacing a broken fence rail, or helping on a guided walk.

We may also be called upon to hunt for lost dogs, help people who are lost, talk to visitors about any management work being carried out, deal with wrong-doers, help injured animals, help the Emergency Services, chase escaped pet rabbits (no joke!). The list is endless.'

◀ Most of a park ranger's job is in the open air

Job opportunities in the leisure industry

OVER TO YOU

Look at the 'situations vacant' section of a local newspaper.

- Identify any job opportunities within the leisure industry.
- For each job that you identify, discuss what skills and qualifications are needed.

KEY TERMS

You should know what the following terms mean:

The leisure industry (page 12)
Leisure (page 14)
Sport and physical recreation (page 14)
Arts and entertainment (page 15)
Countryside recreation (page 16)
Home-based leisure (page 17)
Children's play activities (page 18)
Visitor attractions (page 19)
Catering (page 19)
Leisure centres and health clubs (page 20)
Libraries (page 21)
Video rental shops (page 21)
Cinemas and theatres (page 22)
Pubs, restaurants and take-away restaurants (page 23)
Community centres (page 23)
Museums and galleries (page 24)
Sports venues (page 24)

Theme parks (page 25)
Age groups (page 31)
Culture (page 31)
Special needs (page 32)
Type of household (page 34)
Gender (page 34)
Social group (page 35)
Availability of facilities (page 36)
Availability of transport (page 36)
Customer interests (page 36)
Fashionable trends (page 37)
Influence of family and friends (page 37)
Disposable income (page 37)
Leisure assistants (page 38)
Fitness instructors (page 38)
Lifeguards (page 39)
Ground staff (page 39)
Park rangers (page 39)
Restaurant managers (page 39)

If you're not sure or want to check your understanding, turn to the page number listed in the brackets.

Revision questions

1 In one sentence, explain what is meant by 'the leisure industry'.

2 Identify five different leisure time activities and describe the type of customer that each one attracts.

3 Explain the difference between spectator and participant sports. Give an example of each.

4 List the seven components of the leisure industry. Give an example of each.

5 For each of the components listed in the key terms, identify one organisation in each component, e.g. Catering – McDonald's.

6 Describe two ways in which leisure activities have changed in the last 20 years.

7 Explain what is meant by 'home-based leisure' and give four examples.

8 Identify what products and services a leisure facility might provide.

9 Explain five factors that might influence how people choose to spend their leisure time.

10 Select two jobs within the leisure industry and explain the main duties of each.

Investigation ideas

Assume that a group of students from Sweden are visiting you on a schools exchange visit. They are particularly interested in how the British spend their leisure time and have asked your group to give them a presentation on the subject. They have sent the following list of questions to you:

- What do young people do in their leisure time?
- What sort of leisure activities do families do at weekends, evenings and during holidays?
- What sort of home-based leisure activities do British people enjoy?
- What are the most popular spectator and participant sports?
- How have leisure interests changed in the last 20 years?

As a group prepare and give a short presentation that answers the above questions. Try to make the presentation as interesting and enjoyable as possible – think about what you would like to hear if you were the visiting Swedish students!

REVISION PROMPT

What have I learnt about the leisure industry?

_____

_____

_____

What am I still unsure about?

_____

_____

_____

How am I going to find out the extra information that I need?

_____

_____

_____

The travel and tourism industry in Britain is worth around £50 billion a year. Tourism provides nearly 1.5 million jobs in the UK, making it one of the biggest employers.

The term **'tourism'** refers to temporary travel away from home or work. An important part of tourism is the traveller's intention to return home after the visit. In 1999 the British took 123 million trips of one night or more. Tourism visits almost doubled in the ten years up until 1999. The reasons for a visit might include:

- holiday
- sightseeing
- visiting an attraction
- visiting friends or relatives
- going to a sports event as a spectator or to participate
- business.

Beach holidays are particularly popular with families ▼

Holidays

Holidays are a major part of the travel and tourism industry and range from a short break in a city or a package holiday to a European resort, to a world cruise or a camping holiday.

Holidays are a complex product made up of many other products. A typical holidaymaker will use a range of products such as transport, accommodation, catering and visitor attractions.

Sightseeing

Sightseeing is often part of a day visit to a destination but can also be part of a holiday. Many tourists will sightsee independently. In other words, they will visit a destination and find their own way around the main sights, perhaps using guidebooks and maps. An alternative is to go on an organised sightseeing tour or holiday. A number of organisations provide these services, for example, the company Frames Rickards offers sightseeing holidays and day trips throughout the UK to a variety of destinations.

▲ Frames Rickards' typical sightseeing itinerary

Visiting an attraction

Many people make visits in order to see an attraction such as a museum, theme park, stately home or zoo. This may take up part of a day or the whole day, depending on the size of the attraction and how long visitors stay. Visitors to a large theme park tend to spend the whole day there whereas a visit to a local art gallery may take only a few hours and be combined with a meal out and sightseeing in the area.

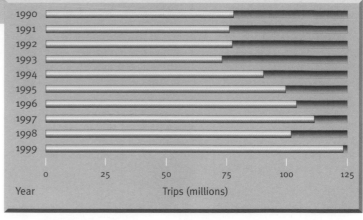

Year	
1990	
1991	
1992	
1993	
1994	
1995	
1996	
1997	
1998	
1999	

0   25   50   75   100   125

Year   Trips (millions)

▲ UK visits in the 1990s

Cycle Fest is a three-day sporting holiday ▶

Visiting friends or relatives

Visiting friends and relatives accounts for a large percentage of the trips taken. Of the 123 million trips taken in the UK in 1999, 42 million were to visit friends and relatives. It is an important part of the travel and tourism industry. Although these visitors do not pay for accommodation they often use a wide range of other travel and tourism products and services, such as transport, restaurants and visitor attractions.

Identify tourist facilities

Think about the travel and tourism facilities in your area. In pairs identify which facilities the following visitors might use:

- a family on holiday in the area
- a day visitor who wants to go sightseeing or visit an attraction
- an elderly couple staying with relatives
- a business person staying in the area for four days to attend a conference.

Sports events

Sports tourism is a rapidly growing area of the travel and tourism industry. People have gone on day trips to sporting events for many years, either as spectators or participants. Recently there has been a growth in the number of organisations offering holidays that are based on sporting events such as international football games and horse racing. These holidays usually include transport, accommodation and entrance tickets to the sporting event.

Business

A lot of the money generated in tourism is through business travel. People travel to attend conferences, meetings or as part of their job, such as salespeople. While the main reason for travelling is not tourism, many of the products and services bought by these business people will be provided by the travel and tourism industry. A business traveller visiting London for a two-day conference will probably stay in a hotel, eat in restaurants and may go to the theatre or a nightclub.

The term travel and tourism covers an enormous range of activities in different situations. The industry is made up of a number of parts or components:

- travel agents
- tour operators
- tourist information and guiding services
- online travel services
- accommodation and catering
- transportation.

▲ Travel agents are found on most UK high streets

Travel agents

Travel agents provide a range of travel and tourism products. While they are recognised as selling mainly package holidays they also offer flight bookings, currency exchange, guide books and a variety of other services.

Airport parking

We can organise your long-stay parking arrangements at all regional airports at very competitive rates. Please ask your Going Places travel adviser for full details.

Airport hotels

Sometimes it can be more convenient to stay overnight at a nearby hotel than travelling long distances to airports in the early hours of the morning. Ask your travel adviser for prices and availability of accommodation.

Airport transfers

If you'd rather not leave your vehicle in an airport car park while you are away, we can arrange for transport to collect you from your home and drop you off at the airport, and then pick you up from the airport for the return journey. Ask in store for full details and rates.

Car hire

Going Places can arrange your holiday car hire needs.

▲ Additional services offered by Going Places

Although there are a large number of small, independent travel agents, the market is dominated by the large multi-agents such as Thomas Cook, Lunn Poly and Going Places. These chains of travel agents have grown rapidly over the last 20 years, to the extent that many of the smaller companies have been forced out of business because they could not compete.

Tour operators

Tour operators are the organisations that put together and sell package holidays. They need to work with transport providers, accommodation suppliers and other services, such as excursion providers, in order to produce a package holiday. They usually sell their holidays through travel agents although some sell directly to the public, such as Portland Direct. As with travel agents, the market is dominated by a few large multinational companies such as JMC (previously known as Thomas Cook Holidays), Thomson Holidays, First Choice and Airtours.

CASE STUDY

The history of Lunn Poly

In 1893, Dr Henry Lunn founded the Cooperative Educational Tours for lecturers and the 'educated classes' to travel throughout Europe, the Middle East and North Africa. Lunn chartered special trains and coaches.

By the late 1890s, Lunn had opened winter sports centres in Switzerland and was operating coach tours. At the beginning of the twentieth century Lunn was offering round the world tours for £220! In 1931 Lunn chartered the first holiday flight from Croydon with 24 passengers on board. The 1940s and 1950s saw the holiday market boom, with package holidays to Spain becoming popular.

In the 1960s, Sir Henry Lunn's company merged with the British Eagle Group and Poly Travel and the company was renamed Lunn Poly.

In 1972, Lunn Poly was bought by the Thomson Holiday Group and became Britain's largest overseas leisure travel group. By 1984, there were 176 Lunn Poly holiday shops, which grew to 505 by the end of 1989. The Lunn Poly chain continued to grow and by 1995 was the leading travel agency, employing 5500 staff.

Lunn Poly continues to develop its products and services to keep pace with change. In June 2000, it opened a new concept in travel agents at Fosse Park in Leicester. It contains five themed travel boutiques including Last Minute Deals, Families, Dream Escapes, Sunseekers and Short Breaks. In December 2000 Lunn Poly opened its first internet café-style store with two internet stations and a touch-screen kiosk for last-minute holidays.

All of the above companies operate under a number of different brand names. They sell package holidays using different brochures with different names to attract different types of customers. For example, the First Choice group includes the following brand names:

- First Choice
- Falcon
- 2wentys
- JWT
- Unijet
- Eclipse
- Sunstart
- Flexiski.

OVER TO YOU

Travel agents as tour operators

Because the work of travel agents and tour operators is so similar, it is not surprising that many tour operators also own travel agencies. It means that they can work together in producing and selling package holidays.

Working in pairs, find out which travel agencies the following tour operators own:

- JMC
- First Choice
- Thomson Holidays
- My Travel (previously Airtours).

The websites of these companies are a good source of information. They might also identify other travel and tourism companies, such as charter airlines, that are part of each group.

Tourist Information Centres and guiding services

Tourists are often in a location that they are not familiar with and will need advice and guidance. A significant part of the travel and tourism industry involves providing information to visitors. Much of this information may be in the form of guidebooks, maps and leaflets. However, many visitors want to speak to travel and tourism staff. One of the main ways in which information is provided to visitors is through visitor information centres. These centres may be in hotels or transport terminals. The largest network of information centres is the ETC-run Tourist Information Centres.

England has a network of 561 Tourist Information Centres providing information for visitors and the tourism industry in England.

The Centres all perform to a national standard and offer accommodation bookings, information on places to visit and transport options, and a wide range of guidebooks. The staff are trained to offer a professional enquiry service to visitors.

Most transport terminals have information centres ▼

Tourist Information Centres are primarily managed by the local authority and may offer a wider range of services than those described. Opening hours vary according to demand.

Visitor information is also provided through guiding services, such as guided tours around tourist attractions or destinations, or on transport such as buses and riverboats. Many large cities have a number of providers who offer organised guided bus tours of the city. The Big Bus Company in London offers visitors a guided tour of London on open-top buses. Visitors may get on and off the bus when they want to. For example, if customers want to stop and watch the changing of the guard at Buckingham Palace they can get off the bus and catch a later one to continue their tour.

FREE RIVER CRUISE AND WALKING TOURS

WINNER SIGHTSEEING TOUR OF THE YEAR 2000

THE BIG BUS COMPANY

LIVE ENGLISH COMMENTARY or A CHOICE OF LANGUAGES

10 YEARS IN FAMILY OWNERSHIP

NOVEMBER 2001 - MARCH 2002

HOP-ON HOP-OFF

◀ The Big Bus Company

Online travel services

With the growing use of the internet, it is now possible to buy almost any travel and tourism product through online travel services, such as:

- accommodation
- transport
- theatre tickets
- holidays.

It is easy to buy a hotel room, holiday or train ticket if you have a computer with internet access.

Accommodation and catering

Recently, the British public are eating out more and more, which is good news for the catering industry, but tastes have changed. Whereas a few years ago few families with young children would have thought of going to a pub for a meal, this is now a favourite choice for many. Likewise, in the 1950s Chinese and Indian food was not widely available and seen as a bit exotic. Now many people see such food as being a regular part of the British diet.

OVER TO YOU

Internet challenge

If you have access to the internet try this challenge. Working in pairs, which of you can find the cheapest flight from Heathrow airport, London, to Charles de Gaulle airport, Paris, for a week on Saturday?

Remember to print out a copy of the web page to prove your findings.

Accommodation	Catering
Hotels	Restaurants
Motels	Cafés
Bed-and-breakfast	Fast food and take-aways
Camping and caravanning parks	Catering at tourist attractions, sports venues and transport terminals such as airports and railway stations
Youth hostels	Inflight catering
Accommodation on transport, such as trains and ships	

▲ Accommodation and catering covers a huge range of different types of provision

OVER TO YOU

Restaurants and take-aways

In April 2001, National Opinion Polls (NOP) carried out a survey of restaurants and take-aways adults used in the last three months. The top ten are listed but not in the right order. In pairs, discuss in which order you think they should be.
1 Burger bar
2 Pub or pub restaurant
3 Café
4 Fish and chip shop/restaurant
5 Kebab restaurant/take-away
6 Hotel restaurant
7 Indian restaurant/take-away
8 Pizza restaurant/take-away
9 Traditional British restaurant
10 Chinese restaurant/take-away

Attractions

Countryside recreation refers to any recreational activities that take place in the countryside.

Visitor attractions play a major role in the travel and tourism industry. In many instances they are the sole reason for a visit. For example, visitors are willing to travel for several hours to the West Midlands for a day out at a large attraction such as Cadbury World or the Black Country Museum.

▲ The Black Country Museum offers a whole day's entertainment

Some visitor attractions facts		
Attractions in the top five categories		
Museums and galleries	1756	28%
Wildlife sites	315	5%
Historic properties	1521	24%
Country parks	290	5%
Visitor centres	489	8%
Farms	247	4%
Gardens	378	6%
Steam railways	106	2%
Workplaces	382	6%
Leisure parks	85	1%
Other	646	10%

A variety of smaller attractions are also important in encouraging visitors to go to destinations.

- There are at least 6215 attractions in the UK; 74 per cent of these are in England.

- Although only 4 per cent of attractions are in London, they account for 13 per cent (52 860 000) of visits.

Numbers of visits

- There were 404 million visits to attractions in 1999 (plus an estimated 12 million to parish churches); 81 per cent were to attractions in England.

- 57 per cent of attractions receive fewer than 20 000 visits per year; 76 per cent receive less than 50 000 visits.

- Attractions with over 200 000 visits make up 7 per cent of all attractions, but account for 58 per cent of visits.

Top ten English tourist attractions charging admission, 1999		
Ranking	**Attraction**	**Visits**
1	Alton Towers, Staffordshire	2 650 000
2	Madame Tussaud's, London	2 640 000
3	Tower of London	2 422 181
4	Natural History Museum, London	1 739 591
5	Legoland, Windsor	1 620 000
6	Chessington World of Adventures	1 550 000
7	Science Museum, London	1 480 000
8	Canterbury Cathedral	1 350 000
9	Windsor Castle, Berkshire	1 280 000
10	Westminster Abbey, London	1 268 215

Admission charges

- 41 per cent (2531) attractions provide free admission.

- In 1999, the average adult admission charge was £3.13. The lowest average was charged by Museums and Galleries (£2.32) and the highest average was Leisure Parks (£7.69).

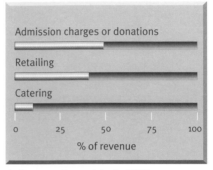

▲ Revenue from visits in 1999

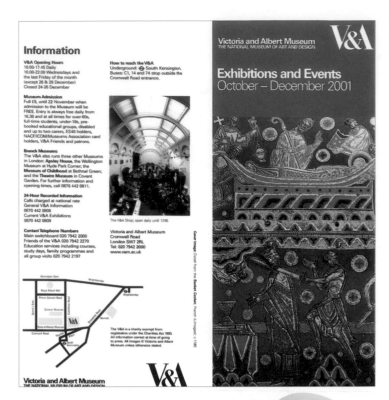

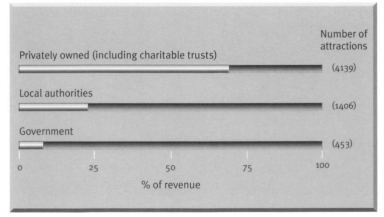

▲ Who owns the attractions?

Employment

- 68 per cent of attractions employ full-time permanent staff; 51 per cent employ part-time permanent staff. The average number of paid jobs at attractions is 18, of which seven are full-time permanent paid jobs.

- On average, 45 per cent of paid jobs at attractions are seasonal, with museums and galleries having the highest proportion of full-time permanent jobs (64 per cent) and leisure parks the lowest. Making allowances for part-time and seasonal work, the 6215 attractions surveyed in 1999 provided an estimated 56 000 full-time job equivalents, supplemented by large numbers of volunteers.

OVER TO YOU

Employment trends within tourist attractions.

As a group discuss the following:

- Why do you think that almost half of all jobs in tourist attractions are seasonal? What would the seasons be?

- Why do you think museums and galleries have the highest number of permanent staff and leisure parks have the lowest?

- Which tourist attractions might have volunteers amongst their staff?

Transportation

Most tourists rely on transport to get them to a tourist destination or attraction. The method of transport that they use could be by air, rail, sea or road. We will look at each of these methods of transport in detail on pages 56–9. It is useful to know which types of transport are favoured by tourists, and the reasons for their choice.

There are four main categories of transport ▼

Different transport needs

OVER TO YOU

One of the points made in the ETC survey is that tourists have different transport needs to commuters. As a group, discuss how you think these needs might be different. For example, would a family of four travelling to London by train for a day's sightseeing have different needs to a businesswoman going to the city for a business meeting?

CASE STUDY

ETC survey on tourist transport

A new survey by the English Tourism Council (ETC) shows that while a third of the population claim to be in favour of using public transport on holiday, the vast majority still used a car to go on their last tourism trip. The volume of tourism trips by car has increased by 58 per cent in the last ten years, compared with 30 per cent growth in bus and coach travel, and 48 per cent in rail.

The survey points out that the ease with which tourists can travel affects their choice of holiday. It warns that unless the capacity of our existing transport systems can be increased, tourists are more and more likely to face congestion on all types of transport. This could reduce their enjoyment of the trip and encourage both UK and potential overseas visitors to seek alternatives abroad.

The survey has found that:

- Tourist travel by road, rail and air has increased dramatically over the last ten years, with tourism trips increasing at a faster rate than transport journeys overall. Further increases are expected in the next decade.

- At the moment, tourists appear to be invisible as far as transport planning is concerned, despite the fact that they account for nearly 55 billion passenger miles in England every year.

- Some of England's best-known tourist destinations are facing particular problems from congestion and poor transport links. They include seaside resorts like Hastings and Great Yarmouth, countryside destinations such as the New Forest and Dartmoor, and historic towns like Canterbury, Stratford upon Avon and Bath.

- Holidaymakers and day-trippers have different transport needs to commuters and other traffic users, but these are rarely taken into account.

ETC chief executive Mary Lynch said: 'Tourists have different travel patterns and needs to commuters but this isn't always taken into account when transport plans are made. We need to 'think tourist'. Better information, facilities and connections would also help to make our public transport system more user-friendly for visitors.'

Source: www.englishtourism.org.uk

Holidays can be categorised in a number of ways:

- package
- domestic
- short-haul or long-haul.
- independent
- inbound or outbound

While day-trippers are an important part of the travel and tourism industry, many organisations focus on providing holidays for the tourist.

Package holidays

A **package holiday** means that the customer pays a set price for a complete holiday. This usually includes transport to and from the destination, accommodation and the services of a resort representative.

Depending on the nature of the package, a number of other services and products might be included, such as meals, entertainment, excursions and travel insurance.

A wide range of different destinations is offered as part of a package holiday. As with any tourism product, certain types are more popular than others.

▲ A typical package holiday to Crete

Tour Operator jargon

There are some terms and tour operator 'jargon' that are useful to know about when looking at package holidays.

- **Self-catering** – This refers to a holiday where meals are not included but the accommodation has facilities for holidaymakers to prepare meals for themselves. The type of accommodation might be in a villa, apartment or studio.

- **Room only** – This usually refers to a package holiday in a hotel where no meals are included. Customers may be able to pay extra in advance for meals. It is also used to describe basic accommodation where no restaurant or self-catering facilities are available, such as on Greek islands.

- **B&B** – Accommodation and breakfast are included.

- **Half-board** – Breakfast and one other meal (usually dinner) are included in the package.

- **Full-board** – Breakfast, lunch and dinner are part of the package holiday.

The ten most popular holiday destinations for UK citizens, 2000

Destination	People (millions)
Spain	9.5
France	6.9
Balearics	5.3
USA	2.6
Greece	2.3
Italy	1.4
Cyprus	1.2
Thailand	0.5
Morocco	0.5
Australia	0.2

Source: *Daily Mail*

- **Fully-inclusive** – Fully inclusive package holidays usually include all meals, drinks and often the use of entertainment, leisure and sporting facilities.

- **Flight supplement** – This is the extra amount that a customer has to pay depending on which airport and flight they choose. Generally they are highest when most people would prefer to travel, such as mid-morning, and lowest at less popular times, such as the early hours of the morning.

- **Occupancy supplement** – Most travel companies charge extra if there are fewer people in the accommodation than it can take. For example, two adults using an apartment that can accommodate four would usually have to pay an accommodation supplement. Likewise a single person may have to pay more for accommodation than a couple.

- **Child discount** – Many tour operators offer free child places or discounts for children under a certain age. The age that qualifies for a discount can vary from between 12 and 16 years depending on the tour operator. It is important to know that if a child discount is offered the child is usually not counted in the occupancy, as explained above. Two adults and two children in an apartment for four people are only counted as two people, which means that there may be an occupancy supplement!

- **Optional extras** – Tour operators offer an increasing number of extras in their package holidays that customers can choose to pay for. These include: pre-booking of flight seats, taxi transfer to the resort accommodation, welcome packs in self-catering accommodation, hire of equipment (such as fans and cots), rooms with sea views or balconies.

KIDS GO FREE! Guaranteed free holidays for children at selected properties, regardless of when you travel or which airport you depart from, as long as the child shares accommodation with two full fare paying adults. Be sure to book early, as they are subject to availability and are very popular.

When all the Kids Go Free holidays are gone, we'll ask you to pay the child's price as listed in the price panel.

Lowest price – guaranteed
Should we be more expensive we will match the lowest available price on identical, bookable holidays in any ABTA brochure in your travel agent.

Group bookings
We offer free places for groups with as few as twelve people. Call our Group Booking Department for details

No supplement for singles
At some of our properties we've negotiated special deals where lone travellers can occupy a single, twin or double room without having to pay a supplement.

Free lunch or dinner
Special deals such as Full Board for the price of Half Board or Half Board for the price of Bed & Breakfast on certain dates and departures.

2 weeks for 1
At some properties, particularly in low season, your basic holiday price is the same for a two week holiday as it is for one week.

Big reductions for room sharers
If more than two people occupy a room, the 'extra' people qualify for a discount (see price panels). Though, be warned, your bed may be a fold-up or a sofa-bed.

Free meals for kids
If two adults pay for half board, up to two kids get half board free or at half the adult price at many properties. The age limit's usually 12, sometimes 16.

OVER TO YOU

Visitor attractions in your area

Collect some tour operators' brochures – you will find the main summer brochures the most useful. Use the brochures to carry out individual research of package holidays and then create a display as a group. Each member of the group should look at some of the brochures and identify the following:

- What different types of accommodation are offered? What facilities are included?

- Where are meals included? Which types of restaurants and what kinds of service are available?

- What facilities and entertainment are included in the package?

- What supplements can be added to the package price e.g. flight, occupancy and optional extras?

When you have completed your individual research of the brochures, create a display as a group showing the range of facilities and services offered in package holidays. Cut out pictures and text from the brochures to make the display more eye-catching.

◄ The tour operator JMC clearly explains holiday costs in its brochure

Independent holidays

While package holidays account for a large part of the holiday market there is a range of other types of holiday that you need to know about.

Package holidays are designed to offer a standard product to a wide range of people. However, some customers have individual needs and interests that they do not feel can be met by a package holiday. These customers frequently take **independent holidays**. They independently choose and book the different parts of their holiday, such as the transport, accommodation, entertainment and catering.

These holidaymakers are all examples of the independent holiday market ▼

' My wife and I are both language teachers so want the children to be bilingual. We usually spend the summer holidays in France. We take the ferry over to France and then travel to different areas each year staying at camping sites.'

' We could not afford a package holiday but an aunt had a holiday cottage in the Lake District that she lent us. We took the train up there and spent the week walking and visiting local attractions. Most evenings we ate at the cottage or went to the local pub.'

' We had been to Spain on lots of package holidays and really liked it, but got fed up with staying in hotels. Two years ago we decided to buy a timeshare apartment there, so now we just book cheap flights and do our own thing.'

' I'd always wanted to see the world before I got too old to enjoy it! Once I'd finished my A levels, a friend and I bought plane tickets and packed our rucksacks, then set off on our travels – Australia, Thailand, New Zealand, Hong Kong (not necessarily in that order!) – the best three months that we'd ever had before settling down to life at university.'

OVER TO YOU

Types of holiday

Read the accounts of the four independent holidaymakers. As a group, discuss why you think each is more attracted to the independent holiday rather than a package holiday.

Domestic holidays

Some people take holidays in the country in which they live. They take **domestic holidays**. Others may take their main holiday abroad yet take holidays in the UK throughout the year. The domestic holiday industry is important to both of these groups. Remember that holidays include visiting friends and relatives and trips taken for business purposes.

Certain areas of the country are more popular for domestic trips than others.

Distribution of domestic tourism in England, 1999	
Destination	Trips* (millions)
Cumbria	3.6
Northumbria	5.1
North West	10.8
Yorkshire	10.4
Heart of England	19.7
East of England	16.3
London	14.8
West Country	19.1
Southern	12.2
South East	13.5
Total for England	123.3

*Trips may add to more than the total because more than one region may have been visited.

Domestic tourism includes: holiday trips, visits to friends and relatives and business trips of one night or more.

Source: UKTS

OVER TO YOU

Tourist attractions

In pairs, select one of the tourist destinations from the table. Each pair should select a different area. Using a map of England, identify the main cities, towns and countryside areas in your chosen area that might attract tourists. Report your findings to the rest of the group.

Inbound or outbound holidays

Holidays are also categorised according to whether they are inbound or outbound. **Inbound** refers to tourists coming into the UK from abroad, whereas **outbound** means UK residents going abroad.

Short-haul or long-haul flight holidays

A **short haul** is generally accepted to mean that the holiday areas are within five hours or less flying time from the UK. **Long haul** means that the flight time is more than five hours. Many tour operators produce different brochures for short-haul and long-haul holidays.

OVER TO YOU

Long-haul or short-haul holidays

Using some tour operators' brochures, identify whether each of the following destinations is a long-haul or short-haul holiday. You may have to work out the flight times using the flight information tables at the back of the brochure.

Destination	Short haul	Long haul
The Balearic Islands		
The Gambia		
Thailand		
Tenerife		
Morocco		
Florida		
Jamaica		
Corfu		
Malta		
Hong Kong		
Turkey		
Dominican Republic		

Transportation is one of the key components of the travel and tourism industry. We identified that the main types of transportation are air, rail, sea, and road (bus, coach, car, taxi).

Air travel

Almost 75 per cent of all package holidays sold in the UK rely on air transport to get their customers to their destination. There are two distinct types of air travel used in package holidays: charter flights (known as ITC or inclusive tours by charter) and scheduled flights (known as ITX or inclusive tour by excursion).

Inclusive tour by charter

A flight can be chartered or hired by a tour operator for a specific time and destination. Charter flights are cheaper than scheduled flights and rely on a high occupancy. They need to be full or nearly full to be profitable. If bookings are low the flight might be cancelled or combined with another flight to increase the occupancy. You may know of someone who has booked a package holiday and then received a letter before the departure date saying that the flight time had been changed. This will often be because there were not enough passengers on the original flight so flights were combined to increase the occupancy.

Airtours are an example of charter flights ▼

Inclusive tour by excursion

An ITX uses scheduled flights that fly to a published timetable regardless of the number of passengers booked on them. This may mean that they sometimes fly with few, or even no, passengers on board. This makes them more expensive to operate than charter flights.

Because fares are usually more expensive, the facilities and services on scheduled flights tend to be better than on charter flights. Seats and legroom may be more spacious and the standard of inflight catering and entertainment is often better. In recent years there has been a rapid growth in budget airlines such as Go, easyJet and Ryanair that offer cheap scheduled flights but with fewer services and facilities.

Some tour operators have realised that customers who buy a package holiday that includes a charter flight may be willing to pay extra for improved services and facilities.

◄ Ryanair aims its products at the budget end of the market

Premiair

First for customer service

- A personal seat-back TV on Airtours International's brand new A330-200 aircraft
- Award winning entertainment
- Bar, duty free† and gift service
- Fun packs for children on outward flights
- Dedicated Airtours check-in areas at Manchester, Gatwick, Belfast and Cardiff
- Celebrating? Then tell us about it! We can arrange champagne, chocolates or a cake (at a charge). Contact your Travel Agent or call our reservations department on 0870 241 2567. Minimum of 10 working days' notice required.

Airtours

Airtours' Premiair Gold service

In 2000, the Airtours tour operating company introduced their Premiair service because, they say, 'We want your holiday enjoyment to start at the moment you arrive at the airport.'

The added benefits of this service are shown in their brochure.

Package holiday survey

Carry out a small survey amongst friends and family who have gone on a package holiday that included a flight. Ask them what was good about the flight and what they think could have been improved.

Following on from your surveys, identify the factors that you think customers are particularly concerned about when travelling by air. For example, which is more important: no delays at the airport, a good inflight meal or lots of legroom?

Discuss your findings with the rest of the group.

Rail travel

Travel by rail is an established means of transport for tourists. In the past, the development of the railways in the UK played a major part in the growth of tourism. Rail links were created to tourist destinations and, in many cases, railway hotels were also built at these destinations to accommodate the visitors. Many towns and cities still have one of these original hotels near to the railway station, usually called something like the Station Hotel.

Rail companies realise the importance of the tourism market and many offer packages that combine rail travel with entrance to tourist attractions and events or accommodation. For example, Scotrail have teamed up with the Our Dynamic Earth attraction in Edinburgh and offer a combined train ticket and entrance to the attraction.

◄ Rail travel is a popular means of transport for tourists

Sea travel

Sea transport covers a range of different types of travel including car and passenger ferries, hydrofoils and hovercrafts.

Since the opening of the Channel Tunnel in 1995, ferry companies such as P&O and Stena have had to improve the onboard services and facilities in order to compete. Although using the Channel Tunnel is more expensive than using a ferry, it takes less than half the time to cross the channel and passengers can stay in their cars – a big advantage for many travellers.

Ferry companies claim that ferry travel gives passengers a chance to relax and have a break from the car. They developed a range of facilities to increase customers' enjoyment. Such facilities include restaurants, bars, shopping outlets and children's play areas.

On longer crossings from the UK, ferries include sleeping accommodation and facilities, and services are more extensive.

OVER TO YOU

Connecting ports and ferries

Using an atlas and working in pairs, work out which which European port is linked by ferry to which English port.

Once you have identified all of the correct ports, draw a map to show the ports and routes.

English port	European port
Portsmouth	Calais
Hull	Santander
Ramsgate	Le Havre
Plymouth	Ostend
Dover	Zeebrugge
Harwich	Cherbourg
Newhaven	Dieppe
Portsmouth	Gothenburg

C A S E   S T U D Y

The Pride of Rotterdam – North Sea Ferries service from Hull to Rotterdam

In May 2001, the *Pride of Rotterdam* came into service on the Rotterdam route. She and her sister ship, the *Pride of Hull* are the next generation of advanced and luxurious Cruiseferries which have set new standards in passenger comfort, accommodation and service. The extensive range of facilities includes:

- Sky Lounge
- Four Seasons Buffet restaurant
- two cinemas
- a variety of shops
- sundeck with bar
- continental café
- two-tiered Sunset Show Lounge
- children's playroom
- Cyber Zone
- wine bar
- casino and piano bar.

Road travel

Road transport includes bus, coach, car and taxi. A large proportion of tourists use road transport either to get to their destination or to travel around the destination once there. Visitors to London may use any or all of these transport methods to visit attractions.

Relative merits of different types of transport

People may use a variety of methods of transport to reach a destination and to travel around the area that they are visiting. A tourist visiting a Greek island might fly to the island, take a boat trip to a neighbouring island, go on a coach tour of the area, and hire a car to explore independently.

The method of transport chosen will depend on a number of factors including:

- cost
- convenience
- availability.

A tourist travelling to Italy might choose to go by plane because of the short journey time and the frequency of flights. However, another tourist might choose coach travel because it is cheaper than flying.

▲ Many tourists hire cars at their resort destination from companies, such as *Avis*

Suitable transport

OVER TO YOU

As a group, discuss which types of transport might be most suitable for each of the following people. You should consider cost, convenience and availability.

- a businesswoman from London who needs to attend a four-hour meeting in Glasgow in the morning and return to London for a further meeting in the late afternoon

- a family of four wanting to tour around the Lake District for a week's holiday

- A couple wanting to go on a 'theatre-break' weekend in Stratford-upon-Avon

- two university students planning to spend the summer touring around Europe.

In tourism, a tourist visits a destination. Some destinations are more popular and attractive to visitors than others. Visitors can be attracted by any number of different features, from the scenery and atmosphere of a location to the facilities offered.

A variety of destinations in the UK are popular with both UK and overseas visitors. These can include:

- coastal areas
- tourist towns and cities
- theme parks
- countryside areas
- sporting venues
- places of historic interest.

Coastal areas

Coastal areas include any destinations that are by the sea. They can range from bustling seaside towns, such as Blackpool, Torquay and Scarborough, to the 44 designated Heritage Coasts in England and Wales, such as some of the Dorset and north Norfolk shores. The attraction of coastal areas to visitors varies according to the type of destination. Different areas will attract a different type of visitor.

OVER TO YOU

Coastal destinations

Read the descriptions of the two coastal destinations. Discuss what types of visitors might go to each. What do you think would particularly attract each type of visitor?

CASE STUDY

The seaside town of Brighton

Brighton and Hove is the most enchanting, exciting, extraordinary seaside city in Britain. However brazen that may sound, it is no exaggeration.

With its cosmopolitan air, oodles of restaurants, feverish nightlife and abundance of culture, the place defies comparison with anywhere else this side of the English Channel.

For centuries it has been regarded as a 'pleasure dome', and that's not about to change. If you love life, welcome to Brighton and Hove, England's loveliest and liveliest city by the sea. Brighton and Hove is fun, cosmopolitan and uniquely eccentric all year round.

Regency architecture, pleasure pier, specialist shops, pavement cafés, lively arts scene and vibrant nightlife – everything's in walking distance, so take time to explore and enjoy.

Source: www.brighton.co.uk

The UK's National Parks

CASE STUDY

The Pembrokeshire Coast Path

Wales' first long-distance route, the Pembrokeshire Coast Path National Trail covers 186 miles (299 km) of the most spectacular coastal scenery in Britain. Opened in 1970 it is one of 14 premier long-distance National Trails in England and Wales, all waymarked by the acorn symbol. Most of the route is within the Pembrokeshire Coast National Park and the National Park Authority maintains the path with funding from the Countryside Council for Wales and the European Union.

National Parks and cities

OVER TO YOU

Using an atlas, identify where each of the National Parks are in the UK. Which National Park would be the closest to people living in the following cities?

City	closest National Park
London	
Manchester	
Exeter	
Norwich	
Cardiff	
Aberdeen	
Newcastle	
Birmingham	

Countryside areas

Any area of the countryside that has attractive landscapes and scenery is likely to develop as a tourist destination. The UK is known for its beautiful countryside, which includes forests, mountain areas and lakes. There are certain areas that are recognised as prime locations and are protected by law – these are known as the National Parks. The National Parks were established under the 1949 National Parks and Access to the Countryside Act. They serve two purposes:

- to conserve and enhance the natural beauty, wildlife and cultural heritage of the National Parks
- to promote opportunities for the public understanding and enjoyment of the special qualities of the Parks.

There are 11 National Parks in England and Wales, including Snowdonia, Dartmoor, the Lake District, the Yorkshire Dales and the Yorkshire Moors. A further four parks are planned in the New Forest, the South Downs and, in Scotland, Loch Lomond and the Cairngorms.

Further countryside areas that are also designated areas and legally protected include:

- Areas of Outstanding Natural Beauty such as the Cotswolds, the Lincolnshire Wolds and the Isle of Wight
- Heritage Coasts such as the Dorset and north Norfolk shores
- Marine Nature Reserves such as Skomer and Lundy
- Forest Parks such as Glenmore
- National and Local Nature Reserves
- Sites of Special Scientific Interest.

National Park statistics, 1998

Park	Designation year	Designation order	Visitor days (millions per year)
Brecon Beacons	1957	10th	7
Dartmoor	1951	4th	4
Exmoor	1954	8th	1.4
Lake District	1951	2nd	22
Northumberland	1956	9th	1.5
North York Moors	1952	6th	8
Peak District	1951	1st	19
Pembrokeshire Coast	1952	5th	4.7
Snowdonia	1951	3rd	10.5
Yorkshire Dales	1954	7th	9
The Broads	1989	11th	5.4

Source: The Countryside Commission, 1998

The National Parks

Yorkshire Dales National Park

Northumberland NATIONAL PARK

NORTHUMBERLAND

Newcastle upon Tyne

NORTH YORK MOORS NATIONAL PARK

LAKE DISTRICT

PARC CENEDLAETHOL ERYRI SNOWDONIA NATIONAL PARK

YORKSHIRE DALES

NORTH YORK MOORS

Leeds

Manchester

Sheffield

SNOWDONIA

PEAK DISTRICT

THE BROADS

Norwich

PARC CENEDLAETHOL PENFRO PEMBROKESHIRE NATIONAL PARK

Birmingham

PEMBROKESHIRE COAST

BRECON BEACONS

Cardiff

Bristol

LONDON

PARC CENEDLAETHOL BANNAU BRYCHEINIOG BRECON BEACONS NATIONAL PARK

EXMOOR

NEW FOREST

DARTMOOR

Plymouth

DARTMOOR NATIONAL PARK

EXMOOR National Park

N

0   km   100

Towns and cities

While many tourists enjoy the peace and tranquillity of coastal and countryside destinations, others are attracted to towns and cities. The UK is renowned for the wide range of tourist attractions and facilities in its towns and cities.

> You can visit London's Tate Gallery in the morning, and be swimming off Brighton beach by lunchtime, before dropping in on the exotic Royal Pavilion for tea. You could be seduced by Manchester's delightful street theatre in the afternoon and enjoying Birmingham's acclaimed Symphony Orchestra, Liverpool's outstanding Royal Philharmonic or Leeds' renowned Opera North in the evening. Beautiful Bristol and Bath are literally down the road from each other, and Cardiff, the handsome Welsh capital, is just over the border.
>
> Only an hour of your time separates Newcastle – that mighty stronghold of the North East – and the world's most famous festival city, Edinburgh. That other great Scottish city, Glasgow, is a mere 40 minutes away, hoarding a spellbinding collection of visual and performance art.
>
> You could see all these individual and original cities in a week – though every one is a treasure trove of contemporary and traditional art, music, theatre, dance and opera, so you will probably want to take longer or make several visits.'

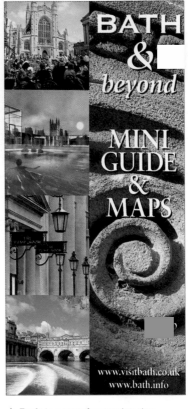

▲ Bath is a popular tourist city

OVER TO YOU

Tourism towns

Select a tourism town or city in your region. In pairs, find out what facilities and attractions it offers to visitors. Present your findings to the rest of the group.

It would be impossible to list all of the towns and cities in the UK that are popular tourist destinations. Some of the traditional destinations include:

- London
- Oxford
- Edinburgh
- Cardiff
- Chester
- Bath
- Stratford-upon-Avon
- York
- Plymouth

In recent years many cities and towns that were not known as tourist destinations have been developed to attract tourists. Cities such as Sheffield, Newcastle, Glasgow and Liverpool have invested a lot of money in new facilities and attractions that cater for the day visitor and short-break market. Many of these cities originally relied on heavy industry, such as shipbuilding or iron and steel. The decline of these industries meant that the cities needed to develop new facilities to attract business. Many turned to tourism as a way of improving the area.

CASE STUDY

Tourism in Yorkshire

There are many examples of towns and cities in Yorkshire that suffered decline in their traditional industries but have since successfully developed the area as a tourist destination. The extracts from the Yorkshire Tourist Board describe some of the attractions of four such destinations.

Bradford

Vibrant, diverse and full of surprises, Bradford City Centre is steeped in Victorian heritage and unique attractions. The Council produces a series of City Trails that provide a revealing insight into Bradford's rich heritage. Bradford is also home to the National Museum of Photography, Film and Television, which houses the 3-D Imax Cinema. Saltaire is a beautiful Victorian 'model' industrial village. It is situated four miles from Bradford. Walk or take a canal boat along the Leeds–Liverpool canal. Visit the beautiful Roberts Park and walk through to Shipley Glen where you can still catch the Victorian Tramway.

Leeds

Don't miss out on Leeds – the chance to enjoy superb nightlife, unrivalled shopping facilities, a range of state-of-the-art attractions, and some of the most breathtaking scenery in the whole of Britain.

Elegant Victorian and Edwardian Arcades, small boutiques and speciality shops meet with modern malls and the top household names – all found in a pedestrianised city centre. Away from the shops is an impressive range of attractions. The Royal Armouries is the first national museum to house part of the Royal Collection from the Tower of London in a £42 million home on the waterfront.

The Thackray Medical Museum is one of Leeds' newest attractions, revealing how medical advances have changed our lives. With its own international airport, excellent rail and road connections, you can be sure of one thing: Leeds is easy to get to, but so much harder to leave.

Hull

Welcome to the maritime City of Kingston upon Hull, the destination with a difference. A wonderful combination of old and new, from the cobbled streets of the Old Town to Princes Quay Shopping Centre. The marina forms an elegant focal point and is just a few minutes walk away from the city's fine selection of museums, shops and attractions. Discover Hull on foot by following one of the self-guided walks.

Wakefield

Heritage, history, shopping and sport are all on offer within the Wakefield District. The centre of the city itself is dominated by the spire of All Saints Cathedral which, at 247 feet, is the tallest spire in Yorkshire. The Wakefield Museum includes new displays and a new setting for the famous Charles Waterton collection. A visit to the National Coal Mining Museum for England will allow you to travel 250 feet underground and experience the conditions endured by coal miners over the years.

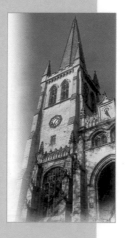

Sporting venues

We looked at some sporting venues on page 24. Many tourists will travel to a particular destination because they want to visit a **sporting venue**. For example, thousands of people go to London each June to watch tennis at Wimbledon.

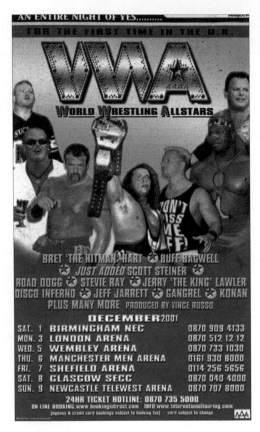

Many large stadiums also stage sporting events as well as other entertainment such as pop concerts. For example, World Wrestling is staged at a number of UK locations.

Theme parks

Because theme parks usually offer a full day's entertainment people are often willing to travel a considerable distance to get to the more popular ones. The creation of hotel accommodation at parks such as Alton Towers and Disneyland has meant that many visitors stay for more than a day at the destination. The main theme parks are spread throughout the UK and are usually situated near to good motorway links, meaning that many people have a park that is accessible.

◄ World Wrestling Association

OVER TO YOU

Locate theme parks

Some of the leading theme parks in the UK include those listed. Find out where each one is located. Are there any areas of the UK that do not have a theme park?

- Alton Towers
- American Adventure World
- Blackpool Pleasure Beach
- Chessington World of Adventures
- Drayton Manor
- Fantasy Island
- Flamingo Land
- Lightwater Valley
- Legoland
- Oakwood Park
- Pleasureland
- Thorpe Park.

Places of historic interest

For many **overseas and domestic visitors** one of the main attractions of the UK is its strong historical and heritage image. In 1999 over 67 million people visited historical properties out of the 219 million total number of visits to tourist attractions – almost one third! Places of historical interest include:

- palaces and castles
- stately homes
- battlefields
- monuments
- ruins
- cathedrals and churches.

THE GREATEST PALACE IN BRITAIN

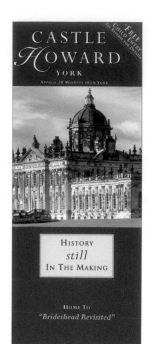

The UK offers a wide range of places of historical interest such as Tower Bridge, Castle Howard and Hampton Court

---

C A S E   S T U D Y

English Heritage

English Heritage is the UK government's statutory adviser on all matters concerning the conservation of England's historic built environment. It is also responsible for the maintenance, repair and presentation of over 400 properties in public ownership.

World heritage sites

To qualify for world heritage status, a site must be of outstanding universal value. The UK currently has 20 World Heritage sites, 11 of which are in England:

- Durham Cathedral and Castle (1986)
- Fountains Abbey, St Mary's Church and Studley Royal Park (1986)
- Ironbridge Gorge (1986)
- Stonehenge, Avebury and associated sites (1986)
- Blenheim Palace and Park (1987)

- Palace of Westminster, St Margaret's Church and Westminster Abbey (1987)
- City of Bath (1987)
- Hadrian's Wall (1987)
- The Tower of London (1989)
- Canterbury Cathedral (with St Augustine's Abbey and St Martin's Church) (1988)
- Castle and Town Walls of Edward I in Gwynedd (1986)
- St Kilda (1986) (natural site)
- Giant's Causeway and Causeway coast (1986) (natural site)
- Henderson Island, South Pacific Ocean (1986) (natural site)
- Edinburgh Old and New Towns (1996)
- Gough island Wildlife Reserve, South Atlantic Ocean (1996) (natural site)
- Maritime Greenwich (1997)
- Heart of Neolithic Orkney (1999)
- Historic Town of St George and Related Fortifications Bermuda (2000)
- Blaenavon Industrial Landscape (2000)

Source: DCMS

Tourism creates jobs and income, as well as providing enjoyment for those who take part in it. However, there can be some less welcome impacts of tourism if it is not managed in a responsible way. These impacts can be:

- social
- economic
- environmental.

Social impacts

There are many social advantages for the people in a tourism area. Job opportunities will usually increase and local people can take advantage of the facilities that are provided for tourists. However, if tourism is badly managed it can have a negative impact on the local community. In attracting tourists, a destination is basically inviting 'strangers' into the area. These strangers may behave in a very different way to the local people. For example, the local people in many British seaside resorts often complain about the drunkenness and rowdy behaviour of young adult tourists visiting their area.

▲ Some tourists are not welcome

Economic impacts

Increased job opportunities are a positive impact of tourism. A negative economic impact can be the loss of traditional employment opportunities. Growing tourism in countryside areas can often encourage local people to leave traditional jobs such as farming to follow careers in tourism. When this happens on a large scale the end result can be the loss of traditional skills and not enough people to fill local jobs.

Another negative impact that some tourism development can have is in increasing the local cost of living. This is a particular problem in poorer areas where the local population has a relatively low income. The development of such an area as a tourist destination will often result in prices rising simply because visitors are wealthier and can afford to pay more for products and services. It also means that the local population is faced with higher prices that they may not be able to afford. Local house and land prices can increase hugely in these areas, making it difficult for the local population. In the 1970s there was a large increase in wealthy people buying holiday homes in areas such as Wales. This caused house prices to rise dramatically. Young local people buying their first home could not afford the prices and had to move out of the area.

Environmental impacts

One of the main concerns in tourism is the harmful impact it can have on the environment. Tourists frequently have to travel some distance to get to tourist attractions or destinations and we can now travel further and faster than ever before. Many people do not mind driving for two hours to visit a theme park for the day or getting on a flight for a weekend in Paris. However, all forms of transport can have a negative impact on the environment. Bicycles and walkers can cause erosion of paths and traffic causes pollution and fuel consumption. Travel also results in noise, traffic congestion of roads, air space and waterways, and the building of transport terminals and car parks.

◀ Cycle paths have been created to encourage visitors to use a more environmentally friendly form of transport

Further environmental impacts come from the sheer number of visitors to an area.

- Overcrowding makes it difficult for locals to use and enjoy the facilities in the area.
- Large numbers of visitors can often create problems with litter.
- Traffic congestion from cars and coaches is a problem in areas that cannot handle a large amount of traffic, such as small narrow streets in historic towns or minor roads in countryside areas. At busy times this can lead to disruption for local road users, damage to roads and verges, and noise and air pollution.
- Increased wear and tear on the physical fabric of buildings or the countryside can be caused by the volume of visitors.
- Large increases in visitor numbers lead to pressure for new developments and problems can arise if these facilities are out of keeping with the setting.

One of the ways in which these harmful impacts can be reduced is through sustainable tourism. We will look at this on page 70.

OVER TO YOU

Impact of tourism

Tourists are often not aware of the damage that they might cause.

The results show that only 15 per cent thought that travel and tourism caused either major or a fair amount of damage.

Carry out a survey of friends and family to find out if they can identify any damage that tourism has on the environment. Ask each person the following two questions:

- Do you think tourism damages the environment?
- Can you give any examples of the damage that it causes?

Present your findings to the rest of the group.

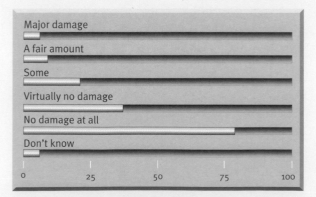

Results of a survey conducted by MORI, 1995

SUSTAINABLE TOURISM

Tourism can have social, economic and environmental impacts. These impacts can be managed through sustainability.

Sustainable tourism means that tourist attractions, facilities and destinations need to be developed in such a way that the existing area, buildings and scenery are not spoilt for future generations. The English Historic Towns Forum states that there are four principles which support more sustainable tourism:

- It must not adversely effect the environment.
- It must be acceptable to the community.
- It must be profitable for businesses.
- It must satisfy the visitor.

Many travel and tourism organisations behave in a responsible way by making sure that their products and services contribute to sustainability. The English Tourism Council gives some examples of Codes of Conduct for visitors that help to ensure sustainability.

The Countryside Code

The Countryside Code is a simple list of points to follow when walking in the countryside, in order to protect the countryside's beauty and paths. The code includes:

- close all gates behind you
- keep your dog under close control
- take your litter home
- keep to public paths across farmland
- use gates and stiles to cross fences, hedges and walls.

Ramblers policy on mountain bikes

The last few years has seen a marked increase in the popularity of the use of mountain bikes in the countryside. At the same time there has been more discussion surrounding the damage and danger they cause. In response to these concerns, the Ramblers Association has produced a policy on mountain bikes. It includes information on where in the countryside mountain bikes can be used and criteria for organising a mountain bike competition at venues in the countryside.

The Waterways Code

This code has been developed by British Waterways to protect the waterways and to consider others who may use them. The code includes:

- keep noise to a minimum
- do not damage the vegetation or water banks
- take home all litter
- leave the site as you found it
- never dump rubbish, sewage or oily bilge water into the water or onto the banks.

▲ The large number of people taking boating holidays on British canals can have a harmful effect on the environment

OVER TO YOU

A possible tourist development

The Gaiety Theatre is a 300-year-old building located on the main street of a historic town in the South of England. For 250 years it was one of the leading theatres in the area, attracting customers from a wide region. However, falling attendances meant that the theatre declined rapidly and was eventually used as a Bingo Hall.

For the last 15 years it has been closed and the building has had no renovation or maintenance. The once beautiful frontage is now an eyesore and the inside of the building needs urgent attention. The local council is worried that the building is getting into such a poor state that it could be dangerous.

A national chain of cinemas has applied to convert the building into a multi-screen cinema with a bar and restaurant. However, local residents are generally against the idea as they feel that the new use as a cinema would spoil the historical importance and appearance of the building.

As a group, discuss the ways in which the Gaiety might be developed as a cinema using the four principles outlined by the English Historic Towns Forum. For example, how could the historic frontage and name of the theatre be kept and preserved by the new owners?

The travel and tourism industry offers a wide range of employment opportunities, some of which you might consider as a future career. The Department of Culture, Media and Sport has found that over the last five years, tourism-related employment has grown by 12 per cent across Great Britain.

Employment opportunities include:

- travel consultants
- conference organisers
- coach drivers
- air cabin crew
- tourist guides
- resort representatives.

The main sectors of tourism-related industries and the numbers they employed in March 2000 ▼

Sector	Number employed
Hotels and other accommodation	349 600
Restaurants, cafés	419 900
Bars, pubs, clubs	459 500
Travel agencies, tour operators	113 200
Libraries, museums, other culture	79 100

▲ There are many opportunities for travel consultants in the tourism industry, including working in a central reservations office

Travel consultants

Travel consultants work in travel agencies or tour operators' reservations departments. They provide advice and services to customers wanting to buy travel and holiday products, such as package holidays or flights. As there is a range of different types of travel agencies, the responsibilities of a travel consultant will vary according to the needs of the business. In some situations a travel consultant may spend most of the working day dealing with customers face-to-face. In other situations, the consultant might deal with customers on the phone or use computerised systems.

AA Appointments
Position: Retail CRS Travel Consultants
Calling all Sabre ticketers and retail CRS travel consultants who want a fresh new challenge in an independent agency. This opportunity will allow you to develop your Sabre skills cross train from another CRS. You will be working as part of a small team issuing tickets on the Sabre system and dealing with some customer enquiries.

Allseasons Travel
Position: Travel Consultant
We are a busy independent agency offering the widest choice to our customers. We are looking for someone who is willing to work hard, can think on their feet and enjoys selling the right product to the right client.

For the suitable candidate we will offer a very competitive salary, uniform, generous holiday allowance and good opportunities for training and educational trips.

◄ ▲ The two job advertisements are from the trade magazine *Travel Weekly* and outline some of the duties of different types of travel consultants

There may be some terms in the advertisements that you do not recognise.

- educational trips – a free holiday to a specific destination offered to travel agency staff by a tour operator. This allows the member of staff to gain product knowledge about the holiday and therefore be able to describe it to customers more accurately.
- Sabre – the name of one of a number of computerised reservations systems used by travel agencies to check availability and book holidays, flights and other holiday products.
- CRS – a computerised reservations system. In hotel companies, CRS stands for central reservations system; it allows customers to book at any of the hotels within the company.

OVER TO YOU

Look at the two job advertisements on page 72. In pairs, discuss how you think the skills needed for each might differ.

▼ The Association of Conference Destinations (ACD) gives this job advertisement as an example of the type of person suited to the role

Conference organisers

The conference industry is a major part of travel and tourism. People who work in this industry often have a background in another area of travel and tourism, such as hospitality, marketing or transport.

A conference organiser holds a senior position that requires a wide range of management skills and experience.

An international company based in London, seeks two people to join its Training and Seminars office. We produce high-level seminars for ministers and senior officials of foreign governments.

Skills required: an analytical mind, ability to work under pressure, attention to detail, experience of seminars or courses, interest in world affairs, knowledge of languages (especially Spanish, Russian, French), excellent written skills and the ability to deal with senior people.

Coach drivers

Transport plays a major part in travel and tourism. Job opportunities within transport include drivers on transport such as trains and coaches. To be a coach driver requires formal training and qualifications, and you need to be over the age of 21 years.

Coach drivers working within travel and tourism will often require additional skills. For example, a driver on a coach package holiday will need good customer service skills because he or she will be in constant contact with the customers during the holiday and will be expected to meet their needs.

◄ Coach drivers need good customer service skills

Air cabin crew

The job of air cabin crew attracts many people into the travel and tourism industry. It is often seen as glamorous. People see it as involving travel throughout the world and perhaps staying in top hotels during stopovers between flights. It is also extremely hard work and requires people with a wide range of skills. Not all air cabin crew spend their working week jetting between America and the Caribbean. Many are on back-to-back flights to European destinations, such as Spain, and hardly have time to get off the plane before they take the next group of passengers home. Because of the large number of young people interested in a career of this sort, the competition is strong.

▲ Airline cabin crew need to be friendly

As an Air 2000 Cabin Crew member, you'll receive comprehensive training in first aid and safety, inflight and customer service, health and hygiene, personal presentation and communicating clearly. With our training programme behind you, you'll have the knowledge and confidence to provide the customer service we're so proud of.

Of course you'll need to be articulate, have a warm and friendly manner and be able to work closely with your fellow crew. Another quality we look for is a good sense of humour – it helps on the busier flights!

Formal requirements:

You will need to be 20 years of age or over, at least 1.58 metres tall, educated to GCSE level and able to swim 25 metres. Any foreign languages and previous experience working with the public are a definite plus.

You must be entitled to live and work indefinitely in the UK and hold a valid EU or UK passport, which permits worldwide travel without restrictions.

OVER TO YOU

Read the Air 2000 requirements for a cabin crew member. Discuss why you think they have the following requirements:

- articulate
- be able to work closely with your fellow crew
- 20 years or over
- at least 1.58 metres tall
- able to swim 25 metres
- entitled to live and work indefinitely in the UK.

Tourist guides

A tourist guide is often an important part of the visitor's experience and can include guides:

- at tourist attractions, such as a stately home or museum
- on transport, such as coach tours and river cruises
- at destinations, such as tours around a city or town.

Many tourist guides work independently. They can be hired by groups of people or tourism organisations to provide a guided tour of a destination or specific attractions. The website www.tourist-guides.net provides a list of registered guides who can be hired throughout the UK.

◄ This is a description of the type of people that the airline Air 2000 are looking for

OVER TO YOU

Read the descriptions of two guides as listed on the www.tourist-guides.net site. Identify some of the specific services that these types of guides might provide.

Annette Kurth

Region: Edinburgh
Languages: English, German (bilingual)
Summary: guide offering tours throughout the year all over Scotland and the North of England.
Interests include: Golf, Food and Whisky, Scottish History, Scottish Heroes, Archaeology, Architecture, Industrial Heritage, Macbeth, The Picts, Roman Scotland.

Frances Brook

Region: Southern England, West Country
Languages: English, French, German, Italian, and Thai
Summary: Tours by car, coach or on foot.
Interests include: Music, Gardens, Stonehenge, Sarum and Avebury, King Arthur, Alfred the Great, Tudors, Cathedrals of the South of England, Isle of Wight, New Forest, Southampton, Portsmouth, Bath, Glastonbury, Wells, Mendips, Devon and Cornwall, Walking tours.

Resort representatives

A resort representative is responsible for meeting the needs of holidaymakers at their resort. One of the largest tour operators, Thomson, outlines the main duties of a resort representative:

'As a holiday representative your main priority will be to ensure our customers have a fun, enjoyable holiday.'

What to do to ensure the customers have a fantastic time:

- find out everything there is to know about the resort, so that you become a local expert on the area
- keep up to date with the local events and activities to pass that on to the customers
- know the excursions and be able to identify the type of clientele each one will be most suited to
- sell the resort excursions and other activities, such as car hire
- spend a lot of time with your customers so you understand how you can best help them to get the most from their holiday.

You will be involved in a variety of activities.

- Hold welcome meetings soon after your customers arrive in the resort. This be your opportunity to promote the accommodation facilities, to tell them all about the great things to do in the resort and to promote the range of excursion activities on offer.
- As well as establishing good rapport with your customers, you need to have excellent working relationships with your hoteliers, hotel staff and other suppliers.
- Another occasion where you will be together with your customers is when you accompany an excursion. It is important that you are visible and attentive to the needs of customers so that the trip meets, if not exceeds, their expectations.
- You may also be involved in escorting your customers from the airport to their accommodation and back.

◄ Many resort representatives work with children and help organise and run children's activities

KEY TERMS

You should know what the following terms mean:

Tourism (page 42)
Holiday (page 42)
Sightseeing (page 42)
Visiting an attraction (page 43)
Visiting friends and relatives (page 43)
Sports events (page 43)
Business (page 43)
Travel agents (page 44)
Tour operators (page 44)
Tourist Information Centres and guiding services (page 46)
Online travel services (page 47)
Accommodation and catering (page 47)
Attractions (page 48)
Countryside recreation (page 48)
Transportation (page 50)
Package holidays (page 52)
Independent holidays (page 54)
Domestic holidays (page 54)

In-bound and out-bound (page 55)
Short-haul and long-haul flights (page 55)
Air travel (page 56)
Rail travel (page 57)
Sea travel (page 58)
Road travel (page 59)
Coastal areas (page 60)
Countryside areas (page 62)
Tourist towns and cities (page 64)
Sporting venues (page 66)
Theme parks (page 66)
Places of historic interest (page 67)
Sustainable tourism (page 70)
Travel consultants (page 72)
Conference organisers (page 73)
Coach drivers (page 73)
Air cabin crew (page 74)
Tourist guides (page 74)
Resort representatives (page 75)

If you're not sure or want to check your understanding, turn to the page number listed in the brackets.

Revision questions

1 In one sentence, explain what is meant by 'the travel and tourism industry'.

2 Identify three different types of holiday and describe the type of customer that each attracts.

3 What is the difference between a travel agent and a tour operator?

4 Describe one way that a customer might use online travel services to book transport.

5 What is the main role of tourist information centres?

6 Describe what is meant by the term 'package holiday'.

7 Explain the difference between short-haul and long-haul flights.

8 Identify three organisations that operate in each of the following forms of transport – air, rail, sea, road.

9 Identify five different tourism destinations (outside your area) within the UK and explain the attraction of each.

10 Select two jobs within the travel and tourism industry and explain the main duties of each.

Investigation ideas

Put together a package holiday in your area for a group of Swedish exchange students. Look at revision page 41. Assume that the students will be staying in the first week of June, arriving and departing on a Saturday.

The package should include the following information:

- Details of a reasonably priced small hotel or guest house. Explain what facilities and services are available.
- Arrangements for breakfast, lunch and dinner on each day. They are particularly keen to sample traditional British food.

- Details of at least one visit each day to a tourist attraction or area of interest. At least one trip should be more than 40 miles from where the group are staying.
- Details of the transport arrangements to take the group on the visits

When you have decided on all of the details, produce a leaflet that can be sent to the Swedish students outlining what the holiday will include. The leaflet could also show a local map, itinerary and pictures.

REVISION PROMPT

What have I learnt about the travel and tourism industry?

What am I still unsure about?

How am I going to find out the extra information that I need?

In this unit we looked at leisure and tourism as two separate industries. You have probably identified that many of the products and services offered by each are linked. For example, accommodation, catering, attractions and transportation are key components of both industries. In addition, both industries rely on each other for customers, for example:

■ a family day out at a visitor attraction is a leisure activity but also involves travel and tourism
■ travelling to an away football match could be considered as both leisure and tourism
■ going on holiday and many of the activities undertaken while on holiday could be considered as both leisure and tourism
■ going to the theatre, having a meal beforehand and staying in a hotel overnight are both leisure and tourism.

Let us look at some examples of the key components of both the leisure and tourism industries and see how they might be linked.

Many city restaurants offer special menus to theatregoers ▼

Leisure industry components

Example	Event	Possible links to tourism
Sport and physical recreation	going to a horseracing event such as the Grand National	spectators will often use public transport to get there and may stay in an hotel during their stay
Arts and entertainment	to see *The Lion King* in London	theatregoers may book a special theatre weekend through a specialist tour operator that includes transport and accommodation
Countryside recreation	a five-day walking tour of the Lake District	walkers may use local Youth Hostels for overnight accommodation and visit tourist information centres for details of local attractions
Children's play activities	a children's residential playscheme	many are provided by specialist educational tour operators
Visitor attractions	a visit to a historic site such as Stonehenge	historic sites are also a key component of the tourism industry
Catering	a family meal at a theme park	catering is also a key component of the tourism industry

Tourism industry components

Example	Event	Possible links to tourism
Travel agents	booking a return flight to Barcelona	the purpose of the flight might be to attend a major sporting event
Tour operators	booking an all-inclusive holiday in Greece	many all-inclusive holidays include a wide range of sporting activities such as water sports
Tourist information centres	finding out information on a local tourist destination	tourist information centres provide information on both leisure and tourism facilities within an area
Online travel services	booking a business conference at a specific destination	conference delegates often use leisure facilities such as theatres and sports centres
Accommodation	staying in a hotel at a popular tourist destination	many hotels attract guests because they are able to offer leisure facilities such as a swimming pool and fitness studio
Attractions	visiting one of the National Parks, such as Dartmoor	most National Parks offer a range of leisure activities such as nature trails and children's play activities
Transportation	taking a guided coach tour of a tourist city	the tour may include leisure activities such as visitor attractions and catering.

Would you visit Paris for leisure or tourism?

Eiffel Tower

Being able to answer these questions will ensure that you have understood the requirements of this unit. You should also be able to deal confidently with the external assessment for this unit.

1 Explain what is meant by 'leisure time'.

2 Describe one sport in the UK that attracts large numbers of both spectators and participants.

3 Identify the main customers for one arts or entertainment product or service.

4 Give two examples of organisations that operate within the arts and entertainment component of the industry.

5 Describe two countryside recreation activities that people may participate in.

6 Describe three different historic buildings or sites within the UK and identify where they are situated.

7 Identify three UK theme parks and explain where they are located.

8 Describe two examples of children's play activities.

9 Identify four examples of organisations that operate within the catering sector.

10 Describe in detail how two leisure activities have changed in the last 20 years.

11 Identify and describe two special-interest museums within the UK.

12 Explain three activities that a community centre might offer.

13 Explain how the use of computers has influenced the home-based leisure market.

14 Describe one leisure time activity that fits into two components of the industry.

15 Explain the range of products and services that a leisure centre might offer.

16 Describe four products that are part of the home-based leisure market.

17 Explain how the following factors might influence how people choose to spend their leisure time:
   a age group
   b special needs
   c gender
   d social group.

18 Explain how the availability of transport might influence the type of customers who use a public leisure centre.

19 Identify two leisure activities that a family with young children might participate in together.

20 Describe how fashion has influenced one leisure activity of young adults.

21 Give one example of how the influence of other family members can affect a person's choice of leisure activity.

22 Outline the main duties of a fitness instructor.

23 What qualifications would be expected from someone applying for the job of a lifeguard?

24 List three services or products that a travel agent might offer.

25 Identify a UK tour operator and explain two types of holiday that it offers.

26 Explain the main services offered by a tourist information centre.

27 Identify an online travel service and describe the products and services that it offers.

28 Identify one organisation that operates in each of the following sectors:
    a hotels
    b fast-food restaurants
    c pubs
    d take-away restaurants.

29 Describe five services that might be offered by a hotel.

30 Explain four elements that might be included in a package holiday.

31 Describe an example of a domestic holiday.

32 Explain what is meant by an 'independent holiday-maker'.

33 Describe an example of an inbound tourist to the UK.

34 Identify two destinations from the UK for a short-haul flight and two destinations for a long-haul flight.

35 Describe a special interest holiday, explaining the type of customer who would be attracted to it.

36 Identify one operator in each of the following transport sectors:
    a air
    b rail
    c sea
    d road.

37 Compare air and sea travel in terms of cost, convenience and availability.

38 Discuss whether the Channel Tunnel is a form of rail, road or sea transport.

39 Identify four popular seaside towns and explain where they are located.

40 Identify and describe three of the National Parks.

41 Name and explain where two (each) of the following are located in the UK:
    a forests
    b mountain areas
    c lakes.

42 Describe three tourist cities in the UK and explain what the attraction is of each.

43 List and explain four sporting venues in the UK.

44 Describe the environmental impact on one tourism destination in the UK.

45 Explain how a destination can benefit economically from tourism.

46 Describe two negative social effects that tourism could have on a destination.

47 Describe the main attributes that someone would need to be an air cabin-crew member.

48 Outline four responsibilities of a resort representative.

49 Describe how a family day out at a visitor attraction is both a leisure activity but also involves travel and tourism.

50 Describe five leisure activities that someone could take part in on a package holiday.

Marketing

Unit 2 is about marketing, an important aspect of today's increasingly competitive leisure and tourism industries. You will learn about:

- getting the right product to the right people in the right place at the right price using the right promotion
- the four key marketing tools – target marketing, market research, the marketing mix and SWOT analysis
- the marketing activities of leisure and tourism organisations
- promotional campaigns.

Marketing is essential for the survival of any commercial organisation. The material that you learn in this unit can be applied to any business or facility that needs to advertise its products or services.

Unit 2 of this book covers Unit 2, Marketing in leisure and tourism, of the GCSE Leisure and Tourism award.

Competition in the leisure and tourism industry is growing all the time. There are more and more organisations offering products and services. This in turn means that customers are becoming more demanding because they have a much wider choice of how to spend their leisure time. For example, 50 years ago a typical family might have gone to the same British seaside resort for their two-week annual holiday each year.

A typical family holiday in the 1950s compared to now

Think of all of the options that families have now: a package holiday to a European resort, Disneyland, Florida, Center Parcs, a city break, or skiing in Austria. Leisure and tourism organisations all hope that customers will choose to buy their products rather than those of a competitor.

The reasons that customers choose to go to Greece rather than Spain, or to the cinema rather than bowling, or eat at Pizza Hut rather than Burger King, vary. Some of the time it may be because of personal choice; they have not been influenced by what they have seen, heard or read. However, in many cases, the reason that customers choose one product rather than another is because of good marketing. For example, customers may:

■ choose to go to Greece rather than Spain because the Greek holiday brochure was better than the Spanish one
■ decide to go to the cinema because they saw the advertisement in a local newspaper
■ decide to eat at Pizza Hut rather than Burger King because they were attracted by the offer of 'eat as much as you like for £4.99'.

All of these reasons are due to successful marketing. Any organisation that does not use marketing well is unlikely to succeed. The methods that organisations use to market their products and services are among the most important factors in their future success. Large leisure and tourism organisations such as British Airways, Alton Towers and Thomson Holidays spend millions of pounds each year on marketing activities. Even the smaller organisations need to use marketing to attract and keep customers.

What is effective marketing?

Effective marketing involves getting the **right product** to the right people in the **right place** at the **right price** using the **right promotion**.

- The **right product** is one people want to buy – the one that specifically meets their needs.
- The **right people** means aiming your products at people who will want to buy them
- The **right place** means that the product has to be accessible to the customer so that they can actually buy it.
- The **right price** is one that people are prepared to pay, but it is also one that allows the company or organisation to achieve its income and profit targets.
- The **right promotion** means that it attracts people to your product and encourages them to buy it.

OVER TO YOU

Effective marketing

Think of a leisure or tourism product that you buy – you are already the 'right person'. Now complete the table. Compare your answers with the rest of the group.

Product	
The right product How does it meet your needs? What do you like about it?	
The right place How easy is it to actually buy the product e.g. can you get there easily?	
The right price Do you think the price is reasonable for what you get? Would you still buy it if it was more expensive?	
The right promotion Think about some advertisements you have seen for the product – did they encourage you to buy the product?	

Market segments

When we talk about the market we mean the group of customers who buy particular products and services. For example, you might be part of the market for organisations offering trainers, teenage magazines, CDs, tenpin bowling, or cinema screenings.

For most organisations the market will be made up of a lot of different types of clients who have different **customer needs** and expectations. These different types are known as **market segments**. The organisation will tailor its products to meet these different segments. For example, a tour operator's general product may be package holidays but it may offer different types of holidays for, families, young adults, retired people, etc. Each type of holiday will have a separate image designed to appeal to the particular segment. This can be seen in some of the brochure examples.

▲ A product aimed at the teenage market

▲ Tour operators offer different types of holidays for different customers

Target marketing means developing and promoting products that appeal to a specific market segment.

Target marketing is an important part of marketing because organisations need to have a clear idea of who their customers are and what they want from the products that they buy. If an organisation knows who their customers are it can use promotion in a way that will attract these customers. For example, Center Parcs and Butlins are aimed at very different market segments even though the product offered might be quite similar. Look at the two advertisements to see how the organisations target different types of customers.

▼ ▲ A similar product may be offered to different market segments

There are a number of ways that the market can be split into segments. Five of the most common are:

- age
- gender
- social group
- lifestyle
- ethnicity.

Match product to market

Look at the leaflets below and discuss which market segments you think each product might be targeting.

Conwy Castle (left), Eureka (centre), Planet Hollywood (right).

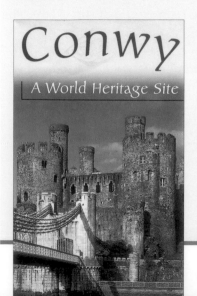

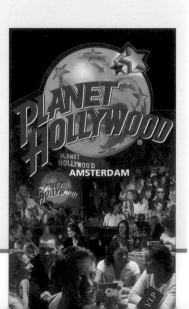

Target marketing by age

One of the main ways in which market segments are identified is by the **age** of customers. Many leisure and tourism organisations aim their products at specific age segments. This allows them to develop products that meet the needs of those age groups. Changes in the age of a population can often affect the products that are developed. For example, the proportion of elderly people in the British population is gradually increasing as people live longer due to better medical services. The graph shows the number of people over 65 years. It is predicted that the number will rise from the current 9 million to over 15 million in the next 50 years. This is an important market for many leisure and tourism providers because retired people have a lot of leisure time and therefore are likely to buy a range of leisure and tourism products.

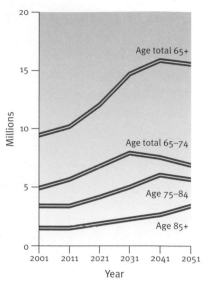

▲ An ageing UK population

C A S E   S T U D Y

SAGA holidays

Companies such as SAGA holidays specifically target people over the age of 50. Traditionally, holidays aimed at the older market tended to be domestic. They were usually in the UK to destinations such as the Lake District and seaside resorts. However, this has changed in the last few years. SAGA now offer holidays to destinations such as Tenerife, Thailand and South Africa.

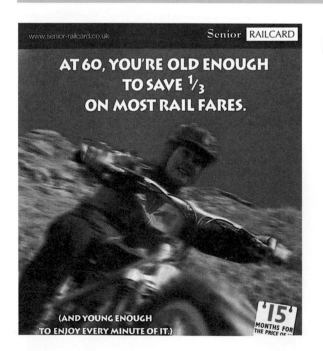

A report published by the English Tourism Council in 2001 showed that since 1993 the number of people aged 55–64 taking foreign holidays had increased by 90 per cent. In contrast, the number taking domestic holidays had increased by only 25 per cent. This means that there is a large market amongst older customers for companies offering foreign holidays. Many tour operators target this market by producing brochures specifically for older people.

◀ Many leisure and tourism organisations realised that one way of targeting and attracting older customers is to tell them that they are still young enough to do what they like

STOP & THINK

Find any other examples of leisure and tourism organisations that try to appeal to the 'younger' side of elderly customers.

Many leisure and tourism organisations target a range of age groups by changing the product to meet the needs of different ages. The advertisement shows how Odeon Cinemas targets children with its Movie Mob Club. Odeon cinemas also target other age groups by screening a range of films at different times.

▼ Odeon's Movie Mob Club

STAR ATTRACTIONS EVERY WEEKEND

ODEON MOVIE MOB BRINGS YOU GREAT VALUE FAMILY FILMS, SPECIALLY PRICED POPCORN AND DRINK COMBO AND SPECIAL OFFERS.

Check for performance times on 0870 50 50 007 or www.odeon.co.uk

TICKETS **£1.50*** *£2 AT SOME CINEMAS

POPCORN & DRINK* **99p**

MOVIE MOB ODEON

CLASSIC AND RECENT FILMS

ODEON FANATICAL ABOUT FILM

IN ASSOCIATION WITH OK! DAILY EXPRESS SUNDAY EXPRESS

Admission price of £2 or £1.50 depending on location 99p special size popcorn and drink combination

OVER TO YOU

Age and sports

Many sports appeal more to certain age groups than others. Look at the list of sports and decide what age groups you think are particularly targeted.

- tenpin bowling
- golf
- squash
- ice-skating
- crown green bowling
- rollerblading
- snooker.

Target marketing by gender

Some products such as rugby or flower arranging classes are aimed mainly at male or female customers, although traditional distinctions are becoming blurred.

In the past, many pubs used to prevent women from being served in the saloon bar and were very male-orientated. Now, they often encourage women and families by providing a wider range of products and facilities. Some leisure and tourism organisations aim products at either male or female markets. For example, there has been a large increase in books, magazines and films aimed at the female market. Examples include books such as *Bridget Jones's Diary* and films like *Coyote Ugly*. The market has become so large that the products have been named 'chick lit' (books) and 'chick flicks' (films)!

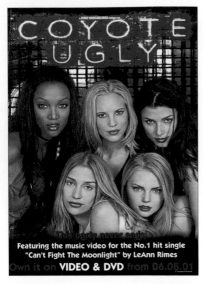

▲ *Coyote Ugly* is typical of the new 'chick flicks'

◄ Some activities attract a particular gender

Leisure activities and gender

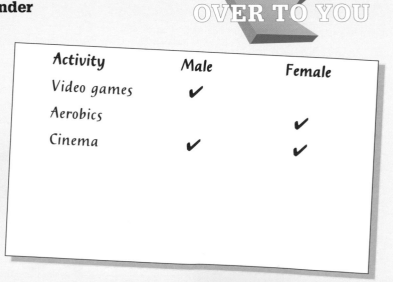

OVER TO YOU

Working as a group, write a list of all of the leisure activities you like to take part in. Include sports, visits to tourist attractions, socialising activities and home entertainment. Now separate the list into three columns. Show whether these activities are done mainly by females, males, or both. Some examples have been given to get you started.

Activity	Male	Female
Video games	✔	
Aerobics		✔
Cinema	✔	✔

Tarket marketing by group

Most people place themselves and others in a **social group** according to their job. A waiter or waitress might be regarded as doing a working class job and a travel agent as middle class. One of the most widely used social class classifications in marketing was developed by the Institute of Practitioners in Advertising. This divides the population into six groups (on right).

Many leisure and tourism products are seen to be attractive to a particular class. For example, bingo is seen as appealing to mainly C2, D and E, whereas opera may be more appealing to classes A and B. This may have changed in recent years because of changes in the amount that people earn. Some manual workers have high incomes and can afford luxury holidays, whereas public sector staff such as teachers and nurses may not be able to afford the same.

Class A	Senior managers and professionals, such as doctors, lawyers and managing directors of large organisations
Class B	Middle-level managers and professionals, such as teachers, accountants and leisure centre managers
Class C1	Supervisory and junior management, such as computer operators, receptionists, fitness instructors and office managers
Class C2	Skilled manual workers such as electricians and hairdressers
Class D	Semi-skilled and unskilled manual workers, such as cleaners, kitchen porters and ride attendants
Class E	Others in low incomes, including casual workers and those on state benefits.

OVER TO YOU

Social groups

Look at the descriptions from holiday brochures.

As a group, discuss which social group you think each one is targeting.

Mallorca

Formentor

HOTEL FORMENTOR

One of Europe's most exclusive and luxurious hotels, the Formentor offers a high standard of comfort and excellent facilities. With a richly-deserved reputation for quality cuisine and impeccable service, the hotel is set in beautiful gardens on the northernmost tip of the island, where tranquillity and seclusion are the order of the day. Relax beside the beautiful lawn-fringed pool or on one of the spacious terraces, or take the opportunity to try one of the watersports on offer from the beach. Pretty Puerto Pollensa is a 15-minute drive

~Blue Ribbon~

Majorca

FROM ONLY £199

Holiday Center Apartments AA
Santa Ponsa

2 FOR 1 *see page 5*   CALVIA MALLORCA *see page 6*
PRICE ATTACK *see page 3*   LONG STAY *see page 5*

ATTRACTIVE, SIMPLE and well situated for local amenities, Holiday Center Apartments are an excellent choice for budget conscious families and couples.

- **Location** Situated 400 metres from local bars and cafes and 550 metres from the sandy beach. The nearest supermarket is only 100 metres away. These apartments are not suitable for customers with walking difficulties.
- **Facilities** Swimming pool • Children's splash pool • Children's playground • Sunbathing terrace • Lobby lounge TV area • Bingo

- **One bedroomed** apartments (Sleep 2 adults and 2 children or 3 adults and 1 child) include kitchenette with cooking rings and fridge, bath/shower, wc and balcony or terrace. Maid service twice weekly.
- **Official Rating** 2 key
- **Board Basis** Self catering
- **Child Age** 2–16
- **Telephone** 00 34971 691461

Target marketing by lifestyle

Lifestyle is a combination of work patterns, income, marital status, family commitments and leisure and social habits, in other words, the way in which we live.

Many people would argue that lifestyle is one of the biggest influences on the type of leisure and tourism products that we buy. For example, a couple with young children is likely to have very different leisure needs than a retired couple or a single, young adult.

Some people's lifestyles can result in them being 'money-rich, time-poor'. People generally work longer hours, so earn more money. However, because they work such long hours they have less leisure time. This means that they will often spend more money on less leisure and tourism products.

Many leisure and tourism providers have recognised this lifestyle market segment and developed products for them. For example, there has been a huge increase in private health clubs, such as David Lloyd centres and Virgin Active. Such clubs are open long hours (sometimes 24 hours a day) and are frequently used by people who want to stay fit but have limited time for exercise.

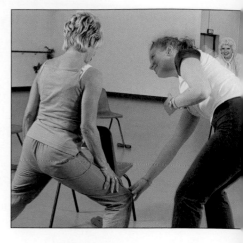

▲ Health clubs cater for people with limited time for exercise

STOP & THINK

More than 5 per cent of the UK's population comes from ethnic minority groups.

OVER TO YOU

Lifestyles and leisure

Compare your working lifestyle with that of an adult. Use the table to record the effect that your lifestyles have on the leisure activities that you do. For example, you might be free every evening and therefore go to the cinema often. The adult might work evening shifts and choose an activity such as swimming that can be done in the morning.

	You	Adult
Working lifestyle lifestyle		
Leisure activities		

Target marketing by ethnicity

Different ethnic groups may have different needs. For example, there is a growing network of cinemas that specialise in showing Asian films, particularly Indian films. Religious beliefs can also mean separate market segments, for example, kosher or halal food menus may be offered by some airlines.

Some organisations are recognising that targeting ethnic groups can be a valuable part of their marketing.

Britain's ethnic composition, 1991 Census ▶

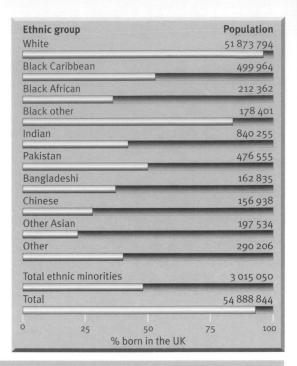

Ethnic group	Population
White	51 873 794
Black Caribbean	499 964
Black African	212 362
Black other	178 401
Indian	840 255
Pakistan	476 555
Bangladeshi	162 835
Chinese	156 938
Other Asian	197 534
Other	290 206
Total ethnic minorities	3 015 050
Total	54 888 844

% born in the UK

CASE STUDY

Coca-Cola – cricket project in Birmingham

In New York, Coca-Cola ran an initiative targeting black Americans, called Project Harlem. It teamed up with local retailers and people to get involved in a range of community activities. The project's success has led the drinks company to repeat the project in the UK where it targets Asian youth in a programme of activities in Birmingham.

The first stage is the foundation of a school cricket league in Birmingham. Coke provides schools with equipment, runs promotions with prizes to see Pakistan and India play, and backs the initiative with materials supplied by local retailers. The cricket initiative will be followed by promotions linked to Bollywood films and a major push to coincide with the celebrations for Diwali, the Hindu festival of light.

Market segments summary

In the last three sections we have looked at the five ways of identifying different market segments: age, gender, social group, lifestyle and ethnicity. Look at the leaflet for the Castle Howard Proms. These concerts are held at night in the magnificent grounds of the castle. Customers take picnics with them; many set up dining tables and chairs with candles and enjoy three-course meals with wine.

In pairs, discuss what market segments would be targeted for this event. Consider:

- age
- social group
- ethnicity.
- gender
- lifestyle

KEY TERMS

You should know what the following terms mean:

Marketing (page 84)
Customer needs (page 86)
Market segments (page 86)
Target marketing (page 87)
Age (page 88)
Gender (page 90)
Social group (page 91)
Lifestyle (page 92)
Ethnicity (page 93)

If you're not sure or want to check your understanding, turn to the page number listed in the brackets.

Revision questions

1 Describe in one sentence what is meant by 'marketing'.

2 Explain why it is important for an organisation to use effective marketing.

3 Complete the following:

Marketing means getting the right ...... to the right ...... in the right ...... at the right ...... using the right ......

4 Explain what is meant by the 'target' in the term 'target marketing'

5 Why is it important that an organisation uses target marketing?

6 Describe what is meant by a 'market segment', giving two leisure or tourism examples.

7 Identify three leisure or tourism products that appeal to specific age segments.

8 Explain one leisure activity that traditionally attracts a particular gender.

9 Describe a typical holiday that might appeal to the social group B/C1.

10 What leisure or tourism products might be aimed at people from specific ethnic groups?

Investigation ideas   OVER TO YOU

For this activity you will need
a display board and copies of a range of colour
magazines. The display board should be headed with
a sign reading 'Target Marketing'.

Look through the magazines and cut out photographs of
a wide range of different people, for example, of different
ages, gender and social group. Stick each photograph
onto a sheet of paper and write the type of market
segment at the top. Then write a list of leisure and
tourism products and services that you think the
particular segment might use. For example, a picture of
a couple with two young children might show theme
parks, family holiday centres, family pubs, pantomime,
beach package holidays and swimming.

Display all the sheets on the board.

REVISION PROMPT

What have I learnt about target marketing?

_____

_____

_____

What am I still unsure about?

_____

_____

_____

How am I going to find out the extra information that I need?

_____

_____

_____

What is market research?

Before organisations begin to think about the products and services that they will develop and promote, they need to have a very clear idea about who their customers are and what they want. It might seem a great idea when people say, 'This town needs a multi-screen cinema – the nearest one is 40 miles away – the locals would love it!' However, how do they know that enough people in the town agree with them? Perhaps none of the large organisations had built a multi-screen because they do not think the local population would go often enough to make it profitable. It becomes clear that the people with the idea need to do some market research.

Market research is the way that organisations find out what their customers really want. If it is done correctly, it means that the organisation can develop and offer products and services that they know will meet customers' needs.

There are many ways in which market research can be carried out. Five of the main methods are through:

- postal surveys
- telephone surveys
- personal surveys
- observation
- the internet.

A leisure and tourism organisation might want to find out about any or all of the following factors.

STOP & THINK

What information might be collected through market research?

Its customers
- Who are they?
- How did they hear about the organisation?
- Why do they buy the organisation's products?
- What do they like and dislike about the products?
- How often and when do they buy the products?
- What other products do they buy from competitors?

Its products and services
- Would customers buy a new product?
- How could existing products be improved?
- Is the price right for the customers?

The competitors
- What products and services are offered by competitors?
- How much do they charge for their products?
- What type of customers are they attracting?

Promotional techniques
- What promotional techniques do the competitors use?
- How effective is the organisation's promotions?
- What influences a customer to buy the organisation's products?

When carrying out market research it is important to identify exactly what it is you want to find out. This is known as setting your market research objectives.

Research objectives for a survey carried out by the National Centre for Social Research

Objectives

1 To measure the extent of participation in leisure day visits
2 To estimate the number and value of trips taken.

Information collected:

- Leisure activities
- Destination and type of location
- Time spent at destination
- Method of transport
- Distance travelled
- Party size and composition.

OVER TO YOU

Market research objectives

Look at the Airport Passenger Embarkation Survey. In pairs, discuss what you think the market research objectives might be for this survey.

AIRPORT PASSENGER EMBARKATION SURVEY

APD

For Official Use Only **A010/**

IMPORTANT: Please complete if aged 18 or over. Please use capital letters. Completed forms *are collected* at departure gates.

Mr ☐ Mrs ☐ Ms ☐   Forename ☐

Surname ☐

Country of residence   AT ☐ BE ☐ DE ☐ DK ☐ ES ☐ FI ☐ FR ☐

Non-E.U.   GB ☐ GR ☐ IRL ☐ IT ☐ LUX ☐ NI ☐ PT ☐ SE ☐

Your home address ☐

Postcode ☐

How many years have you lived there? ☐   Your date of birth D D / M M / 19 Y Y

Your telephone number ☐

email ☐ @ ☐

Your flight number please? (e.g. BA 1234) ☐

Departure airport.................... Destination airport (this flight).....................

Your final destination airport (if different).....................

The purpose of your flight?   Business ☐   Pleasure ☐

Your type of flight?   Your ticket class?   First ☐   Business ☐

Scheduled ☐   Charter ☐   Economy ☐ Package ☐ Seat only ☐ Standby ☐

How much was your ticket?   £ ☐   Don't know ☐

How long ago was this ticket bought?

Under 1 week ☐   1-2 weeks ☐   3-4 weeks ☐   More than 1 month ☐

From where was the ticket bought?

Airline direct ☐   Airline web-site ☐   Travel Agent ☐   Other ☐

How many return flights have you made in the last year?

From all UK airports   2-4 ☐   5-9 ☐   10-15 ☐   16-25 ☐   25+ ☐

From this airport   2-4 ☐   5-9 ☐   10-15 ☐   16-25 ☐   25+ ☐

How did you arrive at this airport today?   Rail ☐   Bus ☐   Taxi ☐   Hire car ☐

Underground/metro ☐   Transit passenger ☐   Courtesy transport ☐   Own car ☐

Are you travelling with?   Hand baggage only ☐   Hold & hand baggage ☐

Were you asked questions about baggage security at check in?   Yes ☐   No ☐

Were you offered a seat selection eg aisle / window?   Yes ☐   No ☐

Please rate this airport for the following

	V.Good	Good	Poor	V.Poor		V.Good	Good	Poor	V.Poor
Time taken to check-in	☐	☐	☐	☐	Concourse shops	☐	☐	☐	☐
Knowledge of check-in staff	☐	☐	☐	☐	Services for the disabled	☐	☐	☐	☐
Courtesy of check-in staff	☐	☐	☐	☐	Direction signs	☐	☐	☐	☐
Security arrangements	☐	☐	☐	☐	Cafes/bars/restaurants	☐	☐	☐	☐
Parking facilities	☐	☐	☐	☐	Toilet facilities	☐	☐	☐	☐
Availability of flights	☐	☐	☐	☐	Cleanliness	☐	☐	☐	☐
Overall convenience	☐	☐	☐	☐	Overall satisfaction	☐	☐	☐	☐

When do you buy foreign currency?   Before arrival ☐   At this airport ☐   Abroad ☐

Do you also purchase with?   AmEx ☐   Visa ☐ MasterCard ☐

Travellers cheques ☐   Diners ☐   Debit cards ☐   Other ☐

Did you buy a newspaper at the this airport?   Yes ☐   No ☐

What newspapers do you read?   Daily .... Sunday ....

Are you?   Married ☐   Single ☐

Are you travelling?   Alone ☐ With business colleagues ☐ With friends/family ☐

Please tick the ages of your children   <1 ☐   1 ☐   2 ☐   3 ☐   4 ☐   5 ☐   6 ☐   7 ☐   8 ☐
  9 ☐ 10 ☐ 11 ☐ 12 ☐ 13 ☐ 14 ☐ 15 ☐ 16 ☐ 17 ☐

Have you visited this airport's web-site   Yes ☐   No ☐

Do you have a home PC?   Yes ☐ No ☐   With internet facilities?   Yes ☐ No ☐

Do you sometimes buy?	At an airport	By internet	By mail/ phone		At an airport	By internet	By mail/ phone
Travel/holidays	☐	☐	☐	Laptops/PCs etc.	☐	☐	☐
Airline tickets	☐	☐	☐	Wine & spirits	☐	☐	☐
Hotel accommodation	☐	☐	☐	CD's/tapes	☐	☐	☐
Perfume/cosmetics	☐	☐	☐	Clothes/fashions	☐	☐	☐
Cameras/films	☐	☐	☐	Travel Insurance	☐	☐	☐
Books	☐	☐	☐	Other financial services	☐	☐	☐

What is your occupation?

Professional/senior manager ☐   Middle manager ☐   Junior manager ☐

Office/clerical ☐   Craftsman/tradesman ☐   Manual/factory worker ☐

Shopworker ☐   Self-employed ☐   Student ☐

Housewife ☐   Retired ☐   Education/medical ☐

What is your household income level £'000's

0-10 ☐   10-15 ☐   15-20 ☐   20-25 ☐   25-30 ☐

30-35 ☐   35-40 ☐   40-50 ☐   50-60 ☐   60+ ☐

Has todays flight been delayed?   Up to 15 mins ☐   15-30 mins ☐   30-60 mins ☐
  1-2 hours ☐   2-4 hours ☐   Over 4 hours ☐

Have you experienced unplanned flight changes?   Today   In the last year

Due to cancellation? ☐   ☐

Due to over-booking? ☐   ☐

In the last year has your luggage been?   Delayed ☐   Lost ☐   Damaged ☐

If you have experienced these last two problems on a previous flight, please state which

Airline? .... Departure airport? ....

Arrival airport? .... Was it a direct flight?   Yes ☐   No ☐

Please tick this box ☐ if you do not want to help with further research on the above.

To which of these travel loyalty clubs do you belong?

BA ☐   British European ☐   Skyteam ☐   KLM/Northwest ☐   Star Alliance ☐

Virgin ☐   Qualiflyer ☐   OneWorld ☐   JAL ☐   Other airline ☐

Hilton ☐   Holiday Inn ☐   Marriott ☐   Hyatt ☐

Starwood ☐   Forte ☐   Intercontinental ☐   Other hotel ☐

Avis ☐   Hertz ☐   Europcar ☐   Budget ☐

Alamo ☐   National ☐   Sixt ☐   Other car hire ☐

Which is your preferred airline? ....

Thank you for your help. The data you have given will be held and processed by Airport Passenger Data within the E.U., and will be aggregated to produce travel research information & statistics.

Please tick this box ☐ if you do not wish the data to be used additionally for third party commercial purposes, which may involve processing outside the E.U.

Postal surveys

A postal survey is done through a questionnaire which is posted to a number of selected people. Many leisure and tourism organisations use this type of marketing research. The information collected will then be used to help improve the service that they offer to their customers.

One of the great advantages of a postal survey is that people can fill in the questionnaire in their own time. Many organisations encourage people to reply by enclosing a return stamped addressed envelope. Some even offer incentives such as prize draws for those who answer. Another advantage of postal questionnaires is that they are relatively cheap to use compared with other methods.

One of the big drawbacks of this method is that very few people return postal questionnaires. Some return rates are as low as 3 per cent, which means that of 1000 questionnaires sent out, as little as 30 may be returned. The organisation then needs to ask if the 30 returned questionnaires truly represent the opinion of all of their customers.

One of the most difficult parts of developing a good questionnaire is writing questions that are easily understood in the same way by all respondents.

Organisations such as Thomson Holidays send out questionnaires to customers who have booked holidays to see whether they were happy with the service that they received ▼

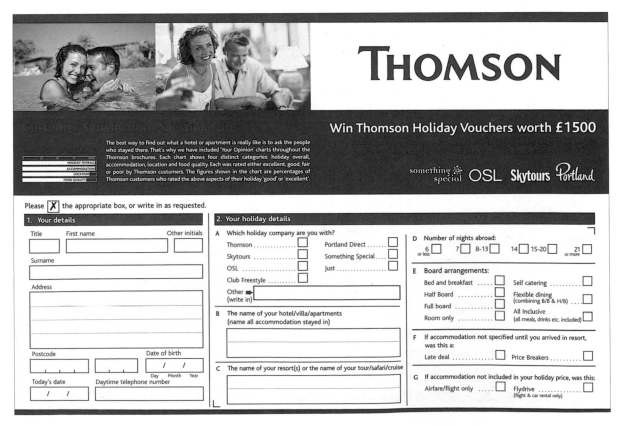

Developing a postal survey

A researcher sent out 5000 questionnaires to the local population, asking if they would use a multi-screen facility if it were available in the town.

- The total population of the town is 43 000.
- 100 people completed and returned the questionnaire.
- 98 per cent (of the 100) say that they would use the facility 'frequently'.

The researcher Idea says that this proves that the facility is needed in the town. What do you think?

- Can we assume from the research that 98 per cent of the local population will use the facility? If not, why not?
- Why do you think 4 900 people did not return the questionnaire? Are they likely to be people who will use the facility?
- What do you think people mean by 'frequently'. Is this important? Why do you say so?
- Draw up a checklist of what might make postal questionnaires unreliable.

General rules for writing questionnaires

- Keep language simple yet specific.
- Avoid jargon, slang or local terms.
- Do not ask more than one fact in a single question.
- Make sure questions are unambiguous, that is, that they cannot be interpreted in different ways by different respondents.
- Do not ask respondents to make complicated calculations or remember events that happened a long time ago.
- Only include questions that are totally relevant to the survey. It is easy to get side-tracked and forget what you are actually trying to find out.
- Do not ask respondents to imagine something that they have not experienced. Their answer will only be a guess and not very helpful.
- Avoid very personal questions. People will either refuse to answer or lie.

Telephone surveys

Leisure and tourism organisations use telephone surveys because it is quick and provides instant information.

Do you have time to answer a few questions?

◀ Conducting a telephone survey

You or your family may already have experienced a telephone survey. Although it is generally more expensive than postal questionnaires, it is cheaper than some other methods. Unlike a postal questionnaire, it allows the market researcher to ask for further explanation when needed.

I'm sorry to hear that you do not like our new fitness equipment. Can you tell me how we could improve it?

However, there are disadvantages to telephone questionnaires. A large number of people will say,

Sorry, I can't talk now. It's not convenient.

Even when people do agree to answer questions, their responses may be quite limited since few people are willing to stay on the telephone for a long time. This means that questions need to be short and to the point. A further disadvantage is that the interviewer and respondent cannot see each other. Apart from the fact that body language cannot be used to help communication, it also means that visual information, such as pictures, cannot be used.

It is much more difficult to follow a long and detailed question when someone is reading it to you than when you are able to read it for yourself. Longer questions might be more suitable for a postal questionnaire.

STOP & THINK

Read this question quickly to someone and see whether that person can answer it.

Think about the last film you saw at the cinema and say which of these best describes your feelings about the experience:

1 It was a great film and I told all my friends to see it.

2 It was a good film and lived up to my expectations.

3 I thought it was going to be better than it was so I was disappointed.

4 It was not very good and I would not recommend it to my friends.

Conduct a telephone survey

Look at the copy of a questionnaire that the tour operator, Olympic Holidays, gives to customers at the end of their holiday. Imagine that you are going to carry out the survey over the telephone.

■ Re-write the questions so that they would be easy to follow on the phone. You might decide to get rid of some of the questions altogether or combine two or more.

■ Once you have written the questions test your telephone survey with a partner. Sit back-to-back when you are doing this so that you cannot use gestures or facial expressions to help.

CUSTOMER SERVICE QUESTIONNAIRE

PLEASE TELL US ABOUT YOUR HOLIDAY

1. Which airport did you fly from

a ☐ Gatwick	b ☐ Manchester	c ☐ Luton	d ☐ Belfast
e ☐ Newcastle	f ☐ Birmingham	g ☐ Heathrow	h ☐ Exeter
i ☐ Glasgow	j ☐ Bristol	k ☐ East Midlands	l ☐ Norwich
m ☐ Other (please specify)_____			

2. Which airline did you fly with

a ☐ Air 2000	b ☐ Helios	c ☐ Monarch	d ☐ Virgin
e ☐ JMC	f ☐ Airtours	g ☐ Britannia	h ☐ Cyprus Airways
i ☐ Other (please specify)_____			

3. Did you book any of the following services   a ☐ Olympic Gold   b ☐ Taxi Transfer

4. Which meal arrangements did your holiday include   a ☐ Full board   b ☐ Half Board   c ☐ Breakfast   d ☐ Self-catering

PRE DEPARTURE

5. How did you book your holiday   ☐ Travel Agent   ☐ Teletext   ☐ Direct

	Excellent	Good	Fair	Poor	N/A
6. Brochure presentation	a ☐	b ☐	c ☐	d ☐	e ☐
7. Brochure information/content	a ☐	b ☐	c ☐	d ☐	e ☐
8. Reservation staff knowledge	a ☐	b ☐	c ☐	d ☐	e ☐
9. Reservation staff helpfulness	a ☐	b ☐	c ☐	d ☐	e ☐

FLIGHTS & TRANSFERS

	Excellent	Good	Fair	Poor	N/A
10. How was your flight overall	a ☐	b ☐	c ☐	d ☐	e ☐
11. Olympic welcome at the airport	a ☐	b ☐	c ☐	d ☐	e ☐
12. Representatives service during transfer	a ☐	b ☐	c ☐	d ☐	e ☐
13. Quality and comfort of your coach transfer	a ☐	b ☐	c ☐	d ☐	e ☐
14. Quality and comfort of taxi transfer (if applicable)	a ☐	b ☐	c ☐	d ☐	e ☐

YOUR REPRESENTATIVE

15. Did you attend the Welcome Getogether   a ☐ Yes   b ☐ No

	Excellent	Good	Fair	Poor	N/A
16. If Yes, How did you rate the Welcome Getogether	a ☐	b ☐	c ☐	d ☐	e ☐
17. Representatives local knowledge	a ☐	b ☐	c ☐	d ☐	e ☐
18. Representatives attention to your needs	a ☐	b ☐	c ☐	d ☐	e ☐
19. Representatives availability as advertised	a ☐	b ☐	c ☐	d ☐	e ☐
20. Representatives smartness	a ☐	b ☐	c ☐	d ☐	e ☐

YOUR ACCOMMODATION

HOTEL ONLY

	Excellent	Good	Fair	Poor	N/A
21. Meals provided by the hotel	a ☐	b ☐	c ☐	d ☐	e ☐
22. Comfort of public areas	a ☐	b ☐	c ☐	d ☐	e ☐
23. Comfort of bedrooms	a ☐	b ☐	c ☐	d ☐	e ☐
24. Restaurant staff/service	a ☐	b ☐	c ☐	d ☐	e ☐
25. Hotel facilities (eg shops/sporting activities)	a ☐	b ☐	c ☐	d ☐	e ☐

SELF CATERING

	Excellent	Good	Fair	Poor	N/A
26. Kitchen equipment	a ☐	b ☐	c ☐	d ☐	e ☐
27. Maintenance	a ☐	b ☐	c ☐	d ☐	e ☐
28. Comfort of accommodation	a ☐	b ☐	c ☐	d ☐	e ☐

ALL ACCOMMODATION

	Excellent	Good	Fair	Poor	N/A
29. Helpfulness of staff	a ☐	b ☐	c ☐	d ☐	e ☐
30. Location of accommodation	a ☐	b ☐	c ☐	d ☐	e ☐
31. Maid service and cleanliness	a ☐	b ☐	c ☐	d ☐	e ☐
32. Childrens facilities (if applicable)	a ☐	b ☐	c ☐	d ☐	e ☐
33. Swimming pool area (if applicable)	a ☐	b ☐	c ☐	d ☐	e ☐

TAKING EVERYTHING INTO ACCOUNT

	Excellent	Good	Fair	Poor	N/A
34. Your journey overall	a ☐	b ☐	c ☐	d ☐	e ☐
35. Your accommodation overall	a ☐	b ☐	c ☐	d ☐	e ☐
36. Your representative overall	a ☐	b ☐	c ☐	d ☐	e ☐
37. Excursions overall	a ☐	b ☐	c ☐	d ☐	e ☐
38. Your holiday overall	a ☐	b ☐	c ☐	d ☐	e ☐

Personal surveys

Personal surveys use questionnaires in a face-to-face situation.

People are usually more willing to respond to interviews that are in person, if only because it is harder to say, 'no' than on the phone. It is also easy to throw away a postal survey.

Answers to a personal survey could be rushed. This is particularly important in a leisure and tourism context. A further drawback of this method is that it is very personal.

STOP & THINK

If you were at a theme park for the day, would you really want to spend 15 minutes answering questions when you could be on the new ride?

CASE STUDY

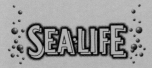

Market research at the Sea Life Centres

The Sea Life Centres are part of the Merlin Entertainments Group, a company with attractions across eight countries and welcoming over five million visitors a year. Its roots lie in the West Highlands of Scotland, where the first Sea Life Centre opened in 1979, on the banks of the picturesque Loch Creran, near Oban. Since then, another 22 Sea Life Centres have been opened – 16 in the UK, with others in Germany, Ireland, Belgium, Holland and Spain.

Now based in Poole, Dorset, Merlin also owns and operates the National Seal Sanctuary in Gweek, Cornwall, and the London and York Dungeons. Merlin is Europe's leading multi-site visitor attraction operator.

Sea Life Centres are famous for producing marine life displays of diverse shapes and sizes, each cleverly themed to mimic the natural habitat of its resident sea creatures as closely as possible. They focus mainly on the environment and sea creatures from their nearest coastlines and also feature special exhibitions that highlight a range of more exotic tropical marine life.

Several Centres, along with their sister attraction, The National Seal Sanctuary, are involved in rescue and rehabilitation work with both grey and common seals. They are also pioneers in the field of captive breeding, particularly with threatened species such as seahorses. Sea Life carries out market research on a regular basis. The selection of suitable methods is largely dependent on which are the most cost-effective.

The company buys information from market research organisations about customer perceptions of visitor attractions. At Sea Life, information is stored on computerised customer databases and regularly analysed. These databases provide a range of information from customer profiles to frequency of visits (e.g. who they are, where they've come from, who they came with, etc.). Valuable data is also collated from the customer details given on completed sales promotions that have been offered, such as discount vouchers.

Each attraction conducts a regular visitor survey using a simple self-completion, multi-choice, 'tick box' format. The questions are designed to evaluate the visitors' perceptions of the attraction and its facilities. Further questions explore how the visitors heard about the attraction and their main reason for visiting. The questionnaire also collects details such as the ages of members of each group, where they've come from, the type of accommodation that they are staying at in the area, and how long they are staying in the area.

◄ The customer is talking face-to-face with a member of staff and therefore may not want to be too critical

Sea Life centres are constantly monitoring visitor response, to ensure you all receive maximum enjoyment. To assist, kindly complete this short survey. Please answer each question fully by ticking the relevant box(es). Thank you.

Visitor Survey

Date of visit ☐

What are the main reasons for this visit?
You may tick more than one box.

To see the sharks (only centres with sharks) ☐
A place to go on a dull / rainy day ☐

To see all the sea life / fish ☐
Promotional offer ☐

Recommended by a friend or relative ☐
Visit a new attraction ☐

Just passing ☐
Family outing ☐

To see the seals (only centres with seal rescue facility) ☐
Enjoyed a previous visit and wanted to visit again ☐
Saw an advertisement ☐

Other (please specify) ☐

Publicity

How did you see or hear about Sea Life before your visit?
You may tick more than one box.

Tourist Info. centre ☐
Television commercial ☐
Posters ☐

Holiday guide ☐
Television news ☐
Radio ☐

Cinema ☐
Local newspaper ☐
National newspaper ☐

Road sign ☐
Sea Life leaflet ☐
Promotional offer ☐

Other (please specify) ☐

If you saw a Sea Life leaflet before your visit, where did you see it?

Hotel ☐
Tourist Info Centre ☐
Self catering ☐

Holiday Park / Camp ☐
B & B / Guesthouse ☐
Pub / Restaurant ☐

Other (please specify) ☐

Did you (or anyone in your party) use a promotional voucher / offer when you entered the centre
Yes ☐   No ☐

If yes, where did you get the voucher?
The Daily Mirror ☐
Other (please specify) ☐

About your visit

How satisfied are you with your overall visit?

Very satisfied ☐

Quite satisfied ☐

Neither satisfied nor dissatisfied ☐

Quite dissatisfied ☐

Very dissatisfied ☐

Would you recommend a visit to friends or family?
Yes ☐   No ☐

Did you talk to any staff as you were going round the centre? (other than in the shop or restaurant.)
Yes ☐   No ☐

Did you or anyone with you buy any goods from the shop?
Yes ☐   No ☐

Did you use the restaurant / catering facilities?
Yes ☐   No ☐

How well did the following live up to your expectations?

	Excellent	Good	Fair	Poor	Very poor	Did not use / see
Restaurant / Catering	☐	☐	☐	☐	☐	☐
Shop	☐	☐	☐	☐	☐	☐
Staff efficiency / friendliness	☐	☐	☐	☐	☐	☐
Talk / Presentation	☐	☐	☐	☐	☐	☐

	Excellent	Good	Fair	Poor	Very poor
Displays / Creatures	☐	☐	☐	☐	☐
Value for money	☐	☐	☐	☐	☐

Observation

Observation is when trained market researchers watch how customers use and react towards an organisation's products and services.

Observation can be particularly useful in giving the organisation a better understanding of how their customers behave and what their needs are. For example, when Madame Tussaud's was originally created, the wax figures were roped off and customers were not allowed to use cameras. Through observation it was realised that what customers really wanted was to be a part of the experience rather than just looking at the figures.

Now the figures are accessible and visitors are encouraged to take photographs of themselves with famous, life-like figures of pop stars, actors and politicians. They can even borrow a camera free of charge.

Observation methods also include focus groups, where a group of customers meet to discuss products or services. Observation methods often result in in-depth information about customers' needs and expectations. However, they can be very expensive because a lot of staff time is required in carrying out the research.

▲ Some people you know might like to have their photos taken with these wax figures

Conduct a survey

OVER TO YOU

In pairs, visit a local fast-food restaurant. Before you start, tell the manager that you are doing a survey for your course. You are going to use observational research to find out how long customers spend eating their meal. You will need a watch, some paper and a pen.

Spend at least an hour in the restaurant and time how long each of the following types of customers spend eating their meal:

- single people
- families and adults with a child or children
- unaccompanied children and teenagers
- adults in groups of two or more.

When you have completed your research, work out which types of customers spend the most and the least time eating their meal.

Using the internet

Developments in technology have meant that marketing research does not just have to be carried out only by post, on the telephone or face-to-face. Many organisations are now using the **internet** to find out the opinions of customers. Most leisure and tourism organisations have customer feedback facilities on their website.

OVER TO YOU

Internet research

If you have access to the internet, see if you can find any other examples of marketing research by leisure and tourism organisations. You might start by visiting some web site addresses.

KEY TERMS

You should know what the following terms mean:

Market research (page 96)
Postal surveys (page 98)
Telephone surveys (page 100)
Personal surveys (page 102)
Observation (page 104)
Internet (page 105)

If you're not sure or want to check your understanding, turn to the page number listed in the brackets.

Revision questions

1 What is meant by the term 'market research'?

2 Explain why it is important that leisure and tourism organisations carry out market research.

3 Give four examples of the type of information that a leisure or tourism organisation might collect through market research.

4 What is meant by the term 'market research objective'?

5 Explain two advantages and two disadvantages of using a postal survey.

6 List three things that you need to remember when writing effective questionnaires.

7 What advantage might a face-to-face survey have over a telephone survey?

8 Explain one way that a leisure or tourism organisation might use observation as a form of market research.

9 What would be an effective method of market research if you wanted to find out in-depth information on customers' opinions about foreign holidays?

10 Explain two ways that an organisation might use the information that they have collected from market research.

Investigation ideas

LOTTERY WINNERS!

OVER TO YOU

Carry out some market research to find out where people would choose to go on holiday if money was not an object. You need to ask each person that you interview to imagine that they have won three million pounds on the lottery!

Ask each person the following questions:
- Where would be the first place that you would go on holiday?
- Why would you choose this particular destination?
- Have you been to this destination before?
- Who would you take on holiday with you?

Each member of your group should try to ask at least 20 people from a range of backgrounds, such as different ages and occupations.

When you have all completed the survey, collect the answers together and work out:
- Which destinations are the most popular? For example, would most people choose somewhere exotic like the Far East?
- What factors make people choose specific destinations? For example, are people attracted by adventure or sunny beaches?
- Who would people take on holiday with them if they could afford it? Might this influence where they would choose to go? For example, would a family choose Disneyland because their children would enjoy it?
- How many people chose a destination that they had already been to?

REVISION PROMPT

What have I learnt about the market research?

_____

_____

_____

What am I still unsure about?

_____

_____

_____

How am I going to find out the extra information that I need?

_____

_____

_____

The four Ps in the marketing mix

There are a lot of different activities involved in successful marketing. It involves getting the right product to the right people in the right place at the right price using the right promotion.

We have looked at how organisations reach people through target marketing, and how they identify market segments. The other activities in the definition include the right product, right place, right price and right promotion. These are known as the **four Ps**.

The four Ps

Product – the goods and services that an organisation offers

Place – where the goods and services are offered

Price – how much the goods and services cost

Promotion – how organisations get people to buy their goods and services

The four Ps work together to form what is known as the **marketing mix**. This is one of the most widely used ideas in marketing and is a useful way of seeing how organisations go about their marketing activities.

Although each factor is important on its own, it is the way that they are combined, or 'mixed', which affects their success. For example, an organisation may have an excellent product but if customers cannot get to it or cannot afford it or have not heard about it then it will not sell. For a good marketing mix, an organisation should:

- provide a product that customers want (product)
- make sure the customer can buy it (place)
- charges a price that the customer is willing to pay (price)
- promote it effectively so that the customer knows about it (promotion).

McDonald's marketing mix

Product

Most people recognise the McDonald's product, largely because it is the same wherever you go. Staff training, food and drink products, packaging, and the design and décor of restaurants are the same in all of their outlets. This means that a customer can be sure of the product that they are buying whether it is in Paris, Palma or Putney.

Research carried out by Interbrand found that the McDonald's product was recognised by more people throughout the world than any other, even Coca Cola. Customers see the McDonald's product as representing:

- fast service
- cleanliness
- value for money
- a 'fun' experience for all of the family.

The McDonald's product in the UK was aimed at the family market by offering catering as a leisure experience. McDonald's have continuously developed new products to meet changing customer needs. Trends in healthy eating and the growing popularity of vegetarianism have seen the introduction of fish and bean burgers. More recently, ethnic influences have resulted in the development of Indian-style products. McDonald's have also targeted children with products, such as the hugely successful 'Happy Meals' offering food, soft drink and a free toy.

Place

McDonald's restaurants seem to be located on every high street throughout the UK. The company has also developed outlets at airports, on ferries, at football grounds and even in hospitals, in fact, anywhere that attracts a large volume of people looking for a fast meal or snack.

Price

The prices charged at McDonald's has always been based on the idea of giving good value for money. Frequent special offers are promoted, such as their very successful 'two for the price of one Big Mac' offer in 1999. This was so successful, that when customer demand for Big Macs increased by 800 per cent McDonald's ran out of burgers and had to put apology advertisements in the national press.

Promotion

McDonald's have always spent a lot of money on promotion. In 1998, the company spent £44m on advertising campaigns compared to the £15.6m spent by their competitors, Burger King. In 1974 the original advertising slogan promised: 'There's a difference at McDonald's you'll enjoy.' This aimed at persuading customers that the company was offering a new and fun product.

Much of McDonald's promotion is carried out through television advertising and national newspapers.

McDonald's also uses what are known as promotional tie-ins, where their product is linked to another product. For example, in 1996 the company reached a ten-year agreement with Disney for the exclusive rights to merchandise based on new Disney films such as A Bug's Life and Pocahontas.

Special offers and posters are also used at outlets to entice hungry passers-by in for a meal.

A typical McDonald's location ▼

Product = goods and service

In marketing, '**product**' includes both **goods** and **services**. Goods are physical objects, such as food and drink, exercise equipment and sportswear. Services involve the combination of skills, information or entertainment, such as the use of facilities or equipment. Examples include sports coaching, hotel accommodation, guiding services at a stately home, and a concert or theatre production. Essentially, goods are something that you can take away with you whereas a service is something that you experience at the time.

Some organisations offer both goods and services. For example, Pizza Hut sells goods in the form of food and drinks and it provides services such as a place to eat and children's entertainment.

▲ Services include the whole museum experience

◀ Goods are physical objects

OVER TO YOU

Identify products and services

Many leisure and tourism products are a combination of both physical products and services. For example, at a pop concert you often buy much more than just a ticket to listen to your favourite band.

- Draw two columns. Label one Products and the other, Services.
- The list shows some of the things that you may expect to be provided at a pop concert. Put each item into the appropriate column.
- Think of any more items that could be added to either column.

- the exciting atmosphere
- programmes
- listening/watching the concert
- First aid assistance
- merchandising (e.g. T-shirts, posters, videos, etc.)
- comfortable seating
- heating and lighting
- refreshments
- clear signposts
- parking
- tickets
- advice from staff.

▲ Pop concerts provide both goods and services

Product or service features

When we talk about a **product's features** we mean the characteristics that the customer recognises as being part of the overall product. For example, the product features of a particular theme park might be:

- exciting rides
- children's attractions
- picnic areas
- catering facilities
- live entertainment
- well laid-out park.

Organisations spend a lot of time making sure the products they offer have specific features that will appeal to their target markets. These features are shown in promotional materials to persuade customers that the product will meet their needs.

▲ The experience of riding the Pirate Falls at Legoland

Conduct a survey

OVER TO YOU

Choose five leisure or tourism products or services that you and your group will have heard about. Take turns to interview each person in your group.

- Ask each to describe three product features that they would associate with the products you have chosen, for example, value for money, good service, etc.
- Record the answers on a table like the one shown.
- When you have completed your survey, give a short presentation on the overall product features that have been identified for each product.

Leisure or tourism product/service	Product/service features

The brand names

The **brand name** is the name given to a particular product or service to distinguish it from other similar products. For example, a product could be sportswear and brand names would be Adidas, Puma, Kappa and Nike.

It is important that a brand name suits the product and sums up the product features. Organisations invest a lot in promoting a particular brand in the hope that customers will automatically think of and buy their product rather than that of a competitor. This is known as **brand loyalty**.

Many organisations combine their brand name with a logo to make it instantly recognisable. A logo is a symbol that helps identify an organisation.

Creating a strong brand is all about getting the customer to trust the brand product. In other words, customers know that the brand will always meet their needs and expectations.

STOP & THINK

Which brand do you automatically think of when buying jeans?

Some of the well-known brand names and logos in leisure and tourism ▶

ENGLISH HERITAGE

CASE STUDY

Europe's most trusted brands

In November 2000, Readers Digest magazine carried out research to find out which brands were most trusted by customers. The five factors that customers were asked to think about were:

- quality
- excellent value
- trustworthiness
- strong image
- understanding customers' needs.

Some of the highest scores were for brands outside the leisure and tourism industry, such as Colgate toothpaste and Persil soap powder.

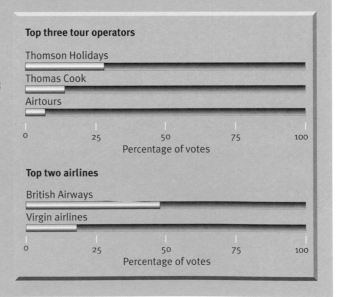

OVER TO YOU

Brand features

In pairs, decide on a leisure or tourism brand that you are both loyal to. For example, it could be a sports shop, fast food restaurant, a cinema, or a sports centre.

- Write a list of what has made you loyal to this particular brand.
- Discuss your ideas with the rest of the group.

Cover for the Unexpected

Because you never know what might happen on holiday, Thomas Cook Travel Insurance covers you for the unexpected. Whether you need insurance for single or multiple trips, we can easily arrange cover together with your booking and other travel plans.

Underwritten by AXA Insurance UK plc - a trusted insurance provider - our comprehensive cover is excellent value for money, and provides complete peace of mind whilst abroad. Another good reason to leave your travel plans to Thomas Cook.

Thomas Cook Travel Insurance

Available for single trips only, this comprehensive insurance policy includes 24 hour medical assistance and covers personal accident, cancellation, baggage and legal expenses.

Thomas Cook Classic Insurance

Available on a single or annual multi-trip basis, this is a premium level of insurance that offers extended cover with the key benefit of unlimited medical cover. It also includes Premier Care Global Assistance - a helpline available 24 hours, 365 days a year - to assist with all types of emergency situations. This puts you in touch with expert, multi-lingual staff fully trained in dealing with emergency situations when abroad.

▲ Travel insurance is another example of after-sales service, offering 24-hour assistance and information to customers who need it

The after-sales service

When a customer buys a leisure or tourism product the buying experience does not always end when the customer leaves. Many customers will need extra after-sales service. Organisations recognise this as being an important part of the overall product offered. You or your family may have bought some home entertainment equipment such as a computer, television, video recorder or camera. Organisations which sell these products understand that many customers may have problems or questions about the product once they get them home. Therefore, they often provide a telephone helpline, as after-sales service, to help you to get the most out of your new purchase.

Computer customers often need some after-sales service ▶

The product mix

Many leisure and tourism organisations offer several different products so that they can satisfy the needs of different types of customers. This is known as the **product mix**.

A public swimming pool, for example, may offer public sessions, 'splash' sessions, lane training, and classes for children, or mothers and babies.

OVER TO YOU

Products and customers

Large tour operators often have quite complicated product mixes with different types of products being sold through different holiday brochures.

- Select one tour operator, such as Thomson or Airtours, and collect a range of different brochures that they offer.
- As a group discuss which particular customers each is aimed at.
- Can you identify any target markets that the tour operator does not cater for?

The product life cycle

The leisure and tourism market is always changing and even popular products can suffer declining sales or fewer customers. For example, the popularity of the cinema reached its peak in 1947, when 1 460 million tickets were sold in the UK. By 1987 this number had fallen drastically to 80 million, due largely to the development of television. However, in the 1990s attendances had once again increased to around 150 million due largely to the development of multiplex cinemas.

In the **product life cycle**, all products pass through four different stages: introduction, growth, maturity and decline.

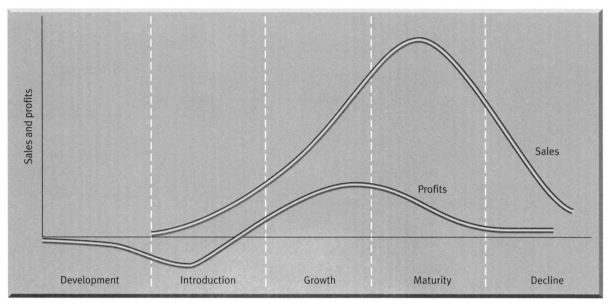

▲ The product life cycle

Introduction	This is when a new product is first introduced. Demand may be low to start with because many people will not have heard about the product. Example: new interactive tourist attractions, adventure holidays in South America
Growth	As more customers become aware of the product, the sales will start to rise quickly if customers like the product. This may be due to word-of-mouth recommendations and the beginning of some customer loyalty. Example: package holidays to Slovenia, children's residential activity weeks
Maturity	Sales are at their highest but tend to remain level. Most of the demand will come from repeat customers who are loyal to the particular brand. Example: package holidays to Greece and Florida, video hire shops, tenpin bowling alleys, family pubs
Decline	Demand starts to decline. This can be for a number of reasons, such as increased competition or changing customer needs. Example: some local theatres, traditional museums, British seaside resorts.

In the product life cycle diagram, each of the stages is shown as being the same length. In reality, each stage may last a different length of time. For example, a basic product such as milk or bread has been in the maturity stage for a very long time. However, something like the skateboard had a short maturity stage and then quickly declined in popularity.

Most organisations try to keep the introduction stage as short as possible as it tends to be the least profitable. A large amount of advertising is needed to attract new customers in this stage, which is very expensive. Many smaller leisure and tourism organisations do not realise the costs involved in introducing a new product. They may go out of business before even reaching the growth stage, as they cannot afford to pay for the advertising. The growth and maturity stages are the most profitable because less advertising is needed as the same customers are returning to buy the product.

Successful leisure and tourism organisations, who understand the idea of the product life cycle, will continually develop and offer a range of different products to ensure that they have products placed at each stage of the life cycle. As a particular product begins to pass from maturity to decline there will be others rising through the introduction and growth stages to take their place.

When a product reaches the decline stage of the product life cycle, the organisation has two choices:

- to stop offering the product and develop a new product for their customers
- to try to 'revamp' the product so that it appeals to existing and new customers.

For example, many traditional seaside resorts such as Brighton, Torquay and Scarborough have attempted to reverse the decline in visitor numbers by revamping products and targeting the conference market.

Some other examples of leisure and tourism products that have been revamped and relaunched following periods of decline, include:

- holiday centres – such as Butlin's Holiday Worlds
- car ferries with limited leisure facilities on board – some car ferries now provide a wide range of leisure facilities and attractions
- museums – many museums have been redeveloped to include interactive displays and simulators.

OVER TO YOU

Conduct a survey

The fizzy drink Lucozade is one product that has come out of the decline stage of the product life cycle. When it was first offered, it was sold as a drink for people who were unwell, with the promise that it would help them get better! Over the years fewer people bought the drink and sales were in a serious decline. In March 1995 the company relaunched Lucozade as a 'sports' drink. They changed the packaging and introduced a number of different flavours and

▲ The changing face of Lucozade

In pairs, carry out a small survey of friends and relatives to find out what image they have of Lucozade. You will probably find out that the older people that you ask will have a different image of Lucozade than the younger ones. This is because Lucozade advertising is now targeted at young people and older people will remember the old image of the product.

The price must be right

The second 'P' in the marketing mix is **price**. It is important that organisations get the price right. If the price is too high customers may not be able to afford the product; if it is too low, the organisation may not make a profit.

The actual selling price

The **actual selling price** of a product means how much the customer is charged. In deciding this, there are four main factors to consider:

- how much it costs the organisation to provide the product
- what customers will pay
- what competitors are charging
- how much profit the organisation want to make (if any).

Prices in leisure and tourism often vary according to the time that the product is offered or the type of customer. When deciding on prices, organisations have to think about peak and off-peak pricing, group and special discounts, and special offers.

Peak and off-peak pricing

Peak times are when there are most customers and off-peak times are when there are fewest customers. Prices are often higher during peak times and lower during off-peak. This is to encourage more customers to use facilities at quiet times.

- Many theatres offer lower prices during weekdays than at weekends.
- Railway companies charge higher fares to travelers leaving before 9.30 a.m. than they do to those travelling later in the day.
- Many public houses offer 'happy hours' when drinks are cheaper.
- Popular package holidays to Europe are most expensive during the school holidays (known as 'high season') because this is when most families want to travel. Lower prices during winter are intended to encourage people to take holidays at a time when demand is low (referred to as 'low season').

▲ The actual selling price of the Heathrow airport shuttle service

Compare holiday prices

- Look through a range of holiday brochures and identify when prices are at their highest and lowest.

- Discuss the reasons for any sudden and short-term rise in prices, for example, prices often rise dramatically at school half-term breaks.

- Compare different types of holidays, such as European winter sports, European summer sun and long-haul holidays (e.g. to the Caribbean, Asia and Africa). You will find that peak and off-peak is not necessarily at the same time of the year for all of them. For example, holidays in Mexico are often cheaper in the summer months because it is the rainy season.

Group and special discounts

Many leisure and tourism facilities offer discounts to certain customers, such as organised groups, school parties, children, pensioners, the unemployed and students. This is to attract customers who might not buy the product usually, or to fill places through bulk (or group) sales which reduces the cost of administration per customer.

◄ The Jorvik Viking Centre in York offers a wide range of different admission charges

2002 admission prices for Jorvik Centre		
Admission charges		
	Jorvik only	Joint ticket (to also visit the Archaeological Resource Centre)
Adult	£6.95	£9.95
Child (5-15)	£4.95	£7.95
Family (2 adults, 2 children)	£21.50	£36.50
Seniors/Students (with proof)	£5.95	£8.95

Premium prices: Tickets can be purchased in advance for pre-booked time slots and during the Jorvik Viking Festivals for an extra £1.00 per ticket. (Pre-booked Family tickets cost £25.00 for the Jorvik Centre only and £40.00 for a joint visit.)

Special offers

A facility may offer reduced prices to all its customers for a limited period. For example, theme parks sometimes offer reduced prices to customers who produce vouchers or discount coupons that have been issued in sales promotions. Likewise, travel agents usually advertise special offers and late availability holidays to increase sales.

Credit terms

Many leisure and tourism organisations offer credit terms that allow customers to pay for a product over a period of time. This is particularly useful for the more expensive products that a customer may not be able to afford all at once, such as a time-share apartment or home entertainment equipment.

Profitability

When setting their prices many leisure and tourism organisations want to make sure that they will make a profit. They need to work out how much it costs to actually provide the product, and charge enough to cover the costs and make a bit more money. The costs include the expense of producing the actual product as well as rent, electricity, staff and advertising.

Organisations try to make a profit when they set their prices ▼

	Direct Holidays	jmc	My Travel (previously Airtours)	Thomson	First Choice
Price per adult	£399	£419	£649	£557	£555
Price per child	One free	One free	One free	£251	£235
Flight supplement	£20 per person	£49 per adult	£95 per adult	-	£83 per person
Free insurance?	No	No	Yes	No	Yes
Other costs	£10 per person	Booking fee £8 per adult transfer	-	Booking fee £7 per person	
Dep. times	07.50	09.30	13.40	08.25	09.15
Ret. times	14.00	15.40	19.50	14.30	15.20
Discounts	-	-	20% + free insurance	£146 discount	£277.50 discount
Total cost	£858	£966	£1206	£1219	1337.50

▲ Tour Operator pricing

Pricing

The prices charged for package holidays are often very confusing for customers. Different tour operators offer different prices, discounts and extra charges. The price you see in the brochure may not be what you end up paying!

- Look at the table which shows the prices charged by five tour operators for a holiday in Magaluf, Majorca.
- Work out how much it would cost for two adults and one child to go with each tour operator.
- Which is the cheapest?

Place = where the customer gets the product

The third P of the marketing mix is place. Place describes how the product or service reaches the customer, in other words, how the customer goes about actually buying it. It includes:

- the types of outlet or facility used
- where outlets or facilities are located
- identifying distribution channels.

With a service a customer usually has to travel to the provider to experience it. For example, if you wanted to swim in a local pool, see a cinema film or eat a restaurant meal, you would have to go to the actual facilities; they cannot be brought to you. This means that the 'place' element of the marketing mix is very important.

The types of outlet or facility used

The location of a leisure and tourism product will often influence the type of outlet or facility used. A sports retailer would have a very different type of outlet in an out-of-town shopping mall than in the high street of a historic town such as Chester or Bath. Choosing the right type of outlet and location will depend on the type of product offered and the target markets. One of the main considerations will be whether the type of outlet or facility fits in with the general image of the organisation and its customers.

Where outlets or facilities are located

The physical location of a leisure or tourism product is often very important. For example, many people suggested that Disneyland, Paris was unpopular when it first opened because it was in a fairly cold and wet area of Europe compared to the Disney parks in Florida and California.

A large number of factors need to be considered when deciding on a suitable location. For example:

- Is there sufficient public transport in the area?
- How much car parking space is there and what does it cost?
- What other facilities nearby attract people to the area?
- Are there already similar facilities and if so, will there be enough customers to support all of them?
- What is the climate like?
- Will the organisation be able to find staff and suppliers in the area?
- Is there sufficient public transport in the area?

OVER TO YOU

Accessible location

Select five tourist attractions in your area. Try to make sure that they are well spread apart. Visit each attraction and evaluate how accessible the location is. You should think about the following:

- the types of outlets or facilities in the area
- public transport to the attraction (including the types available and the times that they run)
- roads for car users (e.g. are the approach roads very busy or is there a complicated one-way system?)
- parking (cost and amount of parking spaces)
- signs to the attraction (would it be easy to find if you were visiting it for the first time?).

Many leisure and tourism organisations give details about their location and how to reach it ▼

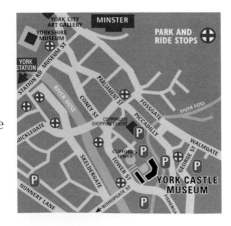

Distribution channels

Location does not only mean where a leisure or tourism facility is but also the ways in which a customer can buy it. This is known as **distribution channels**. For example, if you were going on holiday to Benidorm the location of the product would be Spain. However, you would probably buy the holiday at a travel agency. This is how the tour operator distributes the product. Alternatively, you might buy the holiday directly from the tour operator or over the internet.

You can't beat a Portland Direct Price Checked holiday*

We've Price Checked thousands of holidays in our new Summer 2002 brochure against the equivalent holidays in the brochures from Airtours, JMC, First Choice and Direct Holidays, to make sure we're beating their adult brochure prices. That means you always get the best holiday at the lowest price guaranteed.** This devotion to getting you the right holiday, in and around the Med, at the right price is probably why we're the UK's No. 1 direct holiday company and why we take more people on holiday than any other direct tour operator. So give us a call to find your perfect place in the sun.

Call our 24 hour Brochure Line now on

0845 795 1000

Quote code: NDS2A

We're open 7 days a week. Calls charged at local rate.
or visit us online at
www.portland-direct.co.uk

Portland DIRECT

Price **LESS** holidays guaranteed

▲ Organisations need to supply details of where to buy the product

CASE STUDY

Harry Potter

In some situations it is the actual location that creates the leisure or tourism attraction or facility. For example, locations used for filming television programmes or films often become tourist destinations. The hugely successful books and film of Harry Potter are a good example of this.

HARRY POTTER FILM LOCATIONS

- Alnwick Castle, Northumberland
- Goatland Station, North Yorkshire
- Cloisters of Gloucester Cathedral
- Bodleian Library and Christchurch College, Oxford
- Lacock Abbey, Wiltshire
- London Zoo and Kings Cross Station, London

0   km   150

Potter map to pull in the tourists

Tourist chiefs are counting on Harry Potter to give Britain a multi-million pound boost. They are hoping a map showing places featured in the new film, *Harry Potter and the Philosopher's Stone*, will help lure back thousands of foreign visitors put off by the foot and mouth crisis.

Despite being made with American money, the locations used were English. The apprentice wizards board their magical steam train at King's Cross station and Gloucester Cathedral becomes Harry's famous boarding school of Hogwarts. The grounds of Alnwick Castle in Northumberland will be seen during screen quidditch matches and Durham Cathedral and Lacock Abbey in other school scenes.

Even Goathland, the North Yorkshire moorland village made famous as Aidensfield in TV's *Heartbeat*, gets a showing as Hogsmeade station.

Elliot Frisby of the British Tourist Authority said, 'If Harry Potter is an international success, everyone from local bed-and-breakfast places to tea shops and souvenir shops should benefit. The money generated could run into several million pounds.'

Source: *Sunday Mirror*, 19 August 2001

Promotion = telling and persuading

The fourth 'P' of the marketing mix is **promotion**. This involves telling customers about an organisation's products and persuading them to buy them.

Promotion covers a wide range of activities which are likely to be used in combination as part of a campaign. In the following sections we will look at some of the most commonly used promotional techniques and materials and discuss how they are used effectively in promotional campaigns.

Promotional techniques are the ways in which an organisation promotes its products. All successful leisure and tourism organisations, whether they are multi-national companies or small local providers, will use a range of promotional techniques. Some of the most commonly used techniques are:

- advertising
- direct marketing
- public relations
- personal selling
- displays
- sponsorship
- demonstrations
- sales promotions.

STOP & THINK

What do you usually do when the commercial break comes on during a television programme – make a cup of tea? switch to other channels? have a chat? Unless a promotion can attract the customers' attention and make them watch, read or listen, then it is not going to be effective.

▲ Promotion includes a lot of activities

How to attract attention

Technique	Reason for using
Use unusual or attractive colours	Different colours give different impressions and organisations think carefully about which ones to use. For example, the dominant colours in a summer holiday brochure or advertisement are bright blue and yellow because they are associated with sun, sea and sand.
Attractive fonts or print style	The type of font used can create a strong image about the product. For example, a traditional font such as that used in this text is suitable for a book but may be boring for a promotional title. Promoters will try to use a font that is in keeping with the image of their product. A product aimed at youth markets might choose something like JESPER or KIDPRINT.
Bold titles or headlines	An imaginative headline can often be very effective in attracting the customers' attention.
Pictures and drawings	Customers are often drawn more quickly to a well-chosen picture that sums up what the product is about, rather than a detailed description.
An attractive layout of information	Many organisations pay attention to the way that pictures and text are laid out so that it attracts attention. For example, slanted captions and pictures of varying size and angle all help to make promotional materials more eye-catching and attractive.
Use well-known celebrities to attract specific customers	Many organisations use celebrities in their promotional materials to attract attention. The choice of celebrity will depend on the type of product and the target customers. For example, a boy band would be ineffective in attracting the attention of older customers.
Humour such as a cartoon or funny picture or caption	Humour is used widely in promotional materials. It helps attract attention and puts the customer in a good frame of mind. Many organisations use amusing pictures of young children or animals because they know that this generally raises a smile in the majority of the population.

Using AIDA

Knowing how to design promotional materials that are going to be successful is very important. One of the most common methods used in promotion to make sure it is effective is to use an idea known as AIDA.

AIDA stands for:

- Attention
- Desire
- Interest
- Action.

Attention

Attracting the customers' attention is the first, and probably most important, part of AIDA because if the promotion does not get their attention, the whole campaign is wasted. This is often a lot harder than it seems.

There are lots of different ways that organisations use to make their promotions eye-catching and able to attract their customers' attention.

Interest

It is clearly important to attract the customer's attention but if the content of the advertisement does not encourage them to carry on reading, listening or watching it is likely to be ineffective. Therefore, having attracted the customers' attention the next stage is to keep their interest. This is often achieved by slowly developing the features that originally attracted their attention, rather than bombarding them with lots of information.

Desire

The aim of the content of promotional material should not only be to create interest, but also make the customer want to buy the product. This is the third stage of AIDA. Having attracted their attention and kept their interest, the promoter now needs to create a desire in the customer to actually buy the product. This is done by describing the product in a way that shows how it can meet the customers' needs and expectations. One of the ways in which a lot of leisure and tourism providers create desire in the customer to visit their attraction is to describe it in a way that makes the customer feel as if they are already there. They use lots of descriptive words like 'exciting', 'thrilling' and 'dangerous'.

Attracting attention

Each of the leaflets is a good example of how leisure and tourism providers use various methods to attract the customers' attention to their product. Remember that different methods are effective with different products and different target audiences. Identify how some or all of the leaflets attract the customers' attention.

Action

The final stage of AIDA is to show the customer how they can actually go about buying the product. They create action. Research has shown that the easier it is for customers to buy a product as soon as they have decided that they want it, the more likely they are to buy it. Conversely, the longer the gap between deciding to buy something and actually buying it, the more likely they are to change their minds. Therefore, promotional materials need to make it as easy as possible to buy the product as soon as possible.

Advertising

Advertising is when an organisation pays for the publication, display or broadcast of information that describes their products or services in a favourable way.

Advertising can be carried out in a number of ways. An advertisement can be national and therefore seen across the whole country. It may also be regional, such as only in the London area, in the south of the country, or in Yorkshire. Businesses need to choose the most suitable medium to use for advertising. The medium is the way in which the advertising information is given to the customer and includes:

- radio
- cinema
- newspapers
- magazines
- billboards
- television (both terrestrial and satellite)
- teletext (the information service on commercial television).

All of these may be national, regional or local. However, remember that television and radio advertising can only be through commercial channels, not through the BBC.

In addition to these media, advertising can be found in many other forms, including advertisements on buses, trains and other forms of transport. Advertising can also be found on billboards, electrical signs, as part of loudspeaker announcements at sports grounds and other facilities, and inside programmes, brochures and on tickets.

Advertising channels

Fill in the following table with examples of national, regional and local advertising channels. Some examples have been given to get you started. Replace these with ideas of your own. A line has been drawn in the spaces that do not apply e.g. there is no local television.

OVER TO YOU

Medium	National	Regional	Local
Radio		Radio York	
Television		Anglia	–
Cinema	Warners	–	
Newspapers Evening News			Bolton
Magazines	Readers Digest		

Which is the best advertising medium to use?

With such a wide range of advertising media available, the main problem for organisations is to choose the one which is the most effective. They need to decide at which customers to aim the advertisement and then identify which medium or media these customers are most likely to hear or look at. It is very important to choose the right media because advertising is so expensive.

In 2000 McDonald's spent a total of over £43 million on advertising. The main media used were:
Press: £35 981
Cinema: £780 161
Radio: £2, 920 913
Outdoor: £4 782 681
Television: £33 850 846.

◁ Different customers are targeted at different times of the day ▶

When are products advertised?

OVER TO YOU

Watch a commercial television channel at different times of the day, for example, at breakfast time, during the day, early evening, or mid-evening, and late at night. Keep a record of the products that are advertised at each time. Then discuss the following with the rest of the group:

- How do the advertisements vary according to the time of day?

- Do they vary according to the type of programme that they appear in? Are different products advertised during soap operas compared with during a late night news programme?

- What types of customers are targeted at different times of the day and during different types of programmes?

STOP & THINK

If advertisers wanted to promote their products to you, which magazines and newspapers should they use? Would they be successful if they tried to attract you through radio advertising? If they were to use television advertising, during which programmes are you most likely to be tuned in?

Direct marketing

Direct marketing is one of the fastest growing areas of promotion. It involves sending or giving promotional material directly to individual customers. This can be done by post, over the telephone, or door-to-door.

One of the great advantages of direct marketing is that organisations can target those customers whom they think will be particularly interested in the products on offer. For example, a theatre might send out a direct mail letter about a forthcoming production to customers who have seen similar productions in the past.

▲ Door-to-door direct marketing

Oasis
Forest Holiday Villages

October 2001

Mrs L Taylor

North Yorkshire

48503 / TAYL17 RYO12 5BU / 32333

Another break at Oasis in 2002, do you really need persuading?

Dear Mrs Taylor,

The Oasis experience is something that, once sampled, most people can't wait to repeat.

Some may take a little longer to come back. Perhaps they imagine they can find a similar holiday elsewhere, only to discover that Oasis really is unique. In fact, nowhere comes close.

After all, where else can you stay in luxury in the heart of the forest - no cars, no worries? Where else can you enjoy total relaxation or indulge in over 100 different activities, indoor and outdoor? Where else can every member of your family have exactly the holiday they want?

See overleaf for your early booking offers.

We hope that our 2002 brochure will bring back happy memories, whatever you and your family remember best about Oasis.

Perhaps it's the feeling of being so close to nature, in a forest location which you share with red squirrels and rare orchids. Maybe it's the sheer number of activities you can all do together, as a family, from the World of Water to horse-riding. Perhaps it's the chance of total indulgence with a session in our Health and Beauty Spa. Or is it the opportunity for parents to have some time to themselves while the children have the time of their life, in complete safety?

Continued

O2LT1

The increasing use of computers has greatly helped direct marketing because companies can store huge lists of names, addresses and customer details – known as **customer databases**. Details of particular types of customers can be found quickly. These can be used to provide a mailing list for direct marketing. For example, a hotel might select all guests on their database who have stayed for a Christmas break in the past and send them details about the Easter break package.

◀ Oasis direct mail letter

There is a big disadvantage to direct marketing. Many people have become so used to receiving 'junk mail' or telephone calls from sales people that they simply ignore it. Customers realise that the same letter has probably been sent to hundreds of other people, and so they simply throw it away without reading it. One way of overcoming this is to try to personalise the letter by using the words 'you' and 'yours' as often as possible so that the customer feels as if they are being written to personally. In addition, using the customer's name rather than just 'Dear Sir or Madam' is more effective.

OVER TO YOU

I'm talking to you!

Read the letter shown here. It's fairly impersonal, isn't it? Re-write it using the words 'you' and 'yours' to make it sound personal.

The Occupier
Calendar Cottage
Merrydown
Hants

Dear Customer

Many of our customers use us year after year because they know that we can offer a personal service at competitive prices. Every year we receive dozens of letters from customers telling us how much they have enjoyed the holidays we have arranged for them.

This year we are able to offer a special introductory offer to new customers: Anyone who books a summer package holiday with us receives a guaranteed discount of 20% on the total package holiday price. In addition, we are able to provide holiday insurance and currency exchange at very reasonable charges.

Anyone wishing to take advantage of this amazing offer should call in to our branch in town and produce this letter. Our friendly staff will be pleased to serve you.

Yours sincerely

Manager

Public relations

Public relations (PR) is the planned attempt to create a favourable image of an organisation.

One of the main advantages that most organisations recognise, is that PR is free. It often involves contacting the media (newspapers, radio, television) and persuading them to publicise information about the organisation and its products. This may be achieved by issuing press releases, where 'story' ideas are given to journalists to provide them with ready-written articles or feature material. The general aim is to create a good public image of the organisation and get the name of the organisation well known. Some press releases are good PR for a number of organisations or individuals who may be working together on a particular project or event.

Five million wheel

British Airways London Eye, London's top paid-for visitor attraction, welcomed its five millionth visitor today (24 July 2001).

Secretary of State for Culture, Media and Sport, Tessa Jowell MP, welcomed Hal and Valorie Holzman, of Sacramento, California, and their son Mike, 15, on to the world's biggest observation wheel.

To mark the event the family were given a prize of two British Airways World Traveller Plus return tickets and a private capsule on the London Eye.

Mr Holzman said, 'The London Eye is a famous landmark and was a key part of our trip to Britain. We were surprised and delighted to be the five millionth visitors to ride 450ft up on the Eye. It was a fantastic trip.'

The Right Hon Tessa Jowell, MP, said; 'I am delighted to see the five millionth visitor on the BA London Eye. To reach this number in only 17 months is a fantastic achievement. This year, London was awarded the title of best travel destination in the world. From the top of the Eye on a beautiful day like today you can see why.'

Media requiring further information should contact the British Airways Press Office in London on +44 (0)208 738 5100 (office hours) or +44 (0)208 759 5511 (out of office hours).

Source: British Airways press release

The effects of good public relations can help to increase sales. For example, if a television holiday programme or magazine includes an enthusiastic report about a travel destination, this may be followed by an increase in customer enquiries. Many resorts and holiday companies use PR by giving journalists free holidays in the hope of a complimentary 'write-up'.

PR also includes creating a good relationship with the community by providing support to various groups or events in the area, for example.

Jupiter Hotel is a real star!

The three-star Jupiter Hotel proved this week that not only do they offer some of the best accommodation and food in town but they also have hearts of gold. Having read about the cancellation of the Care Bears Playgroup's Christmas party in last Friday's edition, the Jupiter decided to play Santa Claus.

Readers may remember that Care Bears had arranged a special Christmas surprise for its young members with a party in a local church hall. They were devastated when it had to be cancelled because the hall had been flooded by a burst water pipe. Jupiter chambermaid, Anne Tomlinson, read the article and told her general manager, Bill Soames, about it. Bill offered the playgroup a free room at the hotel for the party as well as providing all of the food and drink for the children. He even dressed up as Santa Claus and distributed presents from the hotel to all of the children.

Playgroup leader, Sue Kirk, said, 'We cannot thank Bill Soames and his staff enough. It is the hotel's busiest time of the year but they still managed to fit us in and gave the children a party that they will be talking about for months.'

Bill Soames was modest about his efforts saying, 'It's Anne who should take the credit, as she was the one who read the article and decided that we should do something. I must admit that putting on a Santa Claus outfit and seeing the look on the children's faces as I handed out the presents was one of the highlights of the year for me!'

OVER TO YOU

Newspaper articles

The article, from a local newspaper, is a good example of how a leisure and tourism provider uses positive public relations. After reading the article, discuss the following points in small groups:

- What general image of the hotel will newspaper readers get from this article?
- How does the use of quotes from Sue Kirk and Bill Soames help to create a positive image?
- What effect do you think the article might have on the following groups of people?
  - existing customers
  - locals who have not used the hotel before
  - existing staff
  - local people looking for employment.
- Find a copy of a local newspaper. How many examples of good public relations can you find in the articles in the paper?

Personal selling

Personal selling involves direct sales contact between an organisation and its customers. It may be carried out face-to-face or over the telephone.

Most employees in the leisure and tourism industry will be involved in selling situations on a frequent basis. Personal selling does not persuade the customer to buy something that they do not want simply to achieve a sale.

The travel advisor in a travel agency is constantly using personal selling skills when booking holidays for customers. However, it is not in the advisor's interest to recommend a holiday that will not meet the customer's needs and expectations. If customers are disappointed, it is likely that they will complain and choose not to use the travel agency in future when booking holidays.

To make personal selling a success, you need to:

▲ Personal selling is an effective form of promotion

- identify the customers' needs and expectations; ask the right questions and listening carefully to their responses
- provide customers with honest and accurate information so that they can decide which product suits their needs
- explain all of the alternatives to the customer so that they can make an informed decision
- do not pressurise customers into buying products that they are unsure about
- describe the products and services in an enthusiastic and positive way; if you are not enthusiastic, you cannot expect the customer to be
- explain to customers how to buy the product that they have chosen
- wherever possible, follow up on the sale to check that customers are satisfied with what they have bought.

Many leisure and tourism organisations train their staff in selling techniques. The Travel Agency Thomas Cook provide their travel consultants with a list of 15 key questions to ask customers when selling holidays.

- What do you like to do on holiday?
- What do the children like to do on holiday?
- What does the other person like to do on holiday?
- What age and sex and are the children?
- What type of self-catering accommodation would you like, for example, studio, apartment?
- How many bedrooms would you like?
- What type of resort would you like, for example, quiet, lively?
- What on-site facilities would you like?

▲ Thomas Cook's key questions when selling

- What amenities would you like close by?
- What time of day would you prefer to travel?
- Would you like to be close to the airport?
- Do you intend to travel around while you are there?
- Are you flexible with your dates and departure airport?
- Do you have a country or resort in mind?
- What kind of temperature are you looking for?

OVER TO YOU

Role-play

Before

Collect enough leaflets or brochures from local leisure and tourism attractions so that each person has a different one. Read the information on your attraction carefully so that you can answer all questions.

During

In pairs, take the roles of a member of staff at the attraction and an inquirer who is interested in visiting the attraction. Role-play the situation with the member of staff using good personal selling skills to explain how the attraction can satisfy the needs of the customer.

The customer should ask at least five questions such as:

- What is there for children to enjoy?
- Is it good value for money?
- I don't have a car, how will I get there?
- What type of refreshments are available?
- Do you have disabled facilities?

The inquirer should think of some specific questions that someone would ask about the particular attraction.

After

As a group, discuss how well the members of staff used personal selling skills and what they could have done to improve their performance.

Displays

Many leisure and tourism organisations use displays to promote specific products and services. One of the most common types of display is to put posters in windows and on doors. For example, a pub might have various posters showing the nightly entertainment on offer, such as karaoke, quiz nights and singers.

Travel agencies use poster displays in their windows to let customers know about special deals and products ▼

Christmas comes early
in many hotels ▶

Many swimming pools use a display board to tell customers about different swimming lessons and forthcoming special events. These types of display are known as a **point-of-sales displays**. Customers can buy the product immediately instead of going away and possibly forgetting about it.

◄ A point-of-sales display

Point-of-sales displays in travel agencies

One of the main types of provider to use point-of-sales displays is the travel agency. Their shop window is very important for attracting customers into the shop to find out more about holidays, travel and other services offered. Depending on the type of travel agency, any number of products can be displayed. Some focus on special 'cheap' deals, whereas others show the wide range of services offered.

Visit two different travel agencies in your area and compare their shop window displays

■ What products and services are displayed in each?

■ What type of products and services seem to be most important e.g. those you see first because of where they are placed in the window?

■ How effective is the point-of-sales display?

■ Suggest any ways in which the display could be improved.

Sponsorship

Sponsorship involves one organisation giving financial or other support in exchange for its name being associated with the product or event. For example, every team in the Premier and Endsleigh football leagues displays the name of its sponsor on the players strip, and the former Football League Cup has been sponsored by several companies in recent years. Many arts and entertainment events are sponsored.

▲ Football clubs have sponsors' logos on their shirts

Sponsoring organisations have to choose carefully with which event or product they want to have their name associated. They use the opportunity to enhance their organisation's image and to strengthen awareness among customers. For their part, event organisers have to think carefully about the public image of a sponsor. For example, many people disagree with sporting events being sponsored by tobacco companies.

Although large leisure and tourism organisations will often pay thousands of pounds in sponsorship, it is just as effective on a smaller scale. Many privately owned organisations will sponsor local causes or contribute a more modest amount to national causes.

Virgin Atlantic supports land speed record

Virgin Atlantic today announced that it is supporting Olympic Gold Medal cyclist Jason Queally in his bid to break a land speed record for human powered vehicles.

To help him with his attempt, Virgin has donated flight tickets and freight space to transport Jason, his crew and his bicycle – Blue Yonder Challenger – to Nevada for his record attempt in October. And Jason should feel very at home in one of Virgin Atlantic's Upper Class seats as Reynard, the same people responsible for his futuristic vehicle, built them.

No stranger to challenging record breaking attempts himself, Sir Richard Branson, Chairman of Virgin Atlantic, said:

'It is a pleasure to be able to send Jason on his way and I will be watching his progress with interest. Most people know that I like to set myself challenges and I certainly wish everyone involved all the best of luck. Jason has already done Britain proud with his Olympic gold and I'm confident he can do the same with this record attempt.'

John Lloyd, Director of Virgin Atlantic Cargo, said: 'It's a pleasure to be able to help Jason by transporting the Blue Yonder Challenger to San Francisco and back for his world record attempt. Jason is such a dedicated and exceptional man. I wish him well and look forward to welcoming him back as the new record holder.'

Source: www. virgin.com

OVER TO YOU

Arranging sponsorship for Hotfoot's

Hotfoot's is a privately owned children's adventure park in South Wales. The manager has allowed £500 in her promotional budget for sponsorship as she feels that it could help to raise the profile of the park and show a caring side to the company. Over the last few months several local organisations and individuals have asked the company to sponsor them. The manager now has to decide how to best spend the £500.

Each of the requests below is for sponsorship of £250. As a group, discuss which two you think Hotfoot's should choose to sponsor, giving reasons for your choice. When making your decision remember what the manager's objectives are in providing sponsorship.

- The Vipers under 15-football team would like sponsorship to enable them to buy a new football strip for all players. They will have Hotfoot's name printed on the front and back of the football shirts.

- The local non-profit making theatre would like a donation of £250 towards their fund to provide programmes printed in Braille for the visually impaired. Three other local organisations have already donated money and all sponsors will be listed in the programme.

- A local group is trying to raise £5000 to enable them to send a 5-year-old child to America for specialist treatment for a rare genetic disorder. The campaign has already had a lot of coverage in the local newspaper and they only need a further £250.

- A part-time catering assistant at Hotfoot's is about to finish her Vocational A-level in Travel and Tourism and plans to work as a volunteer teacher in Sri Lanka for a year before going to University. She needs to raise £2000 in sponsorship.

- The local hospice would like to hold a charity fashion show at Hotfoot's to raise funds. They have asked to use Hotfoot's restaurant on a Saturday afternoon in July and would like the company to provide free refreshments. The event will be heavily publicised in the local press and attended by several hundred local residents.

Demonstrations

One of the problems with many promotional techniques is that the customer cannot really see or experience the product or service. For this reason many leisure and tourism organisations arrange demonstrations and visits to show customers what the products and services would be like if they bought them.

- A leisure centre may invite new customers to try out the facilities before they join as members.
- Time-share apartment companies often take prospective customers on a visit to the time-share complex to allow them to experience the product.
- Tour operators frequently provide travel agency staff with 'familiarisation' visits on package holidays so that they will be able to describe the product more effectively to customers.
- A hotel might invite local business people to lunch so that they can see the conference facilities provided.

STOP & THINK

You might see photographs of a resort in a holiday brochure, but how can you tell what the resort is really like?

You may consider buying a piece of exercise equipment but can you actually tell how easy it would be to use it from looking at the newspaper advertisement?

OVER TO YOU

Creating interest in the theatre

The John Arnold Theatre is situated in a large town in southern England. It stages a wide range of productions from traditional plays, new writers and musical events. The theatre also has a restaurant, coffee bar and souvenir shop. Recent market research has shown that the average age of customers is gradually getting older and that 16-19 year olds rarely, if ever, visit the theatre. The theatre has appointed an Educational Officer, Gianni Ponti, to encourage young people to go to the theatre more often.

Gianni has introduced a number of new ideas, such as Saturday morning theatre workshops, backstage tours and special discounted rates for students and school groups. Despite this the number of young customers has not increased by very much.

You are at the John Arnold Theatre on work placement and Gianni has asked you to help him encourage young people to visit the theatre. He is particularly interested in Leisure and Tourism students – there are 12 schools that ho offer the qualification within an hour's drive of the theatre. As a test run, he has invited a group of 15 Leisure and Tourism students to visit the theatre in two weeks' time. The students will be at the theatre from 1.00 p.m. to 4.00 p.m.

Gianni would like you to suggest a programme for their three-hour visit. Can you think of activities that would appeal to this type of customer and encourage them to visit the theatre again? A small amount of money is available for refreshments – so specify when and how you would spend it.

Sales promotions

Sales promotions are short-term activities intended to encourage interest in a particular product. For example, travel agencies may offer discounts to customers who book a holiday before a specific date. Other examples include:

- free gifts given with products
- money-off vouchers
- discounts
- price reductions
- free samples
- competitions linked to a particular product, or prize draws
- increased quantity of a product for the same price (12 exercise sessions for the price of 10)
- loyalty schemes.

Sales promotions are often used with other promotional techniques. For example, an organisation may use a direct mail letter and include a money-off voucher, or place a newspaper advertisement that includes a competition.

◀ ▲ Examples of sales promotions

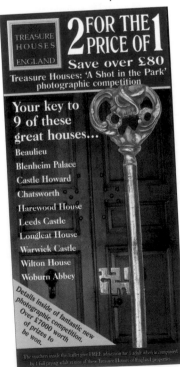

Surf Racers

OVER TO YOU

Rachel Brown is about to open a new jet skiing centre in Wales called Surf Racers. She has a limited amount of money, so has decided to use the local press as her main source of promotion. She has already placed a number of advertisements in local papers and they have all also printed an article about the new centre based on an interview with her.

As the final (and hopefully best) piece of promotion before opening, Rachel plans to use a sales promotion. This is going to be a competition in all local papers offering three prizes of one hour's free jet skiing to the lucky winners. In addition, everyone who enters the competition will receive a 20 per cent discount voucher to use at the centre.

- Design the newspaper competition.
- Think of some suitable questions to help Rachel decide on the winner.
- It may help you to look at examples of competitions in your local paper for ideas.

Promotional materials are the actual pieces of information that the customer sees, hears or reads. They include:

- brochures
- leaflets
- merchandising materials
- videos
- press releases
- internet sites.

Advertisements

Adverts can be used in a variety of media, such as newspapers and magazines, or on radio, television and billboards (poster sites). Remember that the customer may not be willing to spend as long looking at advertisements as with other forms of materials, such as leaflets and brochures. Therefore the information needs to be put across more simply and briefly. Ensure that the design follows the principle of AIDA and is attractive to the target market.

Advertising design

Look at the two advertisements for concerts.

- Identify what type of customers each is targeting.
- How is the design of each advertisement suitable for the target market?

OVER TO YOU

Brochures and leaflets

Brochures and leaflets are one of the most widely used forms of promotional materials in the leisure and tourism industry. Examples include:

- package holidays
- hotel facilities
- sports centre
- theatre productions programmes
- transport timetables
- tourist attraction details
- holiday guides.

Unlike many advertisements, brochures and leaflets often contain a lot more information. Customers see brochures and leaflets as more than than simply promotional material. For example, look at the extract from the leaflet of the Original Tour company which provides sightseeing tours of London. The leaflet provides very detailed information.

WELCOME TO LONDON'S ORIGINAL & BEST OPEN-TOP BUS TOUR!

Tour and Explore "the world's most cosmopolitan city" with London's longest established sightseeing company using open-top "double-deck" buses. With half a century's experience we like to think that we've got it right, but to ensure you make the most of your time with us, you may find the following helpful:

▼ **Will we see all the major sights?** Yes – Our tour routes are the most comprehensive way to see the best that London has to offer including the spectacular panoramic views from seven bridges, the Tower of London, Big Ben, Buckingham Palace, St Paul's Cathedral, Westminster Abbey, Harrods, Trafalgar Square, Madame Tussaud's, London Bridge....

▼ **Will we get a live guide?** Yes – We have a live English speaking guide on every one of our Original Tour buses.

▼ **Will the children enjoy it?** Yes – You can relax and enjoy the tour whilst your children (and everyone else's) are entertained and informed by our highly acclaimed "Kids' Club" commentary and their free London activity packs. "Kids' Club" is featured on our red route service.

▼ **Will we be able to hop-on and hop-off?** Yes – Unlike some other companies, your tour tickets are completely unrestricted. You can travel on any of our tour buses. Each route makes frequent stops – simply hop-off where you want to and return to the same stop to continue your tour.

▼ **Can we tell which route each bus is on?** Yes – Each bus displays a coloured triangle on its front.

▼ **Can we join the tour at any stop?** Yes – But we strongly recommend that first timers board at one of our main departure points where our staff can provide advice about traffic conditions on the day and final departure times. You may then choose to stay on the bus for a complete tour to get fully orientated or hop-on and hop-off at your leisure.

▼ **Can we use our tickets all day long?** Yes – Tickets are valid until the same time the following day for use during our operational hours. Ask our staff when you should board your last bus of the day as times vary seasonally throughout the year.

the ... ? Yes – F... ... our st... the

OVER TO YOU

Design a leaflet

Look at the leaflet for Courtney's Fitness Clubs. You will notice that its main focus is selling the product features and benefits to customers. It shows what customers will gain from joining Courtney's. Customers are told that by using the clubs they will look and feel great, make new friends and enjoy the atmosphere and facilities.

Design a similar leaflet for a leisure or tourism facility in your area. You might choose a nightclub, cinema or sports centre that you use. Think carefully about the product features: why do customers use the facility and what do they gain from it?

Courtney's - the UK's leading chain of fitness centres is now open at Waterworld, York

Do you want to:
Look good and feel great?
Get fit in a relaxed and enjoyable atmosphere?
Achieve your own personal goals?
Meet new friends?
Experience the latest health and fitness products?

If you answered yes to any of the above then you need to join Courtney's

Benefits include:
No Joining Fee
Superb value for money
Free Fitness package to get you started worth £100.00
Free sunbeds
Direct debit easy payment scheme
Free parking

BEST OF ALL - THIS ONLY COSTS £31.00 PER MONTH THAT'S JUST £1.00 A DAY

adidas
Courtney's FITNESS PLUS
CALL 01904 642 162

Merchandising materials

Merchandising materials refers to additional products that are sold or given away to the customer that help to promote the organisation's main products. Usually merchandising materials will include the organisation's name on such things as:

- pens
- bags
- stickers
- drinks mats.
- balloons
- t-shirts
- posters

Merchandising materials are usually given away to customers to encourage them to return and buy the product again. However, in the last few years, a whole new industry has grown from selling merchandising materials associated with a particular product. One of the first organisations to realise the potential of selling merchandising was the Disney Corporation, who now sell such materials at their theme parks, through retail outlets and also through catalogues.

OVER TO YOU

Merchandised products

If you look around your home you will probably find that you have many examples of merchandised products bought as souvenirs of an event or visit. Of the merchandised products you have found, how many examples are associated with each of the following:

- films
- television programmes
- pop groups, performers or concerts
- a local tourist attraction.

Part of the Disney merchandising catalogue ▼

Videos

Many leisure and tourism products are services that customers experience at the time rather than goods that they take away with them. For this reason many organisations feel that printed promotional materials are not enough to show the customer what the experience is actually like. How much of an impression can you get of a foreign package holiday by looking at a few pictures and a written description in a brochure? Would you be able to appreciate how exciting an indoor skiing centre is by reading a leaflet? One of the ways that many organisations have overcome this difficulty is to produce **promotional videos** showing customers actually using and experiencing the services and products.

STOP & THINK

These pictures could be taken from any package holiday brochure. Imagine that it is, in fact, a shot from a video. If you could hear what the characters were saying and see what happened next, do you think that it would give you a better idea of what the holiday experience would be like?

The 'holiday experience' ▼

OVER TO YOU

The video experience

Get hold of a holiday company video. A local travel agency may let you have an out-of-date one or lend you one of their current videos. Some tour operators may send you free videos on request; look for details in the holiday pages of national newspapers.

After watching the video, discuss the following as a group:

- What type of customer was the video aimed at?

- How successful do you think the video would be at persuading these customers to buy the holiday? Give reasons.
- Do you think the video would be more successful than another form of promotion, such as a brochure or poster? Why?
- How was AIDA used to make the video successful?
- Suggest any ways in which the video could have been improved.

Press releases

Press releases can be used as part of public relations (page 130). They are also a part of an organisation's promotional materials. One of the advantages of using press releases as promotional material is that customers are likely to spend longer reading it (because it is not seen as an advertisement). You could therefore include a lot more information. Another advantage, of course, is that it is free. Any organisation, no matter how small, can afford it.

When writing press releases, the same rules of AIDA apply. The press release should read like a proper newspaper article, therefore, it has to be in the third person (for example, The Plaza cinema has recently invested in a brand new coffee shop) rather than the first person (for example, We are pleased to announce that…). You can still say what you think but it needs to be written as if a reporter were interviewing you and writing what you have said. For example, rather than writing:

▲ Potential customers spend longer reading articles than looking at advertisements

We are sure that you will like our new coffee shop.

You would write:

Plaza manager, Gregory Styles said, 'We hope our customers will be pleased with the changes that we have made.'

The press release should include all the relevant details, have a title and date, and not contain any spelling or grammatical errors.

We are orginising a music festival in Greatholm Park in July. We hope that a lot of locle bands will vollunteer to play free of charge as the profits are going to a the childrens ward at the hospital. There will be refreshments and toilets provided. Please come and join us as it will be a grate day for all. If you are a locle band who would be interested in playing at the festival you can contact us on 367289.

Compare press releases

OVER TO YOU

The two examples of press releases have been written by different leisure and tourism groups.

- Which do you think is more effective?
- Which is more likely to be printed by a local newspaper?

15 June 2000

Leisure and Tourism Students Aim For The email Record
A group of GNVQ leisure and tourism students at Greatholm College are hoping to enter the record books. As part of their course they have to organise an event and have come up with the novel idea of trying to enter the Guinness Book of Records for the longest sponsored email session.

Students will work on separate computers, sending email messages to each other. They have set themselves strict rules such as having to reply to messages within 15 minutes, all messages must be a minimum of 20 words and they are not allowed to send the same message more than once to different people.

Student, Mark Evans, said, 'We spent ages thinking about what we could do that would be a challenge but also enjoyable and raise some money for local charities. The email idea came about because we have all had to use computers a lot since starting this course and we wanted to use our new skills.'

The sponsored email session is due to take place from 9 a.m. to 9 p.m. on Saturday 26 July at the college. Sponsors and spectators are welcome!

For further details, course tutor, Maria Combes can be contacted at the college on (01653) 623754.

Are you on the internet?

Most local Councils and many leisure and tourism providers in all areas of the UK have put some of their details on the internet. Some may use a central website with different pages that allow you to find specific types of information, such as accommodation, attractions and transport. Alternatively, different providers may use separate websites.

Use the internet to find out what information is available on your area, or on a large town or city nearby. You might like to find out some specific information such as:

- entertainment available
- museums and Art Galleries in the area
- hotels
- a map of the area
- restaurants.

Afterwards, as a group, discuss how easy you think it would be for a visitor to find information in this way.

Using the internet

One of the greatest advances in producing effective promotional materials has been the widespread use of computers. You may already have used a computer to complete some of the activities in this chapter, such as in designing a poster or leaflet. Even smaller leisure and tourism organisations have access to computers that allow them to design their own promotional materials quickly and cheaply. A further way in which computerisation has changed the nature of promotional materials is through the internet. Many organisations now use the Internet for promoting products.

Use	Example
Provide product information	The Alton Towers web site allows customers to take a virtual tour of the park
Allow customers to 'search' for information that will meet their specific needs	Railtrack asks customers to specify train types and routes that they are interested in before providing the relevant information
Let customers buy or make reservations online	Amazon Books lets customers buy books online, which are then delivered to their home address
Send additional information to past customers by email	Oasis Holiday Centre in the Lake District regularly emails past customers to tell them about special offers

Leisure and tourism organisations often use the internet for promotional materials ▶

So far in this section we have looked at how leisure and tourism organisations use marketing to identify their target markets, carry out market research to identify what products and services they should be developing, and create a successful marketing mix with the right product, place, price and promotion.

The SWOT analysis carried out by the Royal Armouries in Leeds before they opened in 1994 ▶

SWOT analysis of the Royal Armouries in Leeds

Strengths
Attraction of royal status and connections
First national museum to be built outside London
Foremost collection of arms and armour
Wide educational opportunities
Management abilities – commercial and academic
Waterside environment
City centre accessibility
Inspired use of technology
Interactive opportunities
Armouries at three locations

Weaknesses
Arms and armour
Perception of hunting and war
The name Royal Armouries
Lack of appreciation of what Royal Armouries is about
Perception of Leeds
Relevance of the museum in a changing world
Unattractive vicinity
The use of technology off-putting for the over 50s

Opportunities
Large potential target market
Widening the visitor experience through waterside use
Catalyst for development of tourism within Leeds
Innovative merchandising
Joint ventures – tourism and leisure
To generate important funding and sponsorship
International exhibitions

Threats
Political disruption
Competition, especially enhanced regional attractions
Substitutes (sports, shopping etc)
The Channel Tunnel (net exporter)
Change in economic climate
UK continuing to lose tourist revenue
Gun laws

Using the descriptions, facts and figures in the case study, produce a SWOT analysis on Disneyland, Paris.

Disneyland, Paris

During the 1980s the Disney Corporation started to look for a site in Europe for a new theme park because a large number of visitors to their American parks came from Europe. Disneyland, Paris opened in 1992 after the Disney Corporation had considered a number of possible European sites, including Spain and the UK. The chosen site at Marne-le-Vallee, just outside Paris, was on land owned by the French government. The land was offered to the Disney Corporation at a very low price in the hope that it would improve the local area. As part of the deal the French government agreed to improve transport to the area.

Consider these facts about Disneyland, Paris:

- Paris is the most popular European City break destination in Europe
- The weather at Marne-le-Vallee is similar to southern England but they experience quite a lot of rain throughout the year.

- There were initial problems with the French adapting to the 'Disney Magic'. For example, Disney had to introduce wine into their restaurants since the French expected this as part of a restaurant meal.
- One of the big successes of Disneyland, Paris is the business travel market. Facilities are available for conferences from 20 delegates to over 2000. Conference delegates tend to visit at low season and are not affected by poor weather.
- The Disney Corporation has a strong image through their world operations, including films, merchandising, theme parks and other activities. The Disney brand is recognised by more people than any other brand.
- Distribution channels include travel agents, direct sell, tour operators and ticket brokers.
- Disney can afford lots of advertising campaigns that focus on the promise of 'the Disney Magic'. European television advertising tends to be at the end of the season to encourage visitors for the next season.

Analysing performance

Organisations also need to be able to analyse how well they are operating and identify what factors may influence their success. They sometimes use a **SWOT analysis** to identify their:

- **S**trengths
- **W**eaknesses
- **O**pportunities
- **T**hreats.

Strengths and weaknesses are internal factors within the control of the organisation. The organisation could change them they wanted to, for example, the level of customer service or the opening times. Opportunities and threats are outside the control of the organisation and are not easily changed, for example, products offered by competitors or poor weather.

A SWOT analysis allows an organisation to plan its future by answering a number of key questions.

- What are our strengths? How can we build on them to make sure that we offer a better product than our competitors?
- What are our weaknesses? How can we get rid of them?
- What are our opportunities? How are we going to use them to attract new customers or increase the number of products that existing customers buy?
- What are our threats? How are we going to minimise them so that they do not affect sales of our products?

OVER TO YOU

- All staff are involved in testing new rides before they are offered to the public.
- Competition in Paris comes from the well-established Parc Asterix and the Futuroscope centre – both French theme parks.
- About 84 per cent of visitors say that they are very, or totally, satisfied with their visit. 97 pe cent say that they will recommend the park to their friends. More than 30 per cent of visitors have visited the park at least once before.
- Access to the park includes two Paris airports linked by shuttle and rail services to the park, direct motorway access and the channel tunnel link to the UK. Disneyland, Paris has its own railway station.
- The Disney Village provides round-the-clock restaurants, bars and entertainment and is easily accessible from all the resort hotels.
- Customer service is the main priority of the Disney Corporation and all staff are fully trained before beginning work
- Disneyland, Paris resort hotels provide almost 6000 rooms. A further 800 rooms have been added to other hotels in the area to cater to the Disney market.
- Shopping is a major part of the Disney experience and visitors have a vast range of themed retail outlets to choose from.
- In 2001 a large shopping mall and Sea Life centre opened next door to the Disney park in Paris
- More than 50 million people live within a four-hour drive of Disneyland, Paris. Over 300 million are within a short-haul flight designated area.
- Many of the attractions at Disneyland, Paris are covered or heated. Despite the cold weather, Christmas is one of the busiest periods for the park.

Organisations have a large number of different options to choose from when it comes to promoting their products and services. The techniques and materials that they decide to use will depend on a number of factors, such as how much money they have to spend, the type of customers that they are trying to attract and the type of product that they want to promote. In short, organisations aim to achieve the maximum effect by making the best use of their resources. To achieve this there are a number of factors that they need to consider when planning a promotional campaign:

- What is our promotional campaign trying to achieve (its objectives)?
- Who is the target market?
- What promotional techniques should we use?
- What promotional materials should we use?
- How should we to monitor and evaluate the success of the campaign?

What is our promotional campaign trying to achieve?

The objectives of the campaign must be identified before any promotional campaign can be designed or implemented. It must be clear what the campaign hopes to achieve. Objectives will vary according to the type of product and organisation, but could include:

Public swimming pools aim to serve the community ▼

- to make a financial gain, such as an increase in sales or profits
- to achieve a social or community gain; some leisure and tourism organisations provide a service for the community, such as a public library or community sports hall
- to raise awareness where potential customers do not know about the product or the organisation
- to improve, enhance or change the image of a product or the organisation
- to attract new customers
- to maintain existing customers.

Who are the target markets?

Having set the objectives for a promotional campaign, the target markets that the organisation is trying to reach must be identified. It will help the organisation decide which promotional techniques and materials are most suitable. For example, if an organisation's objective was to attract new customers, it would not be effective to use point-of-sales promotions because potential new customers would not see them.

What promotional techniques and materials should we use?

The campaign objectives have been set and and the target markets identified. We now need to establish which **promotional techniques** and **materials** to use. If the market research has been effective, you will have identified the target market and the types of promotional materials that they are likely to see, hear or read. The methods that could be used include:

- advertising
- direct marketing
- public relations
- personal selling
- displays
- sponsorship
- demonstrations
- sales promotions
- brochures and leaflets
- merchandising materials
- videos
- the internet.

These have all been discussed in this unit.

The types of promotional activities and materials selected for a campaign will depend on its nature, the target markets, and the resources available. The decision about which media to be used should be made when target markets have been identified. For example, if a promotional campaign for a local leisure centre aims to attract local customers, there would be little point in advertising in a national newspaper, or on television.

Conduct a promotional campaign

One of the keys to a successful promotional campaign is to choose the right media for your target customers. Often there will be more than one effective medium but some will be better than others.

Look at the list of leisure and tourism products and services below and discuss which media you think would be most effective for advertising each product for the specified target audience. Specify whether you think the advertising needs to be national, regional or local or a combination of two or more of these.

- national coach holidays offered to senior citizens
- a privately owned local sports centre
- luxury wedding package holidays to destinations such as Barbados and the Seychelles
- a pop concert at a major outdoor arena
- forthcoming films at a local cinema
- a national chain of three- and four-star hotels.

Monitoring a campaign

Monitoring a promotional campaign means that those responsible for the campaign need to check that the promotional activities are being carried out in the way that they had planned. For example:

- Has the newspaper organisation printed the advertisement on the correct night?
- Have the Printers produced the information in the brochures as you requested?
- Is someone checking that the point-of-sales display is stocked with leaflets each day?
- Are the posters displayed still in good condition?

When monitoring a promotional campaign an organisation needs to correct anything that is not as it was planned.

The Gemini Restaurant

The Gemini Restaurant paid for an advertisement in the local newspaper to promote their forthcoming Halloween Masked Ball to be held on Saturday 30 October. The event is due to run from 7.30 p.m. to 1 a.m. and includes a five-course meal with wine at £19.50 per person. Live music is being provided by The Ghouls and fancy dress is requested. The manager who monitors the promotional campaign spots a mistake in the advertisement that the newspaper prints four weeks before the event.

- Look at the advertisement and identify what he saw as incorrect.
- What do you think he should do about it to ensure that the campaign is still successful?

GEMINI RESTAURANT
Halloween Masked Ball

Saturday October 30th

7.30 p.m. – 1.00 a.m.

Live dancing to the Ghouls

Five course dinner

Fancy Dress is required

£9.50 per person

Ring: 01532 545611 for further details and bookings

Evaluating the success of a campaign

The final stage of the promotional campaign is to evaluate how effective it has been. Has it achieved the objectives that were set at the beginning? If specific and measurable objectives were set, it should be easy to monitor the success.

Most promotional campaigns are a combination of several different techniques and materials. An organisation may use press advertisements, direct mail and point-of-sale displays to promote one product. This makes monitoring more difficult. Customers could be asked to complete a questionnaire but they may not always be willing to answer questions. It is better to use a promotional technique that lets you know whether the customer has seen it or not. For example, if tour operators advertised on television and gave customers a freephone number to ring for further details, they could count the number of enquiries that they receive and therefore evaluate how effective the advertisement had been. If the advertisement was being screened over a number of nights, they could use a different telephone number each time to evaluate which particular nights were more effective.

CASE STUDY

The tourism brand for England

In June 2000, the English Tourism Council launched a new promotional campaign called The tourism brand for England. The new brand came from research that showed England had many different strengths. The brand reminds British holidaymakers of the reasons for taking a holiday in England and tells overseas visitors what England has to offer.

The logo used for the campaign is made up of four images that show the strengths and benefits of England:

- history, heritage and ceremony is represented by the lion rampant
- culture is represented by the theatrical masks
- tranquillity as found in the English countryside is represented by a country scene
- vibrancy, innovation and youth culture is symbolised by an abstract 'energy rose'.

Campaign objectives

- To ensure that a consistent image of England is presented to both domestic and overseas customers
- To boost awareness of the whole country as a tourist destination
- To use England's uniqueness to create a strong brand that can be used to gain competitive advantage over other destinations.

The target markets

The Tourism brand for England campaign is aimed at a wide range of different market segments:

- city breaks
- country holidays
- coastal destinations
- walking holidays
- birdwatching.

▲ People taking city breaks are an important target market for The tourism brand for England campaign

Promotional techniques and materials

The English Tourism Council has produced a wide range of brochures and leaflets aimed at the different target market segments. There are also examples of display stands, press advertisements and website pages.

A free CD of pictures of England is available for tourism providers. Providers can use these pictures when creating their own promotional materials.

Monitoring and evaluating the success of the campaign

The English Tourism Council accept that it will take some time for the new brand to become widely recognised. The success of the brand depends on everyone involved promoting England with the same words and images in their campaigns.

KEY TERMS

You should know what the following terms mean:

The marketing mix
  (page 108)
The four Ps (page 108)
Product (page 110)
Goods and services
  (page 110)
Product features (page 111)
Brand name (page 112)
Brand loyalty (page 112)
After-sales service
  (page 113)
Product mix (page 113)
Product life cycle
  (page 114)
Price (page 116)
Actual selling price
  (page 116)
Special offers (page 118)
Credit terms (page 118)
Profitability (page 118)
Place (page 120)
Location (page 120)
Distribution channels
  (page 121)
Promotion (page 122)
AIDA (page 124)

Advertising (page 126)
Direct marketing (page 128)
Public relations (page 130)
Personal selling (page 132)
Displays (page 134)
Sponsorship (page 136)
Demonstrations (page 138)
Sales promotions
  (page 139)
Promotional materials
  (page 140)
Brochures and leaflets
  (page 141)
Merchandising materials
  (page 142)
Promotional videos
  (page 143)
Press releases (page 144)
Internet usage (page 145)
SWOT analysis (page 147)
Promotional campaigns
  (page 148)
Monitoring a campaign
  (page 150)

If you're not sure or want to check your understanding, turn to the page number listed in the brackets.

Revision questions

1 What is meant by the term 'the marketing mix'?

2 Explain the difference between goods and a service.

3 Describe the four stages of the product life cycle.

4 Explain how peak and off-peak pricing is used when selling rail travel.

5 Identify five factors that a company might consider when selecting a location for a leisure centre.

6 Describe four distribution channels for the sales of package holidays

7 Explain how a tourist attraction might use two different types of promotional materials.

8 Identify five different methods of promotion and explain how a leisure or tourism organisation might use each.

9 Explain what is meant by the term 'SWOT analysis'.

10 Describe the five stages of a promotional campaign.

Investigation ideas

Your group has an idea of using the school hall as a drama club on two nights a week. You believe that there would be a large amount of interest amongst local children aged 11–16 years and four teachers have agreed to give up some of their spare time to help run the club. You hope to offer sessions on improvisation, acting techniques and stagecraft, and to stage a performance twice a year. You plan to charge a membership fee. These fees, together with profits from the performance tickets, will be donated to school funds. The Head Teacher knows that you are studying Marketing as part of your vocational GCSE and has asked you to present your ideas in the form of a marketing mix. Your presentation should include the following:

OVER TO YOU

Product – What you hope to offer and why you think it will appeal to the target market.

Price – How much you intend to charge and why you have decided on this amount. You might consider discounts for certain types of member and special offers.

Place – Why you believe that the school hall is a suitable location.

Promotion – How you are going to promote the drama club to the intended target market? You might consider advertising, direct marketing, public relations, displays, sponsorship and sales promotions – but remember that you will not have a lot of money to spend!

REVISION PROMPT

What have I learnt about the marketing mix?

_____

_____

_____

What am I still unsure about?

_____

_____

_____

How am I going to find out the extra information that I need?

_____

_____

_____

Customer Service

This unit is about the importance of customer service in the leisure and tourism industries. You will learn about:

- why customer service is so important to the leisure and tourism industries
- the needs of different types of customers and how they are met
- communicating with customers
- the importance of personal presentation
- how to keep accurate records
- the benefits to organisations, their staff and customers of providing excellent customer service.

If you are thinking about a career in leisure and tourism, you will need to practise the skills and techniques outlined in this unit. The ability to provide an enjoyable experience for a customer will encourage repeat custom and ensure the success of an organisation or facility.

Unit 3 of this book covers Unit 3, Customer service in leisure and tourism, of the GCSE Leisure and Tourism award.

What is customer service?

'It's interesting because you see a lot of different people.'

'You feel good because you help people enjoy themselves.'

'It's a challenge dealing with different problems and situations.'

'Because I like meeting people.'

You will meet lots of different people if you work in the leisure and tourism industry and you will definitely experience some unusual situations. However, some of the people you meet and the situations you find yourself in may not be quite as glamorous and exciting as you first imagined.

This unit looks at how to provide excellent customer service. You will look at the skills and knowledge needed and how to improve on existing customer service. In particular, you will learn about:

- the different needs of customers and how they are met
- communicating with customers
- the importance of personal presentation when dealing with customers
- why it is important to keep customer records.

Defining customer service

Customer service means serving the customers. Excellent customer service means serving customers in such a way that they think is outstanding. It includes the way that you meet and deal with all customers as part of your job.

To give excellent customer service you need to be able to:

- put yourself in the place of the customers and think how you would like to be treated if you were them
- put the customers' needs first
- think of ways that you could improve the service you provide to customers.

STOP & THINK

Which customers would you rather not meet?

- the lady who shouts at you because her soup is cold?

- the tourist who has lost his suitcase and wants to know what you are going to do about it?

- the group of children who are making a noise in the cinema and annoying other customers?

These people may be your customers and it is your job to provide them with excellent customer service if you work in leisure and tourism.

Customers who have been delayed will need extra customer service ▼

Customer service can be through direct contact such as when dealing with a customer face-to-face or on the telephone. It can also be indirect, through letters and emails. Customer service includes many different activities:

- providing information
- giving advice
- receiving and passing on messages
- keeping records
- providing assistance
- dealing with problems
- dealing with dissatisfied customers
- offering extra services.

Excellent customer service is not just a part of your work. If you work in the leisure and tourism industry, customer service *is* your job!

You can learn a lot from your own experience as a customer. For example:

- What makes you feel you are well cared for?
- What annoys you and makes you decide not to use a facility?

You need to think and behave with your customers in mind at all times.

If I were my customer would I be totally satisfied with the service that I am giving?

OVER TO YOU

Assessing customer service

Ask a few members of the group to describe the customer service that they had in a leisure and tourism attraction or facility, such as a restaurant, shop, museum, leisure centre or cinema.

- Write a list of their examples of good and poor customer service.
- When you have written the list, discuss how many of the points that you have listed are within the control of the member of staff serving you. You will probably find that most of them are!

OVER TO YOU

A word for service

If you tried to think of all the words to describe good and bad customer service, the list would never end. Here are a few that could be used. Put them into two columns – those that suggest good service and those that suggest bad service. Use a dictionary if you are unsure of the meanings of any of the words.

Accurate	Controlled	Responsibility
Aloof	Discreet	Sincere
Apathetic	Hesitant	Supportive
Attention	Hostile	Tactless
Churlish	Indifferent	Thoughtful
Composed	Ineffective	Vigilant
Concern	Interest	
Confident	Prejudiced	

A common situation in the leisure and tourism industry is the customer wanting information. For example:

- a visitor in a tourist information centre may want to know about entertainment in the area
- a tourist in a stately home may ask the tour guide about the history of the building
- a customer in a travel agency may ask the travel consultant for information about travellers cheques and foreign currency.

Anyone who works in the leisure and tourism industry needs to know the sorts of questions that customers will ask. It is even more important to know how to find the information that is needed. There are a number of sources of information that you can use if you do not know the answer to a customer's question. These include:

- paper-based information
- computer-based information
- colleagues.

Paper-based information

People who work in leisure and tourism rely heavily on printed information when answering customers' questions. A tourist information clerk will use leaflets, brochures, timetables and guidebooks to find out information for visitors. Local newspapers are a good source of leisure and tourism information and many hotels have a copy delivered for the staff to use when looking for information.

The information that you give to customers must be correct. It is always better to say that you do not know something than to guess and give the wrong information. If you give the wrong information, it is likely that customers will be dissatisfied and not trust you in the future.

Newspaper information

OVER TO YOU

Use a copy of your local newspaper (Friday and Saturday editions are best). Imagine that some of your customers have asked you the following questions:

- 'Where is the nearest late-night chemist?'
- 'We'd like an Italian meal tonight. Where can we go?'
- 'Is there anything on at the cinema that is suitable for a family with two children, aged 12 and 14 years?'
- 'What is the weather going to be like tomorrow?'
- 'We love car boot sales and things like that. Is there anything on in the next few days?'
- 'Is there any live music on in the area?'

Find the information for them in the newspaper.

Computer-based information

Some people argue that using computers reduces the level of customer service. However, it is often a quick way of meeting customer needs when asked for information such as opening times, train times or prices.

- Most travel agents provide information on the availability and prices of holidays by using computer systems linked to those of tour operators.
- Many tourist information centres now provide a computerised information system that visitors can use to find out details of local facilities and services.
- All airlines, most tour operators and many hotel groups use computers for making reservations. By using computers they can control the sales of airline seats, holidays and hotel beds on a national or worldwide basis and provide customers with the most up-to-date information.

▲ Computers are becoming more and more important as a way of providing information for customers

Information from colleagues

The easiest and quickest way of finding information for customers might be to ask one of your colleagues. If a customer wanted to know what a local theme park was like and you had not been there yourself, which of the following would be the best source of information:

- give the customer a copy of the theme park's leaflet
- log on to the theme park's website
- ask a colleague who had been to the theme park to describe it to the customer?

It is likely that the customer would prefer to speak to your colleague and ask specific questions. The leaflet is good customer service, but asking a colleague to deal with the customer personally is excellent customer service and shows that you really care.

OVER TO YOU

Giving the right answer

In pairs, look at the situations described here.

For each situation, imagine that the member of staff did not know the answer and just said 'yes'. Discuss what might happen if this was not the right answer.

For each situation say what you think the member of staff should have done.

- 'My son is allergic to peanuts. Do you think the cheeseburger and chips is okay?'
- 'Have I got time to buy a newspaper before my train leaves?'
- 'We want a quiet holiday. Is Benidorm like that?'
- 'Is it safe to swim in the sea today? I don't understand what the coloured flags mean.'
- 'My wife uses a wheelchair. Will she be able to visit all areas of the art gallery?'
- 'My daughter is 15 years old. Is it okay if she has a glass of wine with her meal?'

Giving advice

In many situations customers will want more than simple information – they will expect to be given advice. There is a difference between providing information and giving advice.

A customer wanting information might ask:

▲ Even if written information is available, customers sometimes also need advice

> *What is the hottest month in Greece?*

Whereas, a customer wanting advice might say:

> *I like it warm in the day but cool at night. When should I go to Greece?*

When asking for advice the customer draws on your experience and knowledge to suggest what they do. It is a serious responsibility.

- a customer at a sports centre might want to know which sessions are best for those with mobility impairments
- a customer in a restaurant might want advice on which dishes are suitable for vegetarians
- a visitor to a cinema may ask whether a film is suitable for young children
- a customer in a travel agency may want to know where to go in December that is sunny but not too expensive.

Customers trust you to make reliable judgements, and to give them accurate and honest advice. Therefore, if you are unsure it is always better to ask for help from a colleague or supervisor, rather than give the wrong advice.

Role-play

Different types of customers need different sorts of advice. Customers on foreign package holidays often ask the tour representative for advice on health and safety. This may be because of particular problems or because they are in a strange country and are unsure of 'how things work'. Many tour operators give out safety leaflets for customers but representatives still find that guests will ask them for advice.

Thomson Holidays provide guests with a safety leaflet. Read the extract from this leaflet before starting your role-plays.

In pairs, take turns at playing a resort representative and a package holiday customer. For each of the following situations the representative should give advice to the customer. You may use the leaflet if you need to.

- I am worried that we have a third floor room with a balcony. Our two children are aged 2 years and 5 years. Is it safe?
- I'm not a very strong swimmer but I would love to go in the sea as it looks so inviting. Can I swim safely here?
- My wife got a bit too much sun yesterday and is feeling sick and dizzy. What should she do?
- I've seen lots of programmes about how dangerous foreign swimming pools are. Is the one at the hotel safe to swim in?

- Our hotel lift does not have internal doors, which seems very dangerous. Should I stop my children using it?
- My little girl has adopted a sweet little kitten that keeps coming into our apartment. It's just bitten her finger. What should I do?

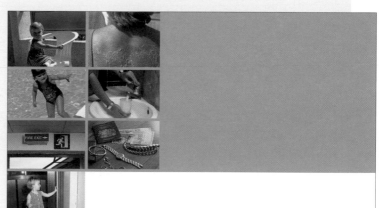

Top Tips for a safe and healthy holiday

Children's Safety
The safety of our younger guests is our biggest concern. Remember that children should never be left alone near swimming pools, balconies or lifts. At children's playgrounds, your children will need to be supervised at all times.

Balconies
Please ensure that children are never left alone on balconies, and keep furniture away from the railings so that they are not encouraged to climb up.

Swimming Pools
Many swimming pools abroad are not designed in the same way as pools in the UK, and may have unusual features. Pools are unlikely to have a lifeguard so please check the layout and depth of the pool at the start of your holiday.

Fire Safety
Familiarise yourself with the location of the nearest fire exit and fire alarm call point to your room or apartment, and read the fire safety information that is provided. Make a mental note of where the fire assembly point is.

On the Beach
Tides and currents can turn the safest beach into a hazard. Check if there is a flag warning system on the beach, and if so then familiarise yourself with it.

Lifts
Never allow children to travel inside any lift without an adult. Do not use the lifts in the event of fire.

Safety in the Sun
Always use a high factor sunscreen that offers both UVA and UVB protection. Take extra care with children.

Road Safety
In a lot of our overseas destinations the vehicles drive on the right hand side of the road, but not in all! The rules of the road can also be very different and drivers are not always obliged to stop at pedestrian crossings, for example. It is therefore essential that you familiarise yourself with local conditions on your arrival, especially when travelling with children.

Drinking Water
Do drink bottled water and make sure that the seal is intact. In hot climates, it is important to drink plenty of water or soft drinks to avoid the effects of dehydration.

Personal Belongings
Watch handbags and cameras when you are out and about in your resort. Only take with you the cash that you will need for that day, and leave valuables in a safety deposit box.

Receiving and passing on messages

On pages 198–201 we will look at the importance of good communication with customers. Good communication includes giving messages to customers and colleagues.

In many situations you will be asked to take and pass on a message to someone. This may be from:

- one member of staff to another
- a member of staff to a customer
- a customer to a member of staff
- a customer to another customer.

It is important that full and accurate details of the message are recorded and passed on as soon as possible. If the message is urgent you need to do everything that you can to contact the person at once. For example, if a message arrives for a holidaymaker that a relative had been in an accident, the resort representative must try to contact the guest at once rather than wait for the daily meeting.

Many organisations have a set procedure for recording messages. They use a specially designed message pad to make sure that the customer gets accurate information.

The way that the message is passed on will depend on the organisation. For example, hotels use a number of ways of passing on messages that include:

- putting the message in the guest's pigeonhole at reception so that they get the message when they collect their room key
- putting the message under the guest's bedroom door
- using a public address system to ask the guest to come to reception for the message
- a flashing light on the bedroom telephone showing that they have a message
- in the more luxurious hotels there are pageboys and girls who go through the public areas announcing who there is a message for.

▲ Bell hops are sometimes required to pass on messages

An example of a message pad ▼

Write down the time you took the message

↓

Record all details accurately

↓

Repeat details back to check that they are right

↓

Write clearly so that the message can be understood

↓

Make sure that the message is delivered straight away

▲ Receiving and passing on messages

Taking and passing on a message

Mr Wood is staying at a residential conference centre for three days to attend a company conference. On his final night's stay the receptionist receives a phone call from Mr Wood's secretary to say that she made a mistake and Mr Wood's flight to Brussels the next day is at 7.30 a.m. and not 8.30 a.m. as she had told him. Mr Wood is not in his bedroom so the receptionist leaves the message in his pigeonhole but notices that his key is not there. She tells the night porter about the message before she goes off duty. The night porter notes that Mr Wood has booked a 5 a.m. wake-up call and decides to tell him about the message then. When Mr Wood is awoken the next morning he is furious about not getting the message earlier. He tells the night porter that he now does not have time to get to the airport to catch the flight.

OVER TO YOU

As a group discuss what you think the receptionist and night porter should have done to prevent this situation happening.

Keeping records

Keeping records is an important part of good customer service. Records make sure that all staff have accurate information about their customers and can therefore give them the best possible service.

OVER TO YOU

Recording information

In pairs discuss what sort of customer information might be recorded in the following leisure and tourism organisations:

- a private health club
- a restaurant
- a theatre
- a travel agency
- a football club
- an airline.

Assisting the customer

In addition to advice and information, a customer may also need assistance. For example, a customer using a wheelchair might not be able to use the stairs, and needs help to reach another floor of the building. Similarly, a visitor to the cinema may expect to receive assistance in finding a seat, and a business person at a conference might need help in operating an overhead projector.

When giving good customer service it is your job to identify any assistance that customers might need and provide it. Just as important is to show that you are happy to assist customers rather than make them feel as if they are a nuisance. Sometimes the level of customer service is let down by the way in which staff do something rather than what they actually do.

The best leisure and tourism organisations try to identify what extra assistance their customers might need and offer it before the customer has to ask. Many shopping centres provide free wheelchairs, pushchairs and baby changing rooms. Theme parks are particularly good at providing extra assistance to customers and are always looking for new ways to improve the service that they offer.

◀ Good customer service includes providing assistance without needing to be asked

C A S E   S T U D Y

Josie Clark and the unhelpful rep

Josie Clark is a single mother on holiday on the Greek island of Crete with her two children aged 18 months and four years. When the coach arrives to take them to the airport for their flight home, it parks at the end of a long driveway. Josie is clearly struggling with the two children, three suitcases and a pushchair and asks the holiday representative for some help. The representative says that she is busy checking guests on to the coach and suggests that Josie puts the children on the coach and goes back for the luggage. Josie explains that the 18-month-old is too young to be left and would probably start crying. The representative tells Josie to wait with her cases and she will help her later.

Once everyone is on the coach the representative carries the cases for Josie, complaining about how heavy they are. During the drive to the airport Josie overhears the representative saying to the driver, 'People shouldn't bring so much luggage if they cannot carry it.' At the airport Josie looks around for the representative to help her get the luggage to the check-in counter. The representative has disappeared into the airport terminal.

- How would you feel if you were Josie?

- What would you have done if you were the representative?

OVER TO YOU

Identify customer assistance

Visit a local train station and collect any information on the services offered to customers. Using the information, identify examples of the assistance that is given to travellers. How much of this service is designed to help the customers help themselves?

▼ The Wild Rivers water park in America helps parents with young children

The radio wrist band that can track lost children

It is a nightmare that haunts all parents – losing a child among the masses of people thronging a sprawling theme park. Dozens of youngsters go missing every day in the world's biggest family fun attractions, including Thorpe Park and Alton Towers.

But now parents at one American theme park are being offered a gadget that could banish the worry of little ones wandering off – miniature radio beam homing devices that will quickly locate youngsters. The SafeTzone system is being launched at the Wild Rivers water park in Irving, near Los Angeles.

Parents are able to rent watch-sized transmitters that attach to a child's wrist or belt. They send out a youngster's location every seven-and-a-half seconds to computerised maps put up around the 15-acre park.

Parents can then log on to the maps and locate everyone in their party. Security experts also believe the devices could be used in other public places, including shopping centres and on cruise ships.

Last night, a spokesman for the Thorpe Park and Chessington World of Adventures said, 'We are always interested in new developments to improve guest care, so we will be watching to see how this works.'

Source: *Daily Mail*, 22 August 2001

Dealing with problems

In an ideal world all customers would buy the products or services you provide, everything would run smoothly and you would not have to deal with any problems. In reality, however, problems often can and do happen. Sometimes this may be within the control of the organisation, such as the fire alarms sounding, or a passenger's cases going astray, or a lift getting stuck between floors. At other times problems may be caused by the customers themselves, such as guests locking themselves out of their bedroom or losing their coat. Whatever the situation it is your responsibility to do everything you can to solve the problem for the customer – even if this means going out of your way to provide service. Remember that customers will often be upset or worried if there is a problem. Sometimes they may also be angry if the problem is the fault of the organisation or staff. You will need to stay calm and reassure these customers while also sorting out the problem.

Different people react in different ways to problems. You need to identify the best way of dealing with each type of reaction. For example, when fire alarms go off in a building:

- some customers may remain calm and simply want to know what to do
- some customers may be frightened and need reassurance
- a few customers may get angry at having to evacuate the building
- other customers may refuse to leave the building thinking that it is a false alarm.

▼ A fire evacuation notice

FIRE INSTRUCTIONS

1 IF YOU DISCOVER A FIRE

IMMEDIATELY break the glass of the nearest fire alarm call point, located throughout the building.

The names of your Fire Warden is as follows:

2 EVACUATION OF PREMISES

FIRST RING *(approx.10 seconds)*
Warning that you should be prepared to evacuate the building. Anybody with a disability should make their way to the Fire Exits at this stage, before the second ring occurs.

SECOND & CONTINUOUS RINGING
Evacuate immediately using the nearest available exit.

ACT QUIETLY
Please do not use: THE LIFTS
THE ATRIUM IN BLOCK 'B'
No-one must re-enter the building until instructed by the FIRE BRIGADE OFFICER.

All persons will assemble at the designated Assembly Points and await further instructions. Fire Warden's must ensure that their floors have been evacuated and report this to the Fire Marshall.

3 HINTS FOR DEALING WITH A FIRE

(i) Shut the doors of the room in which the fire is discovered.
This will prevent draughts and reduce the risk of fire spreading.

(ii) If a person's clothing is on fire, they must immediately be laid flat on the ground and rolled over and over, or muffled in a coat or rug.

(iii) If electrical fittings are involved in a fire, be sure that the current is SWITCHED OFF before they are touched, or the fire is dealt with.

4 IT IS IN YOUR OWN INTEREST AND FOR YOUR OWN SAFETY

(i) To study this notice, to know what to do in the event of a fire and to know how to use the fire appliances.

(ii) To make certain that you are familiar with all means of escape in case of fire and that staircases, landings and other exits are kept clear from obstruction at all times.

(iii) To prevent any possible cause of fire.

EVACUATION MAP PLAN

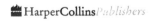

Role-play

This is a role-play that you should carry out in pairs. It would be useful to perform the role-plays in front of the rest of the group so that they can comment on the way you dealt with each of the problems. Different pairs can perform the same role-play to see the various ways of dealing with customer problems.

■ You are a waiter in a restaurant. A customer and his girlfriend have just finished an expensive meal with champagne to celebrate their engagement. Having been presented with the bill the customer says that he has accidentally left his wallet at home and has no money with him – neither does his fiancée.

■ You are a clerk in a tourist information centre. An elderly visitor to the area comes in, clearly in a state of distress. He has parked his car in one of the town's car parks but cannot remember which one it was. He has spent the last two hours walking around looking for it.

■ You are a ride operator at a theme park. A six-year-old girl comes up to you in tears and says she has lost her parents.

■ You work in the ticket office of an industrial museum. It is a very busy day so there are long queues to get in. A customer from the back of the queue pushes to the front demanding to be served straight away.

■ You work at a swimming pool. A customer claims that his wallet has been stolen from his locker while he was swimming. When he returned the locker was open but he thinks he locked it properly.

■ You are an usher at the local cinema. A group of young boys have talked loudly and giggled throughout the film despite the fact that you have asked them to be quiet. They have now started making more noise and other customers are becoming annoyed.

Dealing with dissatisfied customers

Sometimes problems arise which show that the customer is dissatisfied with some aspect of the service. Being able to deal with dissatisfied customers and meet their needs is a very important part of providing excellent customer service. On pages 212–15 we will look at some of the skills you need to deal successfully with dissatisfied customers.

Offering extra service

Leisure and tourism customers usually want no more than other customers, and good staff should find it easy to provide excellent service. However, in some situations customers need more than what is usually offered.

Extra services vary with different customers. They might include:

- a parent who needs baby food warmed
- a theatregoer asking for a taxi to be booked
- a hotel guest asking for help in working the television
- a nervous new member of a beginner's swimming class who needs extra reassurance
- a museum visitor wanting more information on a particular exhibit.

▲ Some customers need extra assistance

In each situation the staff ought to do their best to meet customers' needs – without making the customers feel that they are a nuisance. It may not always be possible to provide the extra service. In these situations you should always be polite and explain why you cannot do something. For example, some organisations do not allow staff to heat bottles of baby's milk because of the risk of accidentally overheating it and injuring the baby. In this situation the staff should explain why they are unable to do it rather than just saying that it is against company policy.

If it is not possible to provide the extra service asked for, you might be able to suggest an alternative. Rather than say that you cannot heat baby's milk you might suggest that you provide a jug of hot water so that the parent can heat the milk themselves.

Leisure and tourism organisations are always looking for ways to improve or add extra services. Until a few years ago the level of service on charter flights tended to be the same on all airlines. However, research shows that customers see the flight as part of their holiday and want it to be enjoyable. Tour operators and airlines realise that offering extra services on flights can greatly improve customer service.

environment relaxing, comfortable and entertaining. Have fun on your flight, and remember that your holiday starts as soon as you board the plane.

New treats

Along with a traditional range of wines, spirits and soft drinks, our new 360 drinks service offers holiday cocktails, a selection of snacks and even a chance to win our Holiday Hunt scratch cards.

The kids are alright

We've captured children's imagination by listening to what they want, and not what we think they want. OBK is their own club, with fun-packed features and activities, meals and drinks, OBK radio and television programmes, and two great OBK magazines with transfers and crayons. If the kids are happy, their parents are too!

The shop in the sky

Skystore offers simply the best in-flight shopping opportunity, with a wide range of duty-free spirits, fragrances, and tobaccos as well as jewellery and gifts with a holiday feel, all at bargain prices.

Real people

Our confident, friendly cabin crew blend approachability with professionalism. The new uniforms they are wearing were created by top fashion designer Elizabeth Emmanuel, who has come up with a look she calls 'classic but funky'.

Plenty to entertain

We've won awards for our approach to in-flight entertainment. We have eight hours of your favourite television programmes and ten radio chanels offering a range of musical styles – and it's all free. On many flights there is even ice-cream for sale and a free national newspaper – all designed to help make your journey a real pleasure.

Thought for food

Having listened to your needs, we've thought up menus to match the time of day, length of flight and destination. There are tasty, traditional breakfasts, Sunday roasts, three- or four-course hot lunches and dinners, cream teas with sandwiches, scones and clotted cream, satisfying suppers and, on longer flights, our snack attack service where you can help yourself to a buffet. And it's all attractively and imaginatively presented.

- List all of the extra services that Britannia Airways' 360 in-flight service offers.
- As a group, discuss which parts of the service you would like if you were travelling as a Britannia passenger.

You should know what the following terms mean:

Customer service (page 156)
Providing information (page 158)
Giving advice (page 160)
Receiving and passing on messages (page 162)
Keeping records (page 163)
Assisting the customer (page 164)
Dealing with problems (page 166)
Dealing with dissatisfied customers (page 167)
Offering extra services (page 168)

If you're not sure or want to check your understanding, turn to the page number listed in the brackets.

Revision questions

1 Explain what is meant by 'excellent customer service'.

2 What is meant by 'direct' and 'indirect contact' with customers?

3 Describe three situations within leisure and tourism where staff might need to provide a customer with information.

4 Explain how a travel agent might use computer-based information when serving a customer.

5 Explain why it is important to be accurate and honest when giving advice to a customer.

6 Describe three ways that a message could be passed on to a customer.

7 Why is it important that a Health Club keeps accurate records about its customers?

8 Describe three types of customer who might need extra assistance from staff.

9 Explain three problems that a member of staff in a theme park might have to deal with.

10 Identify two situations in which a hotel receptionist might offer a customer extra services.

Investigation ideas

You have been asked to give a short customer service training session to a group of new seasonal staff at a local tourist attraction. The manager has suggested that you select a number of different situations where staff provide customer service and act out the wrong way and then the right way of dealing with each situation.

Divide the group into two and let each group work out and perform 'right' and 'wrong' scenarios to the other group:

Group one

- Provide a customer with information about the opening times.

- Advise a customer about whether the attraction is suitable for someone in a wheelchair.

- Pass on a message to a member of staff that a mother needs to speak to her child urgently.

Group two

- Deal with a mother who has asked for her baby's bottle of milk to be warmed in the restaurant.

- Deal with a customer who claims to have been overcharged in the souvenir shop.

- Respond to a customer who has asked the member of staff to call a taxi for them.

After each performance you should ask the audience what was wrong or right with the way that the customer was handled.

REVISION PROMPT

What have I learnt about how customer service is provided?

_____

_____

_____

What am I still unsure about?

_____

_____

_____

How am I going to find out the extra information that I need?

_____

_____

_____

DIFFERENT TYPES OF CUSTOMERS

The leisure and tourism industry includes a very wide range of facilities, attractions and services. Many appeal to different types of customers while others may be aimed at specific customers. Whichever sector you decide to work in, you will probably find yourself dealing with a wide range of customers with different backgrounds, ages, nationalities, interests and specific needs.

Different customers will have different needs. To provide excellent customer service you have to identify what their needs are and decide how you can meet them. Some of the main types of customers that you may have to deal with are:

- individuals
- groups
- people of different ages
- people from different cultures
- non-English speakers
- people with specific needs
- business men and women.

Individuals

You will often deal with individual customers on a one-to-one basis. Someone working in the ticket office of a stately home or at the reception desk in a hotel will deal mainly with individuals. In some ways, this can be one of the easiest types of customer to deal with because you can give the customer your full attention. On the other hand, it can be difficult if the customer is being awkward or you find it hard to understand the person's needs. You may feel somewhat awkward on your own in dealing with the situation.

CASE STUDY

Any tourist resort or destination caters for two distinct groups of customers:

- visitors who come from outside the area – for a holiday, to visit friends and relatives, or on business
- people who live in the area and use the various leisure and tourism attractions and facilities available.

Both groups are equally important. While the visitors may spend more money in a shorter period of time, the residents' spending is spread throughout the year and helps support the area's tourism industry during off-season months.

Groups

Staff in many leisure and tourism facilities will deal with **groups** of customers together.

This situation may save time, but it requires special skills to take into account the individual needs of customers while dealing with the group as a whole. For example, an art gallery guide may have a group of visitors that includes young children, foreigners and art experts and will need to communicate effectively with each member of this group. In some jobs, such as instructors at outdoor pursuits centres, staff members will usually find themselves talking first to a group as they explain and demonstrate the basic techniques, then to individuals as they each try to apply skills. Anyone who has tried this, especially with children, will know that you have to develop 'eyes in the back of your head' to keep in touch with all that is happening.

▲ A guide may have to deal with a varied group of customers

Training courses for guides

To deal with large groups on a regular basis needs training and experience. The Guild of British Tour Guides provides training courses for guides.

- Read the extract from their website.
- Identify the skills that you think a Blue Badge Guide needs.

Blue Badge Guides are selected, trained and examined by the official British tourist boards. The training is detailed and comprehensive, the examinations rigorous and registration an achievement. In London the course lasts for eighteen months.

As well as acquiring knowledge, Blue Badge Guides are trained in the selection and presentation of material. Blue Badge Guides have a wide range of languages, specialities and interests, and can guide on foot, in cars, on coaches, on trains and on boats. They take pride in constantly updating their knowledge to enable their visitors to enjoy Britain's immense, unique and varied heritage. They are practical, punctual, reliable and thrive on the unexpected, welcoming individuals or groups, here on business or for pleasure.

Stamina and good health are essential. The work of the guide is very demanding. Hours can be long, starting say with the arrival of the first aircraft at Heathrow and ending with theatres and pubs at night, with guided commentary throughout the day.

It is absolutely essential to enjoy working with people. Understanding the stresses and strains of the traveller – jet lag, lack of sleep, sickness, hotel and transport problems, loss of valuables or luggage – is all part of the work. The guide may be the only direct human contact.

People of different ages

When working in the leisure and tourism industry you will almost certainly meet people from a wide range of age groups who will have different needs. The ages of customers can be broken down into:

A grandfather enjoys a round of golf with his grandchildren ▼

- children – babies, toddlers, older children and teenagers
- adults – young adults, middle-aged adults, senior citizens.

Leisure and tourism staff will often deal with a group of mixed ages, such as an adult with young children or a senior citizen with grandchildren. You should be able to identify the specific needs of each and satisfy them all.

It is not a good idea to think that a customer expects a certain type of service simply because of their age. Fit and healthy senior citizens might well be offended if you speak to them slowly and loudly just because you think they are old. Likewise, 12 year olds might be upset if you offer them the children's menu when they think they are far too old for such things.

However, different age groups will usually require some different types of service. It is generally safe to assume that older people expect a more formal approach than children and young adults, for example.

Children make up a large part of all leisure and tourism customers. They may visit some attractions and facilities on their own, but more often than not an adult accompanies them. This presents a particular challenge for leisure and tourism providers. The children expect to enjoy themselves and the adult also wants an enjoyable time. In addition, there will often be other adults with no children at the attraction, who expect to have a good time without being bothered by other children. Providers are constantly looking for new ways to offer a service that ensures that all customers are satisfied.

Identify the needs of a mixed age group

Harry and Rosemary Clark are both retired and have their daughter, son-in-law and three grandchildren staying with them for a week's holiday. The grandchildren are Charlie (18 months), Alice (4 years) and Mark (12 years). Harry and Rosemary have decided to take the whole family to a local theme park for the day.

- As a group, discuss what you think the specific needs of each member of the group might be.

CASE STUDY

A class of their own

A nightmare or a brilliant new service? Kids Class is being introduced on some charter flights.

The plan is to segregate five to 12 year olds from other passengers by giving them their own block of seats at the back of the plane where a crew member will have responsibility for entertaining and feeding them. The idea comes from the charter airline Airworld, which is part of Sunworld's operations.

A crew member hands out toys and comics, organises games, and, if needs be, helps the children with their menu of potato letters and chicken nuggets. This has worked pretty well so far, according to Airworld's marketing executives, who say that once-a-week trials on flights to Greece have been so successful that the company hopes to sell Kids Class to many other operators by next summer.

The airline assures us that passengers who want to be seated well away from the children's area can request this, but in any case parents are seated near to their offspring, creating a buffer zone between Kids Class and the rest of the plane.

Source: *Holiday Which?* April 1999

OVER TO YOU

Children on a charter flight

Read the case study about one of the ways that a tour operator has tried to ensure that children, accompanying adults, and adults with no children can all enjoy the experience of taking a charter flight to their holiday destination.

- How effective do you think this approach would be?
- Identify any problems that might arise from this.
- Name any other leisure and tourism services or facilities where customers are separated to ensure that each enjoys the experience.

▼ T.G.I. Friday provides a children's menu, and many fun activities to entertain children while their parents enjoy a meal

Different cultures

When we talk about **culture** we mean the traditions, tastes, opinions and behaviour that influence us. Foreigners might see British culture as including going to watch a football match or a drink at the local pub on Saturdays and families sitting down to a traditional roast meal on Sunday.

When we think about Australian culture, we might imagine them having barbecues on the beach on Christmas day and spending their leisure time surfing ▼

Identify cultural groups

- As a group identify five different cultures – for example, Spanish or American.
- In pairs, write a list of at least three features that make each culture different from the 'British culture'.
- Compare your answers with the rest of the group.

Of course, many of us do not fit into cultural images because we are all individuals. We are now far more aware of other cultures and tend to copy the parts of those cultures that we like. For example, Chinese and Indian take-aways are now more popular in Britain than the traditional fish and chips shops. Likewise, many cultures, worldwide, are influenced by American culture aspects such as theme parks and movies.

It is important to recognise that people from different cultures may have different needs and behaviour. This means that we need to be aware of these differences and provide a service that satisfies the customer's needs. We often take our own cultural background for granted (simply because we have grown up with it) and assume that everyone else does the same as us. They do not!

Did you know...?

- in South Africa a café is a corner shop so do not expect a cup of coffee?
- in Japan you should change into a special pair of 'toilet slippers' before using the bathroom?
- if you take the lift down to the first floor in the USA you will arrive at the ground floor?
- in China it is considered very unlucky to leave your chopsticks in your bowl?
- in India you should never show someone the sole of your shoe – it is a great insult?
- if you enter a Tunisian mosque you must remove your shoes, cover your arms and legs and never walk in front of someone who is praying?
- in Turkey blowing your nose in public is considered very rude?

When dealing with people from different cultures it is important to respect and understand their beliefs and behaviour, but equally important not to make any assumptions based on culture.

One of the key differences between many cultures is in what people find acceptable or unacceptable to eat. This is often based on the religion of the culture. You may already know that Jewish people do not eat pork, but did you also know that they will not eat shellfish, or meat and milk in the same meal?

OVER TO YOU

Cultural characteristics

For this activity you will need to use some reference books to find out as many answers as possible. Working in pairs, identify which religious culture the following statements apply to.

- These people fast during the month of Ramadan.
- For these people all meat must be kosher before cooking.
- These people do not eat beef as the cow is viewed as sacred.
- These people do not eat any meat products at all.

Non-English speakers

If you have been abroad on holiday you may have experienced what it is like to not be able to speak the local language. Perhaps you hoped that the locals could speak English? Possibly you took a phrase book with you and tried to communicate using it? Whatever happened, the chances are that you had some difficulty in communicating.

Many thousands of people visit Britain each year with little or no knowledge of the English language – but they hope that the people providing them with customer service will be able to understand their needs. You may find yourself in a situation where you have to deal with non-English speaking customers. You cannot be expected to be able to speak all foreign languages, but even if you know just a little of the customer's language it shows excellent customer service to use it.

The Jorvik Centre (see page 117) is one of many tourist organisations who provide tourist information in different languages ▶

DEUTSCH

Unter der historischen Stadt York liegt eine noch ältere Siedlung, die Stadt JORVIK aus der Zeit der Wikinger.

Archäologen haben hier die Überreste jenes Ortes gefunden, in dem die Wikinger ehemals beheimatet waren, und haben damit die Ära der Wikinger auf fesselnde und in aller Welt berühmte Weise rekonstruiert.

Nach 20 Jahren Forschung und einem Kostenaufwand von £ 5 Mio. ist es uns gelungen, die Stadt Jorvik noch schöner und besser wieder auferstehen zu lassen, so dass der Alltag der Wikinger noch eindringlicher vor Augen geführt werden kann. Auf dem Gang durch die alten Strassen sehen, hören und fühlen Sie hautnah, wie das Leben in dieser Stadt aus dem 10. Jh. wirklich war.

Deutscher kmmentar zur verfügung.

FRANÇAIS

Sous la ville historique de York s'en trouve une autre encore plus ancienne : la ville de JORVIK datant de l'époque des Vikings.

Là, les archéologues ont découvert les restes conservés d'un lieu que les Vikings considérèrent à une époque comme chez eux. Grâce à toutes les preuves trouvées, ils ont effectué l'une des reconstructions les plus célèbres et passionnantes de l'époque des Vikings.

Après vingt années de recherche et cinq millions de livres d'investissement, nous retrouvons la ville de Jorvik plus parfaite que jamais. Elle rend désormais encore davantage la vie quotidienne à l'époque des Vikings. Un voyage à travers de réelles rues anciennes, où vous pourrez voir, écouter et être touché par les réalités de la vie dans cette ville du Xe siècle.

Commentaire disponible en Français.

NEDERLANDS

Onder de historische stad York ligt een nog oudere stad uit de Vikingtijd: JORVIK.

Hier ontdekten archeologen de vele overblijfselen van de plaats die de Vikingen als hun thuis beschouwden. De reconstructie van de Vikingtijd die ze met behulp van hun vondsten maakten, is een van de beroemdste enindrukwekkendste ter wereld.

Nu, na 20 jaar onderzoek en een investering van £5 miljoen, verbeelden we de stad Yorvik perfecter dan ooit. De tentoonstelling geeft een nog helderder beeld van het leven van alledag in de Vikingtijd en leidt u door echte oude straten, waar u kunt zien, horen en ervaren hoe men deze tiende-eeuwse stad leefde.

NORSK

Under den historiske byen York ligger en annen by som er enda eldre, nemlig vikingebyen JORVIK.

Her oppdaget arkeologene godt bevarte rester av det stedet som en gang var vikingenes hjem, og disse ble brukt til å skape en av verdens mest beromte og spennende rekonstruksjoner av vikingetiden.

Etter 20 års forskning og en investering på over femti millioner kroner har vi nå gjenskapt byen Jorvik bedre enn noensinne, en enda mer levende skildring av hverdagslivet i vikingetiden. Dette er en reise gjennom eldgamle gater hvor du både kan se, høre og bli berørt av livets realiteter i denne byen fra det tiende århundre.

ITALIANO

Sotto il centro storico di York si trova una città ancora più antica risalente all'era dei Vichinghi: la città di JORVIK.

Gli scavi archeologici hanno riportato alla luce i resti ben preservati di questa città, una delle più importanti dei Vichinghi, in base ai quali è stata ultimata una delle più riuscite e interessanti ricostruzioni storiche.

Dopo 20 anni di ricerche e un investimento di 5 milioni di sterline, la città di Jorvik è stata ricreata perfettamente riportando in vita il mondo quotidiano dei Vichinghi. Passeggiare per le antiche strade della città è un vero e proprio viaggio nel passato dove si può vedere, sentire e toccare con mano questo microcosmo del X secolo.

ESPAÑOL

Debajo del centro de la ciudad histórica de York miente otra incluso de mayor antigüedad: la ciudad de la Viking-Edad de JORVIK.

Aquí, los arqueólogos descubrieron el restos preservado del lugar que el Vikings una vez llamó hogar, y utilizaron esa evidencia de para crear una de las reconstrucciones más famosas y cautivadoras de la Viking-Edad en el mundo.

Ahora, siguiendo 20 años la investigación y una inversión £5 millón, hemos recobrado la ciudad de Jorvik más perfectamente que siempre. Es aún más evocador ahora de vida diaria en la Viking-Edad. Un viaje a través de las calles antiguas, donde usted ve, oye y se toca por vida en esta 10ma ciudad del siglo.

Un comentario español está disponible.

JAPANESE

ヨーク市は歴史深い町ですが、その水面下にはさらに古い町が潜んでいます：バイキング時代の名残、ヨーヴィック。

ここで、バイキングがかつて住居と称した遺跡がそのままの形で考古学者たちによって発見されました。発掘された各証拠品を元に世界で最も有名で、しかも魅力の溢れる、バイキング時代を再現する町が建設されました。

20年の歳月をかけた調査と500万ポンドの投資により、今日ヨーヴィック市は見事に再現されています。バイキング時代の人々が送った日常生活が難なく想像できることでしょう。まさに古代という街並みを散策しながら、この10世紀に栄えた町で営まれていた生活事実を学び、探訪してください。

K EARLY AND BEAT THE QUEUE CALL: 01904 543403

OVER TO YOU

Welcome Host

The English Tourism Council runs a number of customer service training programmes for tourism employees called Welcome Host. Welcome Host International combines conversational foreign language skills with cultural appreciation of the needs and expectations of overseas visitors. As part of the programme, trainees practise using basic greetings and phrases in common languages.

Using translation dictionaries work out what the words and phrases in the table are in each of the foreign languages.

Phrase	French	Spanish	German
Hello			
Goodbye			
Please			
Thank you			
Sorry			
Mr			
Mrs			
Miss			
You're welcome			

Even when you and the customer have no language in common it is still possible to communicate with them and provide good service.

OVER TO YOU

Design a sign

Many organisations design signs with pictures and symbols on them that can be easily understood by anyone regardless of their language.

Design a sign for use in a leisure centre that uses only pictures and symbols. The sign should show in which direction the following facilities are:

- the swimming pool
- the exercise studio
- the squash courts
- the cafeteria
- the changing rooms
- the male and female toilets.

Customers with specific needs

Some customers have specific needs that may require special customer service in addition to that provided to meet the general needs of customers. A specific need is anything that may require a bit of extra thought and assistance from staff. This may be because of:

- sight impairment
- hearing impairment
- literacy and/or numeracy learning difficulties
- a need for wheelchair access
- a need for facilities for young children.

If you work in leisure and tourism it is very likely that you will sometimes deal with customers who have specific needs. These customers may have needs that are different from the general customers and require special customer service.

Dealing with this type of customer means understanding their particular needs and acting quickly to ensure that they are able to enjoy the product you are offering. For example, a mother with a baby buggy or a customer in a wheelchair struggling to get through a swing door should not have to ask for assistance – staff who see the situation should react quickly and offer help.

Signed Performances
at the **Stephen Joseph Theatre**
Autumn 2001

All tickets £6.50 for signed performance customers and escorts. When booking, please inform staff that you will be watching the signer.

RolePlay
Friday 16 November at 7.30pm
The Changeling
Friday 16 November at 7.45pm
and Saturday 17 November at 7.45pm
This Is Where We Came In
Friday 4 January at 7.00pm

Our registered qualified signer Steven Conlon has been interpreting SJT shows since 1998

MINICOM: 01723 370555
FAX: 01723 360506

▲ Stephen Joseph's commitment to customers with specific needs

Coping with special needs

OVER TO YOU

Check your own understanding of customers with specific needs by deciding which of the following statements are definitely true.

Statement	True	False
• People who have a visual impairment cannot read.		
• If a customer with specific needs has a companion it is best to talk to the companion.		
• If someone is in a wheelchair you should bend over when talking to them so that you are on the same level.		
• If someone is in a wheelchair you should offer to push them to where they want to go.		
• If someone has a hearing impairment you need to write everything down for them.		
• People who cannot read or write are probably not clever and therefore need things explained to them slowly.		
• People with a learning disability, such as Down's syndrome, will not understand most of what you say to them.		
• People who cannot speak English will only understand you if you can speak their language.		
• People with specific needs require customer service that satisfies their needs without making them feel different to other customers.		

CASE STUDY
Important advice and restrictions at Disney

Big Thunder Mountain
Minimum height: 1.02 m (3'3"). This attraction is not recommended for children under the age of 3. Wheelchair visitors will require a transfer. Visitors must be in good health and not affected by medical problems, which might be worsened by this experience. Pregnant women and visitors in surgical collars are strongly advised not to go on this ride. Guide dogs are not admitted.

Pirates of The Caribbean
A transfer is required for wheelchair visitors going on board. This attraction includes two sudden, quick descents, and visitors with problems liable to be aggravated (such as spinal problems), pregnant women and those wearing surgical collars are strongly advised not to go on this attraction. Unsighted visitors must be accompanied. Guide dogs are not allowed to enter, for their own safety. You may get wet on this ride!

Indiana Jones and the Temple of Peril: Backwards! presented by ESSO
Minimum height: 1.40 m (4'6") Not recommended for children under the age of 8.

In order to join this adventure, our visitors with reduced mobility must be able to move about without wheelchairs, either on their own or assisted by their attendants.

To enjoy this experience, visitors must be in good health and have no medical problems which might be worsened. Unsighted visitors must be accompanied.

Guide dogs are not allowed to enter, for their own safety. Pregnant women and visitors in surgical collars are strongly advised not to go on this ride.

Blanche Neige et les Sept Nains
A transfer is required for wheelchair visitors going on board the carriages. Guide dogs are not allowed to enter, for their own safety. Take care – some scenes may frighten young children.

Star Tours, presented by IBM
Children aged between 3 and 7 must be accompanied. This attraction is unsuitable for children under 3 years old, pregnant women, people wearing surgical collars or orthopaedic devices and anyone with back or heart problems.

Wheelchair visitors will require a transfer. All visitors wishing to go on the Star Tours ride must be in good health without problems which might be aggravated (such as motion sickness). Not recommended for those sensitive to noise and sudden changes in lighting.

Visionarium, presented by Renault.
360° Circle Vision film presentation. Enter by the main entrance where a Cast Member will guide you to the places reserved for disabled guests. Due to the nature of this presentation, guests subject to vertigo may feel uncomfortable.

Source: www. disneylandparis.org

- Identify the specific needs of customers that Disneyland Paris tries to meet.
- As a group, discuss how they meet the needs of individual customers.

Business people

When we talk about leisure and tourism customers we usually think of tourists, holidaymakers or day visitors. However, people visiting an area on business are also leisure and tourism customers since they will often use many of the leisure and tourism facilities and services. They may use public transport to get there, stay in local hotels, eat in the restaurants and spend their spare time at leisure facilities, such as cinemas, pubs, theatres, nightclubs and casinos.

Many leisure and tourism organisations tailor the service that they offer to meet the needs of business men and women. Some hotel chains have special 'business bedrooms' that may include a desk and writing materials. Other services offered in the hotel may be a secretarial service, photocopying, fax, email and internet facilities.

Business tourism has become very important in many British locations. For example, traditional seaside resorts such as Torquay, Blackpool and Scarborough suffered from a decline in traditional tourists over recent years, but they continued to attract people to their conference and exhibition facilities. Conference customers are attracted to these resorts because of the large range of leisure and tourism facilities that are also available.

Business tourism also caters for
conference customers ▼

CASE STUDY

Brighton has been hosting national and international meetings for over a century and now offers organisers an enviable range of meeting facilities and services.

Our own research reveals two key facts: conference organisers enjoy working in Brighton, and conference delegates enjoy meeting here!

Here are some of the reasons why …

- lively, cosmopolitan atmosphere of the south coast's 'London by the Sea'

- shops, restaurants, royal palace, Regency heritage, museums, galleries, theatres and many more leisure activities in and around the city

- easy access by road, rail, air and sea

- extensive range of meeting facilities from the purpose-built Brighton Centre and excellent choice of hotels to non-residential venues and two universities

- a wealth of hotel accommodation from luxury five star to individual, family-run guesthouses

- walkability – all meeting venues, accommodation, shops, restaurants and tourist attractions are within easy walking distance of each other.

Social programmes

There are a number of local commercial companies who can tailor a social programme/accompanying person's package to your own specific requirements. Tour suggestions include the Royal Pavilion, Preston Manor, the Lanes, the English Wine Centre, Michelham Priory, Arundel Castle, Goodwood House, Hever Castle, the Body Shop headquarters and Leeds Castle.

Evening functions

Whether you want to use one of our hotels, the magnificent Banqueting Room at the Royal Pavilion or the splendid Edwardian Preston Manor, we can help. We can provide suggestions and details of other venues such as the Palace Pier, the Sealife Centre, Hove's Engineerium or Greyhound Stadium, country house hotels or many of the 400 restaurants in Brighton.

Source: www. brighton.co.uk

OVER TO YOU

The needs of business people

The website extract about Brighton outlines some of the leisure and tourism facilities that may be used by conference customers.

What other information might customers need? For example, a conference customer might want to know of a restaurant that is suitable for entertaining some important business clients.

What do you think they might expect in terms of customer service? In pairs, discuss what you think their customer service needs might be. Use the following headings:

- providing information
- giving advice
- receiving and passing on messages
- keeping records
- providing assistance
- dealing with problems
- offering extra services.

External and internal customers

External customers are individuals, groups and businesses who use the facility in which you work and to whom your organisation sells goods and services.

Internal customers are other people and departments who work in the same organisation as you do and who may need services from you.

A large part of the day-to-day operations of leisure and tourism organisations involves dealing with customers and satisfying their needs. Therefore providing a high level of customer service will be one of their main aims. When we talk about customers, we mean both external customers and internal customers.

External customers are the most important part of a leisure and tourism business. They buy the product. Internal customers are also very important. They include other people and departments in your organisation, and other organisations that help you to supply your products and services, such as suppliers.

▲ Members of other departments in the company are also customers

It may seem strange to think of your work colleagues as customers, but the way that you treat them and they treat you will affect the way that you work. This, in turn, will affect how you treat your external customers and the overall customer service that you provide. The case study shows how poor service to internal customers can result in poor service to external customers.

CASE STUDY

Lucy works as a part-time travel consultant in a travel agency. One busy Saturday morning she receives a phone call from Mr Charles Holmes who is due to go on a Baltic cruise with his wife in two weeks. Mr Holmes has just received his confirmation letter and is worried because it does not state that he has requested a cabin with disabled access for his wife who is in a wheelchair. Lucy reassures Mr Holmes that she will look into the matter and have a new confirmation document ready for him to pick up when he is in town on the following Tuesday. Unfortunately, Lucy is so busy for the rest of the day that she forgets about Mr Holmes until she is about to go home. She is not due to work until the next Saturday so leaves a note for Amanda, her colleague, that says, 'Please check disabled access on Mr Charles' Baltic cruise – sorry didn't have time to do it, we were so busy.'

When Amanda finds the note on Monday morning she cannot find a file for a Mr Charles so leaves a message asking Lucy to sort it out when she is next in.

On Tuesday morning Mr Holmes arrives for his new confirmation but none of the travel consultants know what he is talking about. He is understandably very angry and says that he will be writing to Head Office to complain.

- What would you have done if you were Lucy?

Good internal customer service is about good teamwork. It means respecting all of your colleagues and treating them in the way that you would like to be treated. You need to ask yourself:

How can we all work together to provide the best possible service to our external customers?

Internal customer service

OVER TO YOU

Think of situations where you have worked with other people. This might be in a part time job or on a project at school. It is likely that you will have found some people easy to work with and others more difficult.

On a whiteboard or flip chart, draw the following table. List the positive and negative ways in which people work together. Some examples have been given.

Good service	Poor service
Being pleasant and friendly to colleagues	Not passing on information

KEY TERMS

You should know what the following terms mean:

Types of customer (page 172)
Individuals (page 172)
Groups (page 173)
People of different ages
   (page 174)
Different cultures (page 176)
Non-English speakers (page 178)
Customers with specific needs
   (page 180)
Business people (page 182)
Internal customers (page 184)
External customers (page 184)

If you're not sure or want to check your understanding, turn to the page number listed in the brackets.

Revision questions

1 Why is it important to identify the needs of different types of customers?

2 Explain three differences between dealing with individual customers and groups.

3 How might the needs of a young adult differ from the needs of an elderly customer?

4 Identify three customers from different cultures.

5 Explain two ways in which a tourist information clerk could communicate with a non-English speaking tourist.

6 What specific customer service needs might a customer with sight impairment have?

7 Explain three ways that a sports centre could provide wheelchair access.

8 What is the difference between internal and external customers?

9 Why is it important to provide good service to your internal customers?

10 Explain how a member of staff could identify the needs of different customers.

Investigation ideas

The Excelsior Conference and Banqueting Centre relies heavily on casual staff. This is because most of their business is seasonal and a lot of staff are needed only when the centre is busy. The turnover of casual staff is very high, which means that the centre constantly has to re-train new staff. Customer service is therefore variable. Interviews with staff who had left show that they do not see The Excelsior Conference and Banqueting Centre as a pleasant place to work. In particular, they complain about how unfriendly and unhelpful the permanent staff are towards casual staff.

One ex-member of staff said, 'I only lasted two weeks. No-one told me what I was meant to be doing and then I got shouted at by the supervisor for making a mistake. The customers were nice enough but the other staff just cut you dead if you even tried to have a pleasant conversation with them.'

You have been asked to give a talk to the permanent staff at the centre on the importance and benefits of good internal customer service. Prepare and give a five-minute talk explaining how they and the organisation could provide good internal customer service.

REVISION PROMPT

What have I learnt about different types of customers?

What am I still unsure about?

How am I going to find out the extra information that I need?

Some of the specific benefits to the organisation of providing excellent customer service include:

- satisfied customers
- more customers through repeat business and recommendations
- a better public image
- an edge over the competition
- increased sales.

External customers are undoubtedly the most important part of any leisure and tourism organisation. Without the customers the organisation would not survive. Good customer service has positive benefits but poor customer service always results in negative effects.

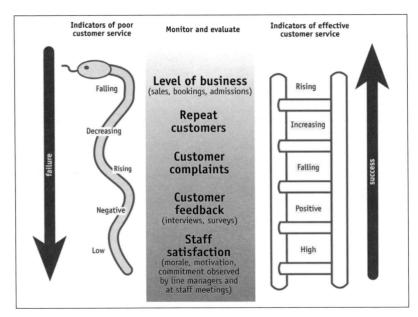

◄ Indicators of poor and effective customer service

Increased sales

If an organisation provides good service, their customers will be satisfied and will want to buy more of their products and services. The organisation will benefit from increased sales.

Poor and excellent customer service

Think about two leisure or tourism organisations that you have used recently – one where you received excellent customer service and one where the customer service was poor. It could be a package holiday, public transport, a cinema, a sports centre or a tourist attraction. As a group discuss the following questions:

- In what ways did the service encourage or discourage you to return and buy more products?
- Did you stay longer and buy more products because the service was good?

Satisfied customers

We know that if an organisation provides excellent service the customers will probably be satisfied. A dictionary defines 'satisfaction' as 'to adequately meet needs and expectations'. However, 'adequate' is not necessarily 'enough'. The word 'adequate' suggests that a minimum has been done to satisfy the customer. Excellent customer service should aim to exceed customers' expectations so that they cannot think of anything more that could have been done to make them satisfied.

Repeat business and recommendations

Customers should have such a good time at a leisure and tourism centre that they will want to come back again and again. Organisations should encourage such customer loyalty and repeat business. Customers will tell lots of other people about how good the product and service is and recommend that they visit.

The opposite is also true. If customers receive poor service they will probably not come back and may tell other people about the bad service. This will discourage others from visiting the organisation in the future. One customer may have been upset by the poor service, but many more have been lost through hearing about it.

1. JOAN: *Hello Sarah. You're looking well, have you lost weight?*

2. SARAH: *Only a few pounds, but actually I'm feeling great since I started going to the Trendsetters Health Club twice a week.*

3. JOAN: *I've seen their advertisement in the local paper and walked past a few times but it looks a bit fancy to me — all those skin-tight leotards in the window and a receptionist who looks as if she's just walked out of Gladiators. I'm sure that they'd take one look at my cellulite and send me packing!*

4. SARAH: *I know what you mean, Joan. I felt a bit like that to start, but once you get there they couldn't be nicer. They're so friendly and helpful.*

5. JOAN: *Are they?*

6. SARAH: *James and Irene who run the club are always around to talk to everyone and advise them on what exercise programme would be best. And the instructors have us all laughing so that you don't feel that it's too serious. In fact, they often come with us for a drink after classes. I started going there to get fit but now it's because I just enjoy it so much.*

A better public image

Leisure and tourism organisations that always manage to provide excellent customer service will find that in time they gain a reputation for good service. Their image is improved with the public. Existing customers will be proud to use the organisation and new customers will be more likely to try the organisation's products and services.

OVER TO YOU

Rate customer service

Select ten leisure and tourism facilities in your area that each person in your group has visited at least once or heard about from someone else.

- Ask each group member to rate the customer service at each of the facilities, based on what they know or have heard. Use a scale of 1 to 10, with 1 being poor and 10 being excellent.
- Add up the total scores for each facility and present them in a list from the highest score to the lowest.

You should now have a clear idea of which organisations have the better public image for customer service amongst your group.

STOP & THINK

Is there much difference in the actual products offered by nightclubs or fast food take-aways in your area?

An edge over the competition

Many of the products offered by leisure and tourism providers are very similar. However, it is the level of customer service offered that varies. In many situations customers will choose one organisation rather than another simply because they provide better service. If your organisation provides better service than your competitors, you will have the edge when it comes to customers deciding which organisation to use.

The competitive edge in fast food?

® Registered Trademark © Kentucky Fried Chicken

Competition in travel agencies

Competition amongst travel agencies is very strong. Most have large window displays showing special offers and deals to tempt customers. However, many customers are more interested in the level of service that they receive. The average customer may spend hundreds or even thousands of pounds on a holiday and expects the customer service to be excellent.

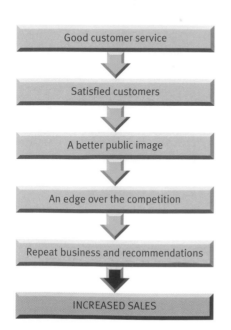

Good customer service

↓

Satisfied customers

↓

A better public image

↓

An edge over the competition

↓

Repeat business and recommendations

↓

INCREASED SALES

▲ The benefits of good customer service are closely linked

OVER TO YOU

Competition in travel agencies

As a group, discuss what you think gives one travel agency a competitive edge when it comes to customer service. For example, some customers may walk out of a travel agency if there is a long queue and go else-where.

List your ideas on a flip chart or whiteboard.

The benefits of providing good service to internal customers

Providing good customer service to internal customers has many benefits, including:

- a more pleasant place to work
- a happier and more efficient workforce
- improved job satisfaction
- improved chances of promotion within the organisation.

There are very few leisure and tourism organisations that employ only one member of staff. Most have a number of employees who work together as a team. They support each other and therefore provide excellent external customer service. Members of the team are known as the internal customers.

A more pleasant place to work

Simply being friendly, helpful and supportive to colleagues creates a more pleasant working atmosphere. It is very noticeable to external customers whether staff enjoy their work and get on with each other.

A happier and more efficient workforce

Staff are happier to carry out their duties if they work well together. Because the whole workforce will be more efficient and happier, members are able to provide excellent customer service to external customers.

STOP & THINK

Think about how your group works together. What do you do to support each other and create a pleasant working atmosphere?

Increase efficiency

Look at the comments from staff who work in the leisure and tourism industry. Draw up a list of how you can increase the happiness and efficiency of the workforce by providing good internal customer service.

▲ Airline cabin crew need to work as a team

Importance of job satisfaction

Job satisfaction means enjoying your work and the duties that you are expected to carry out. Most people are much better at doing things that they enjoy, so the more job satisfaction you get from your work the better customer service you are likely to give. In fact, if you enjoy your job and therefore give good service to customers, then the customers are likely to be nice back to you, which makes you enjoy your job even more. Good internal customer service will therefore lead to job satisfaction.

'The Entertainments Manager is really good at letting us know what's going on. We have a daily briefing meeting each morning and if anything changes during the day, she tells us straight away.'

Jason, Holiday Camp Host

A few months ago I had lots of problems at home and had to take time off at short notice. The other staff were great – covering for me when I couldn't get in and always asking how things were at home.'   **Raschid, Waiter**

When I first started working here I used to really panic when it got busy – especially on Saturdays. But now I know that there is always someone around to give a hand if I need it. We all look out for each other and step in if someone needs help.

Stacey, Sports Equipment Shop Assistant

Like anyone, I sometimes make mistakes in my work but the manager is always very understanding, so I'm never afraid to own up when I've done something wrong. He will always help me sort out the problem and then spends time showing me how to do it properly next time.

Karen, Advanced Reservations Computer Operator

Importance of chances of promotion within the organisation

The better you are at doing your job the more likely you are to do well in your career. Staff in more senior positions in organisations will always need to be able to prove that they can provide good customer service. They will also be responsible for encouraging the staff who work for them to follow their example. Therefore if you are able to give good service you are far more likely to be promoted to a position with more responsibility.

OVER TO YOU

Poster design

Design a poster to be displayed in the staff canteen of a tourist attraction. The title of the poster is:

Customer service – what's in it for me?

- Concentrate on one benefit to staff of providing good customer service.
- Make the poster as eye-catching as you can. Persuade staff that giving good customer service can benefit them.

◄ Customers will be nice to you when you give good service

KEY TERMS

You should know what the following terms mean:

Benefits of customer service (page 188)
Increased sales (page 188)
Satisfied customers (page 189)
Repeat business and recommendations (page 189)
A better public image (page 190)
An edge over the competition (page 190)
A more pleasant place to work (page 192)
A happier and more efficient workforce (page 192)
Job satisfaction (page 192)
Promotion, job (page 193)

If you're not sure or want to check your understanding, turn to the page number listed in the brackets.

Revision questions

1 Describe three ways in which poor customer service might harm an organisation.

2 Why do sales often increase if an organisation provides excellent customer service?

3 Describe a situation in which excellent customer service would result in customer satisfaction.

4 Why are repeat business and customer recommendations important for an organisation?

5 Describe a leisure or tourism organisation that has a better public image because it provides excellent customer service.

6 How can excellent customer service result in an edge over the competition?

7 Describe how good service to internal customers can create a more pleasant place to work.

8 Why would poor customer service result in less job satisfaction for staff?

9 Why is it important that all members of staff give a high level of service to each other?

10 How could an organisation persuade staff to give good service to each other?

Investigation ideas

The cleaning staff at a leisure centre have recently been told that they are to receive training in customer service because they come into contact with customers. William, the cleaning supervisor, and his staff are not impressed. 'We are employed to clean the centre not deal with the customers. Why should we give up our time to go to some useless training session?'

In fact, the cleaning staff are so annoyed that a meeting has been arranged between them and the management team to discuss the issue.

Four members of your group should play the role of cleaners and three are the management team. The rest of the group should observe the following role play:

The management team should explain to the cleaning staff why it is important that they understand what is meant by good customer service and how they can provide it. They should also explain the benefits to the organisation and staff of providing good customer service. The cleaning staff can be as uncooperative as they like and should think of as many arguments as they can for not doing the training. Can the management team persuade the cleaning staff that the training is a good idea?

REVISION PROMPT

What have I learnt about how customer service is provided?

_____

_____

_____

What am I still unsure about?

_____

_____

_____

How am I going to find out the extra information that I need?

_____

_____

_____

Contact with staff can be:

- face-to-face
- on the telephone
- in writing.

Most people who work in leisure and tourism will be in contact with customers at some time. For many staff this will be a large part of their job. Whichever method of contact is used, customers will expect you to be able to communicate clearly and effectively.

▲ Tour guides staff use face-to-face communication most of the time

Face-to-face communication

For most leisure and tourism products and services the customer has to visit the organisation in person to enjoy what is offered. A lot of the communication is face-to-face.

Face-to-face situations have many advantages if you understand how to use them well. For example, your appearance can help to create a positive impression. You can also use facial expressions and gestures to help you to communicate more effectively. See the section on body language on page 199.

▲ Telephone communication

Telephone communication

Most organisations use the telephone to provide part of their customer service. Some organisations, such as hotel central reservations offices, use the telephone as the main method of communication in dealing with customer enquiries. With good telephone skills, we can usually meet or exceed the standard of service that customers expect. Many of the skills needed are already used in customer service situations, such as being polite, friendly, attentive and efficient. However, additional skills are needed when using a telephone because you and the customer cannot see each other. Any expressions or gestures that you use to help the communication process cannot be seen. You must rely on your voice and your ability to listen carefully.

Using the telephone effectively

- Speak clearly. Do not eat, drink, chew gum or smoke while on the telephone as this will distort or muffle the sound of your voice.
- Take notes. Always write down full details of what the customer wants, particularly if the message is for someone else.

- Identify the caller's needs. Remember that the caller is paying for the call and wants to be dealt with quickly and efficiently.
- Listen carefully. Do not interrupt the caller.
- Explain what is happening. If you transfer the caller to someone else, state what you are doing.

Written communication

In leisure and tourism it is rare for written communication to be the only method of contacting customers. However, it still plays an important part in the overall service offered. For some organisations, written communication is the main way in which they keep in contact with customers. For example, many customers rarely visit a branch of their bank to talk to staff. They will get money from a cash dispenser and receive details of their accounts by letter. Much of the image that they have of the service offered by the bank will depend on written communication.

▲ Excellent written communication from the Dean Court Hotel

Examples of written communications used by leisure and tourism organisations include:

- menus
- tariffs or price lists
- letters and bills
- brochures and leaflets
- advertisements
- signs and notice boards
- programmes
- tickets
- faxes and email
- timetables.

The same standard of care needs to be given to written forms of communication as to any other aspect of customer service. The quality of written communication will affect the customer's image of both you and the organisation. Guests in a hotel may be very impressed by the friendly, enthusiastic attitude of the receptionist but that impression may change if they are handed an illegible handwritten message on a scrappy piece of paper. However, if the message is presented in a professional manner the positive impression will be reinforced.

OVER TO YOU

Communication

How would customers use each of the following kinds of communication in the different leisure and tourism facilities? List three examples of each.

For example, tourists visiting a stately house might telephone in advance to find out the opening times, communicate face-to-face with a guide during a tour of the house and use the printed guide to find their way around the grounds.

Facility	Face-to-face communication	Telephone	In writing
A travel agency	1	1	1
	2	2	2
	3	3	3
A theatre	1	1	1
	2	2	2
	3	3	3
A leisure centre	1	1	1
	2	2	2
	3	3	3

At some time in the leisure and tourism industry you will be in contact with customers and need to know how to communicate with them effectively. Some situations will be expected, such as a receptionist or waiter. Other situations may be unexpected, such as a cleaner being asked for assistance. Whatever the situation, you need to develop good communication skills to deal with the customer effectively.

The importance of language

Understanding the best language to use in customer service situations is very important. We all use different types of language and words depending on whom we are talking to. Some situations may require a more formal approach, such as when dealing with a complaint or talking to a business person. In other instances it may be appropriate to be less formal, such as when talking to children or young adults. Likewise, when dealing with a customer you may have to change the type of language that you would normally use to suit the customer and their specific needs.

▲ Customers often ask the cleaners at Disneyland Parks questions

◄ Dealing with children is less formal

STOP & THINK

What different words might you use when talking to a friend? a tutor? your doctor? an elderly relative?

Using appropriate language

Three of the most common communications that you will have with customers are:

- greeting customers
- asking customers what they want
- thanking customers.

OVER TO YOU

As a group, brainstorm the different phrases that could be used in these three situations. List all the phrases that you can think of, even if they are slang, such as 'hiya' and 'ta'.

Decide which phrases are the most appropriate when providing excellent customer service.

OVER TO YOU

Changing tone

In pairs repeat the phrase to each other several times:

Good morning sir, how may I help you?

Each time use a different tone and pitch to your voice so that you sound one of the following and see if your partner can guess which one it is:

- bored
- angry
- nervous
- impatient
- happy to serve the customer.

Pitch and tone of voice

Sometimes you may find that staff in leisure and tourism say the right words but the tone and pitch of their voice spoils the good impression. They may sound bored, disinterested or even aggressive.

The use of pauses and silences

Communication is more than just how we talk to others. It is as important to understand how the other person can communicate back to you. By using pauses and silences it gives the customer the chance to ask you questions and also allows you to show that you are listening. Being a good listener is a skill that improves with practice. You have to learn to know when the customer might want to ask a question or make a comment. Sometimes you will need to encourage the customer by saying perhaps, 'Does that answer your question?' or 'Is there anything else I can tell you about?'

Body language

Body language means the way that we communicate with others using posture, gestures and facial expressions. It is important to know how much is communicated between people in this way. Generally body language can be put into two categories – open and closed.

Open body language is when your expression, posture or gestures show that you are interested, relaxed, confident and friendly. This would include good eye contact, smiling, relaxed posture and confident gestures, such as using your hands to emphasise a point. Closed body language shows that you are unfriendly, ill at ease, hostile and disinterested. This might include avoiding eye contact, tightly crossed arms, hands in pockets, expressionless face and nervous fidgeting.

OVER TO YOU

Body language

Look at the cartoon drawings shown here. What can you tell about the person's attitude from the body language?

Working accurately

When dealing with customers it is very important that you work accurately. Make sure that you record correct information about the customer and also give the customer correct information. If you are in any doubt, ask the customer to clarify the details – even if it is just how to spell their name. Incorrect details are usually worse than having no details at all. Imagine how Mr Tollet will feel if you send him a letter addressed to Mr Toilet!

Listening and responding to customers' questions

When dealing with customers you will find that they often have questions that they expect you to be able to answer. You should be ready to listen to and respond to these questions as they arise. Remember to listen carefully to what the customer is saying and then to answer appropriately.

▲ A travel agent needs to get the details right

Getting just one detail wrong, such as the time of the flight, could ruin the customer's holiday ▼

Asking appropriate questions

You will need to ask the customers appropriate questions to ensure that you understand exactly what they want and can meet their needs. You may also ask questions to make sure that you have accurate customer details, when making a reservation for a holiday, concert or hotel stay, for example.

Questions need to be asked in an appropriate manner. Customers should not feel as if they are being put through a standard process. Look at the difference in the way the following questions are asked:

- 'What name?' and 'May I take your name, sir?'

- 'Method of payment?' and 'How would you like to pay for the tickets, Mrs Graves?'

- 'Estimated arrival time?' and 'What time do you expect to arrive, Mr Jones?'

CASE STUDY

A conversation between a customer and a receptionist in a Sports Centre.

Customer: *Hello, I'm thinking about taking up aerobics as I suffer from a bad back and thought it might be good for me. I've not done an exercise class before. What would you suggest?*

Receptionist: *We have an excellent beginners aerobics session on a Monday at 6.00 p.m. which is ideal for people who have not done aerobics before. Would you like me to book you a place?*

In the conversation the receptionist has not listened to the customer properly. She has ignored the customer's comment about a bad back. Advising the customer to start an aerobics class could be dangerous as it might make the back problem worse. The receptionist should have asked the customer to check with a doctor that an aerobics class is a suitable form of exercise.

When asking questions it is important to understand the difference between open and closed questions. An **open question** allows the customer to give an explanation. A **closed question** usually results in a short answer. A response to the open question, 'What type of accommodation are you looking for?' invites customers to explain fully what they want. In the closed question, 'Do you want to stay in a hotel?' the answer could only be 'yes' or 'no'. You will need to listen carefully to what customers say and ask further questions if necessary.

OVER TO YOU

Open and closed questions

Look at the list of closed questions in the table.

In pairs re-write them so that they are open questions.

Closed question	Open question
Have you had a nice day?	
May I help you?	
Would you prefer a daytime flight?	
Have you been to Spain before?	
Did your children enjoy the theme park?	
Is your bedroom OK?	

Talking about good communication is not the same as actually putting it into practice. Everyone needs to learn good communication skills and continually try to improve on them. In this section you will practise using communication skills in role-play situations.

Practising through role-play

The purpose of this role-play is for you to practise and evaluate your communication skills. It might help your evaluation to record your face-to-face and telephone role-plays either with a video camera or tape recorder – most of us are surprised to find out how we sound and look to others. To carry out the role-plays you will need a range of leisure and tourism leaflets, brochures and maps of your area. You can get these from a local tourist information centre, train station or hotel.

Carrying out the role-plays

Imagine that you are working in a tourist information centre in your area. A visitor who has not been to the area before would like some information on local facilities and attractions that he or she could go to. In pairs, role-play the visitor and information clerk – make sure you both try each role. Remember to use open questions and listen carefully to the customer before responding.

Face-to-face

Try the role-play first in a face-to-face situation. Imagine that the customer has come into the centre and approached the clerk at the desk.

Telephone

Now try sitting back to back to each other and role-play as if you were on the telephone. In other words, the visitor has telephoned the tourist information centre for information.

In writing

Imagine that you have received the letter shown here from the visitor. Write back with a suitable response.

> Dear Sir or Madam
>
> I am planning to visit your area in July with my family for a week's holiday. We have already booked a hotel but would like some information on local attractions and suggestions for days out. My children are aged 3 and 7 years and like to be doing things all the time! We are travelling by car so can get around the area. I am particularly concerned about what we can do if the weather is not good.
>
> I look forward to hearing from you.
>
> Yours faithfully
>
> T R Walton

Evaluate your communication skills

After the role-plays, evaluate each person's communication skills using the chart opposite.

ROLE-PLAY EVALUATION SHEET

Pupil's name: _____

Date: _____

Description of the customer/s:

_____

Description of the customer service situation:
What type of communication was used?

_____

Was the language, tone and pitch of voice used appropriate
to the type of customer and the situation?

_____

How did you use pauses and silences to help you
communicate with the customer?

_____

How did you use open body language to help communicate
with the customer?

_____

Did you use any closed body language and, if so, what effect
did this have on the customer?

_____

What was particularly good about the way in which you
communicated with the customer?

_____

How could you have improved the way in which you
communicated with the customer?

_____

KEY TERMS

You should know what the following terms mean:

Communication (page 196)
Language (page 198)
Pitch and tone of voice (page 199)
Pauses and silences (page 199)
Body language (page 199)
Working accurately (page 200)
Listening and responding to
  customers (page 200)
Open question (page 201)
Closed question (page 201)

If you're not sure or want to check your understanding, turn to the page number listed in the brackets.

Revision questions

1 What are the main advantages of face-to-face communication between staff and customers?

2 Describe three ways in which telephone communication might be used in the leisure and tourism industry.

3 Identify three ways in which members of staff can make sure they communicate clearly on the telephone.

4 Identify five different ways that a hotel might communicate with its guests in writing.

5 Explain a customer service situation where you would be expected to use more formal language.

6 Why is the tone and pitch of voice sometimes more important than the actual language used?

7 Explain why it is important to use pauses and silences when communicating with a customer.

8 Describe what is meant by the term 'body language'.

9 Identify three examples of open body language.

10 Why is it usually better to use open rather than closed questions when talking to customers?

Investigation ideas

One of the keys to successful communication is being able to ask the right questions – questions that allow you to identify and meet your customer's needs effectively.

For this activity each member of the group should think about an ideal holiday – you need to decide where the destination would be, who you would go with, what type of accommodation you would stay in and what you would do while you are there. Write down a detailed description of the holiday but do not show it to anyone else at this stage.

Next, work in pairs and take turns to try and find out the details of your partner's ideal holiday. You have five minutes each.

It may sound easy but your partner is only allowed to answer 'yes' or 'no'! The partners can, however, use body language when answering your questions, so look out for facial expressions.

At the end of both five-minute questioning sessions, find out which of the group was able to identify the holiday that most closely matched the description that their partner wrote down.

Ask the most successful member of the group to describe the questions that they used to identify their partner's holiday needs.

REVISION PROMPT

What have I learnt about how customer service is provided?

_____

_____

_____

What am I still unsure about?

_____

_____

_____

How am I going to find out the extra information that I need?

_____

_____

_____

Because such a large part of your job in the leisure and tourism industry will involve dealing with people, the way in which you present yourself is very important. The first impression that the customer gets of both you and your organisation is largely to do with the way that you present yourself. First impressions are very important. Your personal presentation says a lot about the sort of person you are and how you feel about your job. It will have a big effect on your customer's satisfaction.

Dress

The correct dress for any job will depend on what your job actually is. Some jobs call for more casual clothing, while others require you to wear a uniform. For example, a sports instructor would look out of place in a suit and tie but you would not expect to see a travel agency consultant in a tracksuit.

◄ Both are dressed appropriately

STOP & THINK

How would you feel if the pilot flying your plane wore dirty jeans and T-shirt and smoked a cigarette?

Whatever you wear for work you should always take care with your appearance. If someone is not appropriately dressed, you would probably think that he or she was not very professional. You might also worry that he or she could not do the job properly. In the case of an untidy pilot, you would probably think badly of the airline company and the rest of the staff that it employed.

A smart appearance tells customers how members of staff feel about their job, the organisation they work for, themselves and the customer. A neat and tidy appearance is likely to reassure customers that staff are professional in their attitude and can do their job well. It also has a direct influence on your customer's enjoyment, your job satisfaction and the future success of the organisation that employs you.

▲ The pilot you'd rather not meet

Many leisure and tourism organisations give new staff instructions on how they should look at work. This may be a printed list or included in the staff handbook.

Imagine that a cinema is writing instructions for new staff. The cinema provides staff with black trousers or skirt, black waistcoat and a white shirt.

Fill in details in the table to show what standards are expected, for example, making sure that clothes are properly ironed.

OVER TO YOU

Dress	male staff	female staff
Uniform		
Shoes		
Tights, socks, stockings		
Make-up		
Hair		
Jewellery		

Personal hygiene

Appearance does not only mean a clean and tidy uniform. It also involves personal hygiene and cleanliness. Hopefully you always make sure that your personal hygiene is good whether or not you are at work. You certainly would not want to be one of the members of staff described by these customers.

Remember that in some leisure and tourism situations, good personal hygiene is a legal requirement for health and safety reasons. In catering, for example, staff are required to wash their hands often and thoroughly. They should also keep their hair tied back.

Personality

The word **personality** means 'having a distinctive character'. However, we usually use it to mean that the person is likeable, outgoing and good to be around, as in 'He has lots of personality'. It is very important that the customer sees you as someone with a pleasant and caring personality.

Different jobs require people with different types of personality. For example, a resort representative for holidays aimed at young adults would need a different type of personality to a representative who looks after elderly customers.

OVER TO YOU

Personality

Write down all the things that you like about your personality. When you have done this, compare notes with the rest of the group and write a list of all the positive features of a good personality.

▲ Different jobs suit different personalities

You may already have an idea of the sort of job that you would like in the future. This is probably based largely on your type of personality. You might think: 'I could never work with young children; I don't have the patience', or 'I'd like to work in a busy airport because I'm confident when dealing with new people'. Understanding your personality and the type of job that it is suited to is important. It means that you can pick a job where your personality will allow you to give excellent customer service.

OVER TO YOU

Matching personalities to jobs

Look at the descriptions of four different types of personality and decide which one is closest to your own personality. Each description is based on a particular job in leisure or tourism.

Which job?

1

'I enjoy working under pressure and never panic if there is a lot of work. I am patient and don't mind doing routine jobs and paperwork. Angry customers don't worry me at all – in fact I quite like the challenge of trying to calm them down. If they shout and swear at me I can be very firm and stick up for myself – I don't take any nonsense! On the other hand, I am always very polite and welcoming to customers.'

2

'I am very patient which makes me good at dealing with older customers. I get asked the same questions over and over again but don't mind, as I'm good at explaining things to people. I'm very confident which is important, as I often have to speak to large groups of people. I like routine – no sudden surprises. I'm good at taking responsibility which is useful as I work on my own most of the time!'

3

'I'm very energetic and outgoing so like lots happening all of the time. I rarely lose my temper – which is important in my job because the customers can be very demanding. I think what makes me good at my job is that I can be a bit silly at times. My friends say I'm just a big kid. I always enjoy what I'm doing and can keep going with a smile on my face even when I'm really tired.'

4

'I like everything in place and orderly. My worst job would be where you didn't know what was going to happen from one minute to the next – I'd get nervous that I wouldn't be able to cope. I'm very methodical so great at administration and like the fact that my work is quite routine – that's not to say that it's boring. I'm dealing with customers all the time. Generally they are all very nice and it's a pleasure to serve them!'

Attitude and behaviour

Your **attitude** and **behaviour** towards customers are a very important part of your overall personal presentation. Customers are very sensitive to the ways in which staff react and behave towards them. The way you feel and the level of interest you have in the customers will affect how you act towards them.

▲ It's not nice to be ignored!

You have probably been in a situation where you felt that a sales assistant in a shop was not really interested in serving you. If so, then you will know that no matter how good the product was that you bought, you went away as a dissatisfied customer and probably did not go back to that shop.

There are many ways in which you can show customers that you really want to serve them. You can:

- attend to them straight away
- show that you are interested in what they have to say
- ask them questions to make sure that you know exactly what they want
- ignore distractions and concentrate on them all the time that you are serving them
- be friendly and encouraging
- smile!

▼ Smiling keeps you young!

The importance of smiling at customers cannot be stressed too much. A smile instantly tells customers that you are happy to serve them. It will usually make them smile back at you, which makes your job more enjoyable. It takes less effort to smile than to frown – you use seven face muscles to smile and 43 to frown.

All aspects of personal presentation – dress, hygiene, personality and attitude and behaviour – apply to any customer service situation, whether you are dealing with the customers face-to-face, over the telephone or in writing. Even though the customer on the other end of the phone or a letter cannot see whether you have ironed your shirt or washed your hands, it is part of being professional and always maintaining excellent personal presentation to have done so.

Role-play: a welcome meeting

A resort representative holds a welcome meeting for new holidaymakers when they first arrive in their destination. A typical meeting will explain a bit about the resort, facilities, attractions and optional excursions. The resort rep will also be available to answer customers' questions and give advice.

▼ The welcome meeting

Preparation

As a group, decide on a uniform for your resort reps. You do not need to buy new clothes for this but must agree on similar clothing for everyone.

Decide on which resort you are in and read some brochures so that you know a bit about the resort and can describe it. You could use a young adults holiday brochure, such as Club 18–30 or Escapades.

Decide who is going to present each of the following sections of the meeting:

- welcome to the resort
- local attractions and facilities
- local food and drink
- optional excursions
- health and safety advice.

If your group is quite big, you may share some of the categories so that everyone has something to present.

Do the role-play

Take turns at presenting your part of the welcome meeting. The rest of the group should play the part of the holidaymakers and ask questions.

Evaluate the role-play

At the end of the role-play, as a group discuss each person's personal presentation in terms of:

- dress and personal hygiene
- personality
- attitude
- behaviour.

Customer complaints

Dealing with customers is largely a pleasant and interesting experience – it will probably be the part of your job that you enjoy most. However, no matter how good you are at providing excellent customer service there will be times when you have to deal with a customer complaint. This may be over the phone, in a letter or perhaps face-to-face with the customer. Customers may complain about a number things:

- poor or slow service
- faulty products or products that do not match up to their expectations
- the behaviour of other customers, such as rowdy football spectators.

Often a customer will complain about a combination of issues, which makes it even more difficult to deal with.

▲ Not all customers are satisfied

> 'Your brochure said that the resort was quiet and peaceful and the travel agent assured us this was true. However, the noise from the nightclub and other guests singing and shouting kept us awake for most of the night. When we complained to the rep she said that there was nothing she could do.'

In this complaint there are four issues that need to be answered:

- inaccurate brochure description
- poor advice from the travel agent
- noise from the nightclub and other guests
- lack of help from the resort representative.

No one enjoys dealing with complaints but knowing how to do it properly can make the experience a lot easier. Most organisations train their staff to deal with complaints and some have a set procedure for staff to follow. Organisations realise the damage that can be done when a customer's complaint is not resolved effectively. For a start, it is likely that the customer will not return and in addition, they will probably tell others about their bad experience which will discourage new customers from visiting.

If complaints are handled well, customers will feel satisfied and impressed by the level of care and attention that they received. Therefore they are much more likely to return as well as tell others about how good the service was. When dealing with a complaint, see it as an opportunity to show the customer just how good your service really is.

CASE STUDY

The wrong way of dealing with complaints

TechnoWorld is a new interactive science museum in the south-east of England. It has been designed to appeal to the family market, particularly to children aged 5–14 years. Since opening it has been very busy during the school holidays and at weekends. One Saturday morning there is a long queue of customers at the ticket desk waiting to get in.

The two members of staff working at the desk have had to deal with a number of customers who are angry at the long wait. They explained that they are short staffed and are working as fast as they can. A customer and his wife on their way out of the museum make a complaint.

They had waited for more than an hour to get into the museum. When they went inside they found that many of the exhibits were out of order. The customer says that he thinks that he should have a refund, as they did not get what they paid for.

The ticket clerk points out that the brochure says that some exhibits might not be working. The customer asks to see the Duty Manager who arrives after 15 minutes. The customer and the Duty Manager have a heated argument about the closed exhibits, in front of the waiting queue. The Duty Manager refuses to give the customer a refund but offers him two free tickets for a return visit.

OVER TO YOU

Complaints

As a group, discuss the following points:

- How well do you think the ticket clerks and Duty Manager dealt with the dissatisfied customer?
- How could they have dealt with the complaint more effectively?
- How many customers do you think might have got a bad impression of the organisation, following the complaint?

Customers are often dissatisfied if they have to wait for a long time ▼

The eight basic steps

There are eight basic steps to handling complaints effectively. This applies to all situations.

1 Listen carefully to the customer.
2 Apologise in general terms for any inconvenience caused.
3 Let the customer know that the matter will be fully investigated and, if possible, put right.
4 Try to see the problem from the customer's point of view.
5 Keep calm and do not argue with the customer.
6 Find a solution to the problem.
7 Agree the solution with the customer.
8 Make sure that what you promised to do gets done.

Steps 1 – 4

1 Listen carefully to the customer.

If you do not know and understand all of the details of a complaint, you cannot do anything about it. It is also important to show customers that you are listening. Maintain good eye contact, make sure that your body language is positive and, above all, do not interrupt the customers when they are talking. This is often quite difficult to do, particularly if the customers are very angry.

▲ Angry customers are not easy to deal with

OVER TO YOU

Role-play: the angry customer

In pairs play the customer and member of staff standing up, face-to-face. The customer is very angry and shouting. (Add more detail if you like.) The customer uses aggressive gestures such as pointing a finger at the member of staff.

Customer: I think you and your company are an absolute disgrace. I've never had such bad service. Don't think you've got away with it because I will be writing to your head office to complain. I'll have you sacked if it's the last thing I do.

■ After the role-play discuss what your natural reaction was when you were the member of staff being shouted at. For example, did you look away because you were embarrassed, or cross your arms in a defensive gesture?

■ Discuss what you should have tried to do to show that you were listening.

2 Apologise in general terms for any inconvenience caused.
It is very important to offer a general apology as soon as you know that the customer is dissatisfied. You must show that you are concerned that the customer is unhappy. Perhaps say something like:

'I'm very sorry to hear that you are disappointed about… I'm sure that I can do something about it.'

However, do not apologise about specific details of the complaint until you have had a chance to investigate the situation thoroughly and found out what happened.

3 Let the customer know that the matter will be fully investigated and, if possible, put right.
Sometimes you will be able to solve the problem immediately and the customer will be satisfied. For example, if a customer complains that he has been waiting for twenty minutes for his order to be taken, you would apologise and serve him straight away.

However, in many situations you will not be able to solve the problem straight away. When this happens you need to reassure the customer that you will look into the matter and make contact once you have done this. You will need to write down all of the details, such as:

- the nature of the complaint, including the day and time that it happened
- customer's name
- contact address and telephone number.

4 Try to see the problem from the customer's point of view.
As with any customer service situation it is always important to think of how the customer feels and see the problem from the customer's point of view. Put yourself in the customer's position and think about what you might do.

Design a complaints book

Many leisure and tourism organisations have a complaints book for staff to record details of a customer complaint.

Design a page layout for a complaints book which staff could fill in when they are dealing with a complaint. Remember to include boxes for the name of the person dealing with the complaint and the action that was taken.

◄ If I were complaining about this how would I feel and what would I want done about it?

The eight basic steps (continued)

Steps 5 – 8

5 Keep calm and do not argue with the customer.

The reason that customers complain to you is that they expect you to be able to do something about it. Two of the worst things you can do is panic or lose your temper and argue with the customer. This shows that you have lost control of the situation and is likely to make the customer even more dissatisfied. In fact, if you argue with customers they are likely to get angrier, which would make the situation far worse.

6 Find a solution to the problem.

Finding a suitable solution to the problem will depend on the customer and the nature of the complaint. Sometimes the customer may require nothing more than a sincere apology and a promise that the problem will not happen again in future. Other complaints may require further action, such as offering a refund to the customer or replacing a product. If it is within your power to solve the problem straight away then you should do it. It is always better to act quickly rather than letting the customer leave without knowing what action is going to be taken.

▲ Arguing with the customer is very bad customer service

7 Agree the solution with the customer.

To make sure that customers are satisfied you need to agree the solution with them. Make sure that they are happy with what you are going to do. If you promised to look into the matter and contact them later, it is important that you let them know when you will be in touch.

8 Make sure that what you promised to do gets done.

Most organisations keep a complaints book to record customer complaints. This ensures that management is fully aware of dissatisfied customers and can take action to improve the level of customer service. It also makes sure that every complaint is followed up to ensure that the customer is satisfied.

Sometimes you may not be able to deal with a complaint on your own. For example, you may not be allowed to give a customer a refund without the permission of your supervisor. When you first start working in the leisure and tourism industry, you are probably not expected to solve customer complaints on your own. In fact, many organisations train their staff to contact a supervisor if a customer complains. This is because supervisory and management staff will be more experienced in dealing with complaints and usually have more authority to put things right.

Ask your supervisor to help if you feel that you cannot deal with a complaint on your own. It shows that you are handling the complaint very well by making sure that the customer is dealt with properly.

▲ Ask for help if you cannot deal with the complaint yourself

Role-play: Dealing with complaints

You have been given the opening sentences of complaints spoken by customers to a member of staff. In pairs, role-play each situation making up all further details about the customers' complaints.

Take time at the end of each complaint to discuss how well the complaint was handled and what, if anything, could have been improved.

'We've already been waiting three hours and now you are telling me that the flight is delayed by a further two hours at least. My young children are tired and I've run out of English currency to buy any food.'

'When I rang up yesterday I was told that this film was suitable for young children. My two sons were absolutely terrified – they spent most of the film hiding behind the seat in front.'

'When I booked to go on the Greek night I was told that there was unlimited free wine. Well the stuff you've been serving tastes like paint stripper. I think it's a big con!'

'You advertised these aerobics lessons as a way to get fit and lose weight. I've been coming for six months now and I still weigh 12 stone.'

'The brochure said that the weather was hot and sunny at this time of the year. We've had 12 days of solid rain and spent all of our holiday money on warm clothes.'

'I was just getting changed in my bedroom when the hotel maintenance engineer barged into my room. He said that he knocked but I certainly didn't hear him.'

'I made it quite clear when I booked the table that three of my party were vegetarians. What do you mean you can only do them a plain omelette?'

'I've been waiting to pay for these trainers for the last 15 minutes while you've been talking on the phone. Why didn't you tell the customer that you would ring them back and serve me first?'

If you're not sure or want to check your understanding, turn to the page number listed in the brackets.

Revision questions

1 Explain why personal presentation is important when dealing with customers.

2 What are the advantages of an organisation providing its staff with uniforms?

3 Explain why personal hygiene is important for someone employed as waiting staff in a restaurant.

4 Describe how a member of staff's attitude and behaviour can affect the level of service that they provide to customers.

5 Why is it important that staff handle customer complaints effectively?

6 Explain how members of staff can show that they are listening to a customer who is complaining.

7 Why should you never argue with a customer who is complaining?

8 Explain why a member of staff might need to ask for help from a supervisor when dealing with a customer complaint.

Investigation ideas

You are on a work placement at a privately owned travel agency and are surprised to find out that the travel consultants do not receive any training on how to deal with a customer complaint. The owner/manager, Neil, explains,

'They do not need to know how to deal with complaints because they have strict instructions to call me if a customer is not happy – and I deal with it myself. If I am not available they take the customer's address and phone number and I get in touch with them as soon as possible.'

You suggest that knowing how to deal with a complaint is part of good customer service for all staff and that training his travel consultants would result in a higher level of customer satisfaction. You also accept that it is sometimes better to call a supervisor to deal with the situation.

Neil asks you to write a short report outlining what you suggest his travel consultants should do when a customer has a complaint. He stresses that he would still rather deal with all complaints himself but is concerned about the way in which his staff handle the situation initially and, particularly, if he is not available immediately. He asks you to include a suggested checklist for staff on how to handle a complaining customer.

REVISION PROMPT

What have I learnt about the leisure industry?

_____

_____

_____

What am I still unsure about?

_____

_____

_____

How am I going to find out the extra information that I need?

_____

_____

_____

KEEPING CUSTOMER RECORDS

A large part of good customer service involves writing information down so that it can be used by other staff as well. Customer records give organisations a clear picture of its business and help them to plan for the future. Most leisure and tourism organisations keep records on their customers. Knowing how to maintain and use these records is an essential part of excellent customer service. Records may be kept in any number of situations and for different reasons, for example:

▲ Keeping records is an important part of customer service

- a travel agency will keep files containing the customer's holiday reservation details as part of their work in progress
- a theatre may keep files on existing customers showing what performances they have attended for future marketing
- a health club will have details on customer's including any medical conditions in case of emergencies
- a hotel will have records of guests who have stayed before and any special requirements for marketing
- any organisation may have records of past customer complaints and the action taken to satisfy the customer for future staff training sessions.

But no one asked me if I could swim!

I definitely said a coach for 53 not 33!

I asked for a double room with sea view not a single!

I reserved a non-smoking table, but...!

Incorrect records can have disastrous results ▶

Create a customer record

Organisations that use customer records will have standardised procedures for creating them. They will have a system that allows staff to record necessary information. These systems may be paper-based or on computer. You need to know how to create and store these records for customers. If you are unsure of how to do this, ask another member of staff for help rather than guessing.

Surname	First names/s	Address	Tel number	e-mail	Date of birth

▲ Coverdale Sports Centre Customer Record

OVER TO YOU

Create a record

The Coverdale Sports Centre has offered a special membership deal to teenagers in the area and you have all decided to join! They plan to enter all customer details on a computer database. A record sheet from this database is shown here.

- Make enough copies of the blank records so that you and each person in your group has two copies.
- Ask each member of the group for their personal details – they will need to make some up. Record each person's details.
- Once you have each person's details, re-write the database so that it is in alphabetical order.

Find and change existing records

Customer details are always changing, which means that you need to know how to find and change existing records. Records may be kept in a filing cabinet, on a computer database, on record cards or in books and files. Organisations often keep different types of records in different places so it is important that you know where they are. For example, reservations may be written into a diary, customer complaints may go into a complaints book and customer details may be stored on a computer.

Be just as careful when changing customer details as you are when creating the original customer record. This is particularly true when you change details on a computer.

Accuracy and confidentiality

The details in customer records are only useful if they are completely accurate. If they are only partly accurate then all of the information is useless – you do not know which details are true and which are not. Everything you enter in a customer record must be correct. Always double check before you enter information if you are unsure.

Personal records often contain personal information about customers. When customers give this information to the organisation they trust you not to pass it on to anyone else. Make sure that you keep this information confidential. If you do not, you risk causing the customer embarrassment or difficulty. Even a casual remark to customers in front of others about something that you have read on their record could result in them being extremely dissatisfied.

An elderly gentleman contacted his travel agent to say that his wife had unfortunately died, so could they take her name off any future letters that they sent to him. The eager new receptionist found his file on the computer and typed in 'died' after the wife's name. The computer automatically addressed all further letters to Mr and Mrs (died) Johnson.

Do not make these kind of casual remarks:

- I'd never have guessed that you were 50.

- Have you had any luck in finding a new job yet?

- Our fitness programme must be working; I see you're down to 15 stone.

- Have you fully recovered from that little accident that you had in Tenerife?

Most organisations will have strict rules about which staff can and cannot see various customer records. Therefore they will make sure that the records are stored securely and only certain staff will have access to them.

CASE STUDY

The Gemini Restaurant's records

The Gemini Restaurant keeps the following customer records:

- A written reservations diary of advance bookings for the restaurant – the details recorded include name and telephone number of customer, number of diners, time of arrival and any special requests, such as vegetarian, or preferred table. Each page of the diary is organised into tables to make sure that the restaurant does not become overbooked on any night.

- Details of regular customers are recorded on a computer database. This includes business people who regularly entertain clients at the restaurant and people who have attended special themed nights, such as Christmas parties. Letters are often sent out to these customers telling them of special offers or events that might interest them.

- A file of customers' complaint and compliment letters together with the reply sent to the customer by the restaurant – a separate book is kept to record telephone and face-to-face complaints.

- An accident book.

Restaurants use a number of customer records ▼

Advantages of customer needs

OVER TO YOU

As a group discuss the advantages to the customer and the organisation of keeping these records. Use the table to record your answers.

Advantages of customer records		
Record	Advantages for the customer	Advantages for the organisation
Reservations diary		
Customer database		
Complaints file/book		
Accident book		
You're welcome		

KEY TERMS

You should know what the following terms mean:

Keeping customer records
  (page 220)
Creating a customer record
  (page 221)
Finding and changing existing
  records (page 222)
Accuracy and confidentiality
  (page 222)

If you're not sure or want to check your understanding, turn to the page number listed in the brackets.

Revision questions

1 Describe three examples of customer records that might be kept by leisure or tourism organisations.

2 Why is it important to keep details of customer records confidential?

REVISION PROMPT

What have I learnt about customer records?

_____

_____

_____

What am I still unsure about?

_____

_____

_____

How am I going to find out the extra information that I need?

_____

_____

_____

FURTHER STUDY

PGL holidays

Young adult and children's activity holidays are an important part of both the leisure and tourism industry. One of the main providers in this market is PGL.

The PGL Company takes its name from the initials of the man who started it in the 1950s and who is now Chairman of the PGL Group of Companies – Peter Gordon Lawrence.

In 1950, Peter went on holiday to Austria, bought a folding canvas canoe and set off down the Danube. He enjoyed this so much, he wanted to share this experience. In 1957 he started canoe camping trips for small groups of young adults down the River Wye on the border between England and Wales. From this small beginning has grown the company we know today as PGL.

Gradual expansion throughout the 1980s confirmed PGL's position at the forefront of the adventure market. The range of activities now includes a host of other watersports in France, skiing for schools and teenagers, language programmes at PGL's own French Chateau and even 'Baywatch' life-saving courses. In 1999, over 120 000 guests enjoyed a PGL experience, either as part of an organised school trip or an individual holiday.

Source: www. pgl.co.uk

OVER TO YOU

PGL is a good example of the strong links between the leisure and tourism industries.

- Read the description of one of their holidays
- Identify and describe the specific aspects of the holiday that are either leisure, tourism of both.

Source: www. pgl.co.uk

Sights, Lights and City Nights

Sights, Lights and City Nights is an amazing holiday that includes daily excursions to the most exciting attractions and sights in Paris. PGL's new Chateau is a brand new PGL centre. The Chateau boasts the very best in facilities with two outdoor heated swimming pools, a full size football pitch, volleyball court, five tennis courts, two boules pitches, and a games room.

All guests on the full-week holiday will enjoy two full days at Disneyland Paris to make the most of the rides and the shows, and a full day-visit to famous sights in central Paris, including the Eiffel Tower and a Seine river cruise. After that it's time to make a splash at the Aquaboulevard, a massive indoor water fun park. Guests will also visit La Villette Science Park that combines technology with leisure and entertainment and includes a Planetarium, the Geode cinema and Cinaxe – a motion simulator!

Accommodation includes four-bed rooms with ensuite bathroom facilities. Bedding supplied.

Travel by luxury coach from Manchester, Birmingham, London or Dover. Ferry from Dover included. Stops are made en route to purchase meals/snacks.

Historical interest – an exercise

Historical interest

The descriptions of some of the UK's famous stately homes, castles and palaces have been taken from the website www.dlc.fi/~hurmari/castles.html.

From the statements that follow, can you identify each attraction and find where it is on the map of the UK?

This is said to be the largest castle ruin in England and was built in 1120.

This castle was destroyed by two Civil Wars and a great fire in 1816.

The National Motor Museum is housed here – with more than 250 vehicles.

This castle was destroyed by a large crowd in 1831 who looted its treasures and set fire to the building.

Mary Queen of Scots was crowned Queen in this castle in 1543.

Queen Victoria was the first ruler to live in this palace in 1837.

This hall is home to the Marquess and Marchioness of Hertford.

This stately home was voted the most popular in 1996 and 1999.

This house was built by a rich merchant in the fourteenth century.

This Hall was given to the National Trust in 1967 by the Vernon family.

The television drama, Brideshead Revisited, was filmed at this large castle.

King Edward VII made this stately home his residence.

The Egerton family lived in this home from 1598–1958.

This magnificent palace was the birthplace of the Prime Minister Sir Winston Churchill.

Stirling Castle

Located in Fife, Scotland, the former Scottish Royal Residence and perhaps the grandest of all Scotland's castles. It has strong links to Mary Queen of Scots, who was crowned here in 1543.

Castle Howard

This castle is in North Yorkshire. Built by Sir John Vanbrugh, it provided the location of *Brideshead Revisited*, and has an impressive Great Hall and fabulous collection of art.

Tatton Park

Tatton Park is in Knutsford, Cheshire. Home of the Egerton family from 1598 to 1958; it is now owned by the National Trust. Tatton Old Hall was built around 1520 and enlarged to its present size in the 1580s. In the early nineteenth century its appearance was changed to the fashionable neo-classical style. There are fine collections of pictures, books, china, glass and furniture and there is an extensive park.

Aberconwy House

Built by a prosperous merchant in the fourteenth century in Conwy, Gwynedd, it is the oldest remaining domestic medieval structure in town. The furnishings reflect changes in styles and use since the seventeenth century.

Belvoir Castle

Originally built in Leicestershire in the eleventh century and destroyed by two Civil Wars and a great fire in 1816. The present castle is owned by the Duke of Rutland and has belonged to his ancestors since the time of the Normans. It has magnificent collections of ancient arms, fine furniture and outstanding paintings. The Queen's Royal Lancers Regimental Museum is in the castle.

Sandringham House

This is a private Country House of the Queen, built in 1870 in Norfolk. It has been home to the Prince of Wales, later King Edward VII. The grand and imposing neo-Jacobean house now also has a museum full of Royal memorabilia.

Sudbury Hall

The original old manor house was replanned and rebuilt in Derbyshire in the 1660s by George Vernon. Richly decorated, it has a collection of family portraits and a magnificent carved staircase. The Great Staircase is one of the finest of its kind in an English house. In 1839, the family moved to their beloved Italy for the next three years, letting the house to tenants. Among these was Queen Adelaide, William IV's widow, and The Queens Room was appropriately named after her. Sudbury remained as the home of the Vernon family until gifted to the National Trust in 1967.

Kenilworth Castle

This is reputedly the largest castle ruin in England, was founded in 1120 in Warwickshire. It was constructed for defence with walls six metres thick; in the fourteenth century the castle was transformed into a palatial home. During the English civil war Cromwell's troops demolished the castle.

Ragley Hall

This is the home of the Marquess and Marchioness of Hertford, in Alcester, Warwickshire. It was designed in 1680 by the versatile scientist, Robert Hooke, as one of the first Palladian country houses. Ragley has 6000 acres of land; the gardens were designed by 'Capability' Brown.

Blenheim Palace

This Oxfordshire palace is the home of the Duke of Marlborough, birthplace of Sir Winston Churchill, and the unique park of 'Capability' Brown.

Beaulieu Abbey

This has been the Hampshire home of Lord Montagu's family since 1538, and the Gardens and the National Motor Museum, with over 250 vehicles.

Buckingham Palace

This is the official residence of Britain's sovereigns in London; it was originally a town house owned by the Dukes of Buckingham. King George III bought Buckingham House in 1761 for his wife, Queen Charlotte, and Queen Victoria was the first sovereign to take up residence in July 1837. The State Rooms are open to the public each year in August and September; the Royal Mews is open throughout the year.

Chatsworth

This Derbyshire, palace-like ancestral home of the Duke of Devonshire was built in the late sixteenth century by Elizabeth Hardwick and her second husband, William Cavendish. There are outstanding painted ceilings, a library of over 17 000 volumes, and 'Capability' Brown's exceptionally fine garden. Chatsworth was voted the public's favourite house in 1996 and 1999.

Kathleen Kennedy, the sister of the late President Kennedy, was married to tenth Duke's elder son William, who was killed in action in World War 2 in 1944, and Kathleen died childless in an aeroplane accident in 1948 at the age of 28.

Nottingham Castle

This is one of the first castles built by William the Conqueror in Nottingham, Nottinghamshire, just after the Battle of Hastings. The castle was destroyed during the Civil War, but rebuilt soon after that as a Palace by the Duke of Newcastle. The Ducal Palace was gutted during the Reform Riots in 1831 by a large crowd who smashed or looted everything and finally set it ablaze. The castle remained as a blackened shell for almost 50 years until it was bought by the Nottingham City and restored as the first Provincial Museum of Fine Art, which was opened by the Prince of Wales in 1878.

Website directory

Trade organisations and government bodies

www.bha-online.org.uk
British Hospitality Association

www.hcima.org.uk
Hotel and Catering International
Management Association

www.htf.org.uk
Hospitality Training Foundation

www.toursoc. org.uk
The Tourism Society

abtanet.com
Association of British Travel Agents

www.artscouncil.org.uk
Arts Council

www.visitbritain.com
British Tourist Authority

www.baa.co.uk
British Airports Authority

www.culture.gov.uk
Department for Culture, Media and Sport

www.english-heritage.org.uk
English Heritage

www.nationaltrust.org.uk
National Trust

www.wisegrowth.org.uk
Sustainable tourism

www.ilam.co.uk
Institute of Leisure and Amenity Management

www.englishsports.gov.uk
Sports England

www.staruk.or.uk
Star UK (statistics)

www.employtourism.com
Employ Tourism

www.britishresorts.co.uk
British Resorts Association

www.countryside.gov.uk
The Countryside Agency

www.marketing.haynet.com
Marketing magazine

National and Regional Tourist Boards

www.englishtourism.org.uk
English Tourism Council

www.visitscotland.com
Visit Scotland

www.tourism.wales.gov.uk
Wales Tourist Board

www.ni-tourism.com
Northern Ireland Tourist Board

www.golakes.co.uk
Cumbria Tourist Board

www.visitnorthumbria.com
Northumbria Tourist Board

www.visitnorthwest.com
North West Tourist Board

www.yorkshirevisitor.com
Yorkshire Tourist Board

www.visitheartofengland.com
Heart of England Tourist Board

www.eastofenglandtouristboard.com
East of England Tourist Board

www.londontouristboard.com
London Tourist Board

www.westcountrynow.com
South West Tourism

www.southerntb.co.uk
Southern Tourist Board

www.southeastengland.uk.com
South East England Tourist Board

www.jersey.gov.uk/tourism/index
Jersey Tourism

Transport

www.britishwaterways.co.uk
British Waterways

www.thetrainline.com
The Trainline

www.pti.org.uk
UK Public Transport Information

www.virgin.com
The Virgin Atlantic

www.bhx.co.uk
Birmingham International Airport

www.britishairways.com
British Airways

www.easyJet.com
Easyjet

www.manairport.co.uk
Manchester Airport

www.ryanair.com
Ryanair

www.stenaline.co.uk
Stena Line Ferries

www.pogroup.com
P&O Ferries

Travel Agents and Tour Operators

www.lunn-poly.co.uk
Lunn Poly Travel Agents

www.thomascook.co.uk
Thomas Cook Travel Agents

www.going-places.co.uk
Going Places Travel Agents

www.airtours.co.uk
Airtours

www.jmc-holidays.co.uk
JMC holidays

www.Thompson-holidays.com
Thompsons Holidays

www.firstchoice.co.uk
First Choice Holidays

Leisure and Tourism Organisations

There are hundreds of different web sites covering the range of organisations in the leisure and tourism components, – a few of which are listed below. One of the easiest ways to find information on a specific component is to search through a directory such as the first two on the list below or to use the search facility on the Regional Tourist Board sites.

www.sightseeing.co.uk

UK Sightseeing Directory

www.dlc.fi/~hurmari/castles
British Castles, Stately Homes and Houses

www.alton.towers.co.uk
Alton Towers

www.bplltd.com
Blackpool Pleasure Beach

www.butlins.co.uk
Butlins

www.centerparcs.com
Center Parcs

www.thorpepark.co.uk
Thorpe Park

www.british-museum.ac.uk
British Museum

www.nationalgallery.org.uk
National Gallery

www.nmsi.ac.uk
National Museums of Science and Industry

Maps, facts and figures at a glance

Each chapter of this book contains a wide range of statistics, facts and figures for you to use and evaluate. The information in this section provides some further information that you may find helpful.

1 Employment

Employees in employment (thousands)	Sept 1996	Sept 1997	Sept 1998	Sept 1999	Sept 2000	Sept 2001	Change Sept 2000/01
Hotels and other tourist accommodation	421.7	400.6	427.3	403.5	413.6 (R)	410.9	-0.6
Restaurants, cafes and snack bars	462.9	479.2	489.2	536.6	547.9	556.2	+1.5
Public houses, bars, night clubs and licensed clubs	515.8	577.2	563.0	559.0	541.8 (R)	528.0	-2.5
Travel agencies/ Tour operators	93.8	105.1	107.5	136.9	137.8 (R)	140.9	+2.2
Libraries, museums, and other cultural activities	80.4	83.6	80.6	81.7	80.3 (R)	81.8	+1.9
Sports and other recreational activities	379.3	377.1	365.9	377.2	407.4 (R)	414.6	+1.8
Total of which:	1953.9	2022.7	2033.5	2094.9	2128.8 (R)	2132.4	+0.2
Self-employment jobs	231.8	228.1	178.6	148.9	167.0	176.6	+5.7
Employee jobs	1722.1	1794.6	1854.8	1946.0	1961.8	1955.8	

Source: Office for National Statistics

2a Tourism spending, 2000

Category	UK Residents
Total	£26,132 million
	%
Package trip	5
Accommodation (non-package trip)	25
Travel	20
Services or advice	2
Buying clothes	8
Eating and drinking	22
Other shopping	7
Entertainment	7
Other expenditure	4
Total	100

Source: UK Tourism Survey

2b Top UK cities and towns visited by foreign visitors, 2000

	City/Town	Visits (thousands)
1	London	13 150
2	Edinburgh	910
3	Manchester	560
4	Birmingham	520
5	Glasgow	430
6	Oxford	410
7	Cambridge	370
8	Bristol	360
9	York	310
10	Bath	300
11	Brighton/Hove	260
12	Cardiff	240
13	Inverness	220
=14	Liverpool	190
=14	Nottingham	190
16	Newcastle-upon-Tyne	180
=17	Stratford-upon-Avon	170
=17	Coventry	170
=17	Reading	170
20	Bournemouth	150

Note: Includes visits for all purposes: holidays, visits to friends and relatives, business and work and other purposes.

Source: *UK Tourism Survey*

2c Type of tourist destinations, 2000

Tourism trips by destination		
Trips	Million	%
Town	902	72
Seaside	81	6
Countryside	278	22
All trips	1,261	100

Source: *UK Tourism Survey*

2d UK conference market, 1999/2000

	2000	1999
Urban/airport hotels	43	54
Educational establishments	22	14
Purpose-built centres	14	5
Rural hotels	8	13
Unusual venues	7	8
Multi-purpose venues	4	3
Residential centres	2	3
Total value	£6.6 Billion	£1.7 Billion

Source: *British Conference Trends Survey 2000*

3 Accomodation used by UK residents, 2000

	UK Residents			
	All trips	All expenditure	Holiday trips	Holiday expenditure
	%	%	%	%
Hotel/Motel/Guesthouse	25	39	23	34
B&B/Farmhouse B&B	7	8	7	8
Rented house/Flat/Chalet	5	8	8	12
Hostel/University/School	1	1	1	1
Friends/Relative's home	47	27	40	25
Second home/Time-share	1	1	1	1
Camping	2	1	3	2
Towed caravan	3	2	4	3
Other	12	11	15	13

Note: Figures may be greater than the sum total
due to more than one accommodation type being used during a trip.

Source: *UK Tourism Survey*

4 Main leisure activities of visitors, 2000

	All visits	Town/City	Countryside	Seaside/Coast
	%	%	%	%
Eat/drink out	22	23	24	7
To go shopping	16	21	5	5
Visit friends/relatives	15	15	14	9
For entertainment	12	15	4	3
Leisure attraction	6	4	9	11
Walk/ramble	4	1	12	

Source: *UK Day Visits Survey*

5 Main transport used by visitors, 2000

	All tourism trips	Town/City	Countryside	Seaside/Coast
	%	%	%	%
Car	71	67	85	77
On foot	10	12	7	6
Bus/Train	12	16	1	9

Source: *UK Day Visits Survey*

Main rail companies

Anglia Railways
Company operates throughout East Anglia, and links East Anglia to London, Feltham (for Heathrow Airport, Hampshire and Surrey.

Arriva Trains Northern
Rail company operating local services in the north of England and Trans-Pennine Express services.

c2c
Operator of local train services between London (Fenchurch Street), Southend and Shoeburyness via Basildon, Grays or Lakeside Shopping Centre.

Central Trains
Rail company serving mid- and west Wales, and England from the Welsh border in the west to the Lincolnshire coast in the east. Has an extensive network of services in the Midlands, centred on Birmingham, and connects the Midlands directly to Stansted Airport.

Chiltern Railways
Operates train services between London and Birmingham, via the M40 corridor through the Chiltern Hills.

Connex
The main rail operator in the south-east of London, Kent, Sussex and parts of Surrey

Eurostar
Official web site for the Eurostar London/Ashford-Paris/Brussels rail service

First Great Eastern
Rail company operating services between London and Essex and parts of Suffolk.

First Great Western
Inter-city rail company operating between London and the West Country and South Wales.

First North Western
Rail operating company, serving the North-West of England and North Wales.

Great North Eastern Railway (GNER)
Inter-city rail company operating between London and West Yorkshire, the North-East and Scotland.

Hull Trains
Official site for the rail service connecting Hull, Brough, Selby, Doncaster, Grantham and London.

Midland Mainline
Midland Mainline operates trains serving Yorkshire, the East Midlands and London St Pancras, and is a part of the National Express Group.

Scotrail
Rail company operating most services in Scotland and also providing the overnight rail service between London and Scotland. Sells tickets on-line – UK rail tickets as well as Caledonian Sleeper berth inclusive.

Silverlink Trains
Operator of rail services around North London, and serving Birmingham, Bedfordshire and Luton, Hertfordshire, Buckinghamshire and Milton Keynes, Northamptonshire and parts of Warwickshire.

South Central Trains
Operator of train services in south London, Surrey, Sussex and parts of Kent and Hampshire.

Thames Trains
Rail company connecting London to the Thames Valley, Oxfordshire, the Cotswolds, Hereford/ Malverns and Stratford-on-Avon. Also links Oxford to Bristol.

Thameslink
Rail Company linking Bedfordshire and Luton Airport to London, Gatwick Airport and Brighton.

Leading UK ferry companies

Brittany Ferries
Ferry operator sailing to France from Portsmouth, Poole and Plymouth, and also operating Plymouth-Spain.

Condor Ferries
Ferry operator linking the Channel Islands to the UK mainland and France.

Fjord Line
Ferry company operating from Newcastle to Bergen (Norway).

Hoverspeed Fast Ferries
Company operating seacat services between the UK and France/Belgium (from Dover and Newhaven).

Irish Ferries
Ferry company operating Holyhead-Dublin, and Pembroke-Rosslare. Also information about P&O European Ferries service Cairnryan-Larne.

Norse Merchant Ferries
Ferry operator running from Liverpool to Dublin and Belfast.

P&O Irish Sea Ferries
P&O subsidiary, operating services between Scotland and Northern Ireland (Cairnryan-Larne) also Fleetwood-Larne and Liverpool-Dublin.

P&O North Sea Ferries
P&O subsidiary, operating services to Belgium and the Netherlands from Britain's east coast (Hull).

P&O Portsmouth
P&O subsidiary, operating western cross-Channel ferries from Portsmouth.

P&O Scottish Ferries
P&O subsidiary, operating services to the Orkney and Shetland Islands (from Aberdeen and Scrabster to Stromness and Lerwick).

P&O Stena Line
P&O/Stena Line joint venture, operating UK-France cross-Channel ferries from Dover.

Sea France
French-based operator of cross-channel ferries from Dover.

Stena Line
UK ferry operations of the Stena Line ferry group. Serves Stranrae-Belfast, Fishguard / Holyhead-Ireland, Harwich-Netherlands.

Swansea Cork Ferries
Ferry company operating between Swansea, in South Wales, and Cork, in western Ireland

DFDS Seaways
Ferry company operating between the UK and Scandinavia, Germany and Holland (serving Harwich and Newcastle).

UK airports

UK motorways

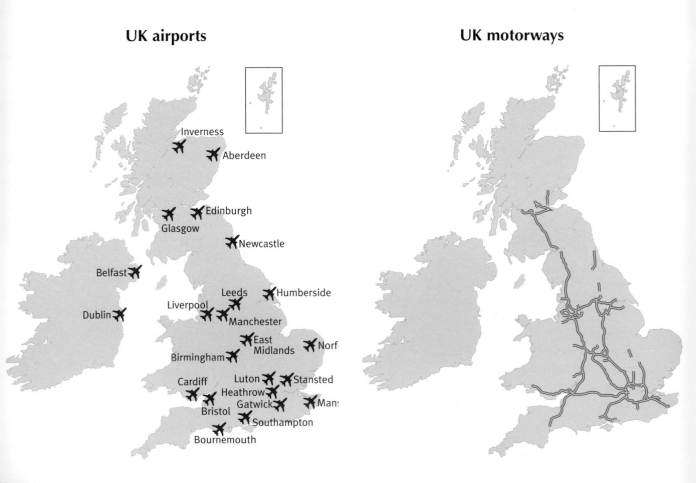

INDEX

Numbers in red show the page on which the word is defined or used as a key word

Published by HarperCollins*Publishers* Limited
77–85 Fulham Palace Road
Hammersmith
London
W6 8JB

www.CollinsEducation.co.uk
Online support for schools and colleges

© HarperCollin*Publishers* Limited 2002
First published 2002

10 9 8 7 6 5 4 3 2 1

ISBN 0 00 713810 5

Lindsey Taylor asserts the moral right to be identified as the author of this work.

British Cataloguing in Publication Data
A cataloguing record for this publication is available from the British Library

Almost all the case studies in this book are factual. However, the persons, locations and subjects have been given different names to protect their identity. The accompanying images are for aesthetic purposes only and are not intended to represent or identify any existing person, location or subject. The publishers cannot accept any responsibility for any consequences resulting from this use, except as expressly provided by law.

Series commissioned by Graham Bradbury
Series design and cover by Patricia Briggs
Book design by Sally Boothroyd
Cover picture by Telegraph Colour Library
Pictures researched by Thelma Gilbert and Sarah Clarke
Illustrations by Jerry Fowler
Index by Marie Lorimer
Project managed by Melanie McRae and Kay Wright
Production by Jack Murphy
Printed and bound by Scotprint, Haddington

www.fireandwater.co.uk
The book lover's website

Sulston, Sun Cheo-Yeh, Lisa Sutcliffe, Jim & Moira Sutherland, Soren Svendsen, Jakob Swezinna, Patrick Szymkowiak **T** Alaa Taher, Maria Talboys, Steph Tamlyn, Estelle Tant, Caroline Tasker, Steve Taylor, Martin Tazky, Bill Tedds, Hanna Tettenborn, Nigel Thomas, Paul Thomas, Severde Thomas, Kerri Thompson, Nell Thompson, Alan Thornton, Susanne Thulin, Brian Tiernan, Joe Tighe, Jessima Timberlake, Bob & Rhonda Todrick, Rhonda Tomlin, Ben Tompkins, Hayden Torr, Cara Torrington, Anabel Tournaire, Becky Tranter, Sinead Treacy, Martina Triner, Karen Tsui, Amanda Tucker, Judy Turnbull, Maria Tusa **U** Rebecca Uccellari, Marieke Uitentuis **V** Isabel Heim Vadis, Maria Vagunda, Christine Valade, Miranda van Damme, Mike van de Water, Daphne van der Mark, Jordy van der Star, Frank van Hilten, Kris van Kooten, Kim & Jan van Rijbroek, Suzan van Wezel, Anthony Veale, Michael Vejlgaard, Bas Verhelst, Thomas Verschuuren, Clem Vetters, Maria Giovanna Villari, Brice Villion, Sven Visser, Lea Vivarelli, Tatiana Vogt, Ann Marie Volpe, Beat & Frances Vonarburg, Mattias Vossen, Caroline Voy **W** Chris Waddington, Stefan Waibel, Jeanette Wain, Keila Waksvik, Naomi Wall, Adrian Walls, Ross Walsby, Paula & Tom Warmerdam, Tjebbe Warnink, Adrian Warren, Anthony Warren, Suzanne Wartenbergh, Melissa Watson, Jenny Watts, Mary Weeder, Gavin Welch, Helen Weld, Irene Weldon, Ken Wendle, Penny Werner, Sebastian Werner, Annelies Wessels, Catherine Whatley, Steve White, Daniel Wickie, Cajsa Wikstrom, Erin Wilcox, David Wilkins, Paula Wilkinson, Samantha Wilkinson, Susanne Willems, David Williams, Lawrie Williams, Alan Williamson, Bob Williamson, Jodie Williamson, Bill Wills-Moren, Andy Wilson, Catherine Wilson, Mickie Wilson, Pamela Wisley, Mijke Witbraad, Rachel Withers, Kerry Woodcock, Dennis & Trevor Woods, Wyn Woods, Tim Woodward, Deanne Wright, Jennie Wright, Miriam Wright, Sally Wright **Y** Cara Young, Caroline Young, Ivan Young, Saffron Young, Shane Young **Z** Eric A Zeliff, Jolanda Zwetsloot

ACKNOWLEDGMENTS

Many thanks to the following for the use of their content:

John Stainton, Best Picture Show Company, for helping to source the Steve Irwin boxed text on p441, and Angela Sharpe at AQIS.

Index

000 Map pages
000 Location of colour photographs

000 Map pages
000 Location of colour photographs

MAP LEGEND

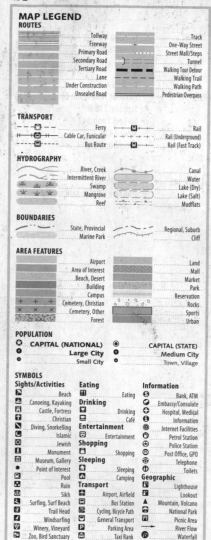

ROUTES

Tollway	Track
Freeway	One-Way Street
Primary Road	Street Mall/Steps
Secondary Road	Tunnel
Tertiary Road	Walking Tour Detour
Lane	Walking Trail
Under Construction	Walking Path
Unsealed Road	Pedestrian Overpass

TRANSPORT

Ferry	Rail
Cable Car, Funicular	Rail (Underground)
Bus Route	Rail (Fast Track)

HYDROGRAPHY

River, Creek	Canal
Intermittent River	Water
Swamp	Lake (Dry)
Mangrove	Lake (Salt)
Reef	Mudflats

BOUNDARIES

State, Provincial	Regional, Suburb
Marine Park	Cliff

AREA FEATURES

Airport	Land
Area of Interest	Mall
Beach, Desert	Market
Building	Park
Campus	Reservation
Cemetery, Christian	Rocks
Cemetery, Other	Sports
Forest	Urban

POPULATION

◎ **CAPITAL (NATIONAL)**	◉ **CAPITAL (STATE)**
● **Large City**	◎ **Medium City**
● Small City	◦ Town, Village

SYMBOLS

Sights/Activities	Eating	Information
Beach	Eating	Bank, ATM
Canoeing, Kayaking	**Drinking**	Embassy/Consulate
Castle, Fortress	Drinking	Hospital, Medical
Christian	Café	Information
Diving, Snorkelling	**Entertainment**	Internet Facilities
Islamic	Entertainment	Petrol Station
Jewish	**Shopping**	Police Station
Monument	Shopping	Post Office, GPO
Museum, Gallery	**Sleeping**	Telephone
Point of Interest	Sleeping	Toilets
Pool	Camping	**Geographic**
Ruin	**Transport**	Lighthouse
Sikh	Airport, Airfield	Lookout
Surfing, Surf Beach	Bus Station	Mountain, Volcano
Trail Head	Cycling, Bicycle Path	National Park
Windsurfing	General Transport	Picnic Area
Winery, Vineyard	Parking Area	River Flow
Zoo, Bird Sanctuary	Taxi Rank	Waterfall

LONELY PLANET OFFICES

Australia
Head Office
Locked Bag 1, Footscray, Victoria 3011
☎ 03 8379 8000, fax 03 8379 8111
talk2us@lonelyplanet.com.au

USA
150 Linden St, Oakland, CA 94607
☎ 510 893 8555, toll free 800 275 8555
fax 510 893 8572, info@lonelyplanet.com

UK
72–82 Rosebery Ave,
Clerkenwell, London EC1R 4RW
☎ 020 7841 9000, fax 020 7841 9001
go@lonelyplanet.co.uk

Published by Lonely Planet Publications Pty Ltd
ABN 36 005 607 983

4th Edition – August 2005

First Published – January 1996

© Lonely Planet 2005

© photographers as indicated 2005

Cover photographs by Lonely Planet Images: Lifesaver at Noosa Beach, Olivier Cirendini (front); Hiking through the rainforest at Bunya Mountains National Park, Chris Bell (back). Many of the images in this guide are available for licensing from Lonely Planet Images: www.lonelyplanetimages.com.

Printed through Colorcraft Ltd, Hong Kong.
Printed in China.